10.00.

Playback

PLAYBACK: *Canadian Selections*
Jack David and Michael Park, Editors
McClelland and Stewart

McClelland and Stewart Limited
The Canadian Publishers
25 Hollinger Road, Toronto

Design: David Perry

Printed and bound in Canada
by John Deyell Company

Canadian Cataloguing in Publication Data

Main entry under title:

Playback

ISBN 0-7710-2560-2

1. Canada—Civilization—20th century—
Addresses, essays, lectures.* I. David, Jack,
1946-   II. Park, Michael.

FC95.4.P53 971.06'44 C78-001108-2
F1021.P53

27,832

CONTENTS:

BIEN SÛR QU'IL ME PLAÎT! MAIS, DIS DONC, EST-CE QU'IL EST BILINGUE?

New C.B.C. symbol costs us $250,000.

Le nouveau symbole de Radio-Canada nous coûte un quart de million.

CARTOON ACKNOWLEDGMENTS ON P. 239...

Fast Foreword:

This is an unusual collection of Canadian articles and essays.

It is also an unusual textbook for the teaching of Canadian writing, rhetoric, and style. It omits the standard clutter of headnotes, footnotes, biographical notes, analyses, and obscure questions that even the teachers can't answer. In short, *Playback* doesn't boss you around. What matters are the articles and essays themselves, and in place of notes you will find cartoons.

Playback is also unusual because if you read the weekend magazine in your local newspaper, then you may have already read some of the contents. Or you may recognize some of the authors' names, like those of novelists Mordecai Richler and Margaret Laurence, or journalists June Callwood and Barbara Frum. But even if you haven't read the articles or heard of the writers, you know the subject matter: abortion, capital punishment, exams, ESP, and rock and roll. Moreover, the topics are up-to-date. What other textbook discusses punk rock, McDonald's, international hockey, and Quebec separation?

But interesting themes can go only so far. The articles – sometimes traditional in approach, sometimes radical – are by people who write for a living, and that means you can understand what they say.

Some people might even suggest that *Playback* is unusual because it's 100 percent Canadian. These people, though, probably live in the United States, where textbook essays are about Harlem, the Texas Longhorns, or Disneyland. If you're from Canada, however, you'd likely prefer articles about Vancouver, the Toronto Argonauts, or the CBC. Well, here they are.

Canadian people, Canadian ideas, Canadian experiences – that's what you'll find in *Playback*. And for most of us, that's unusual.

I

GROWTH

JOANNE KATES

The New "Nonviolent" Childbirth Method

A small, gentle, Parisian doctor has decided babies deserve soft, gentle, blissful births— without trauma, without violence.

You were in a dark warm place, so secure and so quiet, all sounds from the outside gently muffled by its walls. The place was so small that your body had to be curled up like a snail all the time, but you got used to that and it became comfortable. So did the constant lulling motion of the walls. It was a calm, unchanging world.

Suddenly, your world exploded. Bright lights burned your eyes that only knew darkness. Your ears were assaulted by crashing new noises. Your back, so used to being curled up tight, was wrenched straight. You'd been naked for months, touched only by warm, satiny waters; now cold cloth felt like sandpaper on your tender skin. But what made you panic most was air. They cut the cord, your lifeline, and you had to take your first breath into lungs never yet used. It was like breathing fire. And then, less than 10 minutes after your world exploded, they left you alone on a cold, hard, unmoving surface, so alien you cried and cried.

Birth doesn't have to be that painful, but, according to Parisian obstetrician Frédérick Leboyer, who is fast making newborns a *cause célèbre,* it usually is in the Western world. It's not as if babies begin to live the moment they pop out of the birth canal: the fetal senses develop long before the journey to our world begins, and those senses are accustomed to the gentlest world there is. The pace of fetal life is slow; even the journey down the canal goes inch by inch.

And how do we welcome this newborn who's nothing more than a bundle of sensitivity, not yet equipped to filter out stimuli? Like an object. We hang him or her upside down like a prize fish. We wrench the baby from her lifeline, her mother, and expose her at the hectic pace of the delivery room to terrifying new sensations, then leave her alone in a crib.

Leboyer feels that "for the child, each sensation is new and each sensation is so powerful because it is the first time. What makes a horror of birth is the immensity of the experience, its frightening variety."

We've never read emotions into a newborn's crying, but Leboyer says that's only because we've never listened. The first cries tell us that the reflexes are normal, that the machine is functioning: one scream, two screams, that's enough.

Why should this yelling, this weeping, go on and on and on? If you look at newborns, Leboyer writes in his book *Pour une Naissance sans Violence,* you'll see that the crying is not that of a little machine. We interpret the feelings of mutes and monkeys and foreigners. Why not newborns? Look at any newborn. Eyes screwed up tight, feet curled in tension, flesh that's all spasms and twitches. New babies don't talk? It's we who don't listen. And interpreting their sobbing as a mere physical act devoid of feelings is, to Leboyer, like equating a woman crying over raw onions to a woman crying because her husband has sued for divorce.

Since publishing his book in France in early 1974, Leboyer has made "soft childbirth" his cause. The book, which came out in English in the U.S. and Canada the following year, met with furious controversy, and yet Frédérick Leboyer is like the eye of a hurricane—calm and quiet.

I pursued Leboyer from Paris to Frankfurt and finally caught up with him in Munich. Before he flew to Spain to publicize the Spanish edition of the book, we talked about his theories, Leboyer switching easily between English and French. He showed me his eloquent photographs of babies born in the regular way and Vietnamese children scorched by napalm—and yes, the expressions were painfully similar. When he pulled the next two pictures out of his portfolio I was convinced—the Leboyer new born wore the same blissful expression as a sculpture of the Buddha.

Put briefly, Leboyer has designed a simple ritual for the first 10 minutes of a child's life. The oldest children born Leboyer's gentle way are now eight years old, and are being studied psychologically and physically.

To soften the tidal wave of birth sensations, he makes the transition from internal life to external life gradual, by prolonging some of the feelings of life in the uterus and introducing the new ones slowly and smoothly.

In the womb, sounds are absorbed and muffled by the amniotic fluid and the mother's stomach walls, so the first step towards making birth less shocking is quiet. No one may talk above a whisper in the delivery room. During delivery, if the mother absolutely must scream, so be it. But if she's had proper breathing training she'll know how to use the tendency to scream, to breathe deep and hard, or pant, as in the Lamaze natural childbirth method.

Babies delivered the normal Western way open their eyes as soon as they pop out, only to shut them in defence against the bright light. Though they're too young to see it as we do, with understanding, they're sensitive to light, and it probably makes them feel the way bulls do when held in the dark for a week, and then released into a sunny arena for the kill: "blind" with panic.

So no spotlights glare in Leboyer's delivery room. He wants enough light to gauge the condition of mother and child, but not the bright lights that terrify a baby who's lived so far in darkness. Newborn babies are not pretty to look at. Leboyer recalls: "Very often I've seen women looking at the newborn and saying, 'He's so ugly.' Then they say, 'All right, we'll still love you.' But the feeling is not there and the child can sense it. And hard to believe as it is, these impressions remain, both with child and mother." In the dim light of the Leboyer method, the first contact between mother and newborn is not the distant intellectual one of looking, but the intimate introduction of touching, of starting life together with loving caresses.

When babies arrive they're covered with a layer of slippery fat and mucus, which makes them as hard to hold as live fish. So for safety, doctors hold them by the ankles, upside down. Snap! Suddenly the baby's back is straightened and there he is, upside down and dizzy. Imagine how the abrupt straightening shocks the spine of a little creature whose back has been curled and compressed by his mother's womb and then by the tight birth canal. Leboyer holds babies just as safely under their armpits and he supports their backs.

Cutting the umbilical cord as soon as the baby comes out is cruelly inhumane, according to Leboyer. He keeps the cord intact until it stops pulsing; just five minutes or so till it beats no more, but those five minutes, insists Leboyer, "give the newborn time to get used to this world. The cord substitutes for the fetus' lungs—the mother breathes for him as she does everything for him, and just as he'll need her to hold on to when he takes his first steps, he needs her to help him make the breathing transition. When the cord is cut right away the newborn's lungs start working out of panic, danger. He must breathe or die and the first gulps of air burn like fire. If you let nature set the pace, and respect the rhythm of the newborn, his lungs will take over comfortably. The change will be gentle instead of brutal. And the baby hardly cries!"

As soon as the baby comes out, Leboyer puts him naked on the mother's belly. He and the woman hold the baby, creating a cosy little womblike cradle for him. For the child it's very much like the uterus: mother's stomach rises and falls with a familiar rhythm; her smell is the same; her warmth protects him from the chill of the delivery room, which is about 20 degrees colder than the womb; the feel of her supple skin is security personified, and of course proximity allows the cord to stay intact.

Leboyer wants the baby to straighten his back slowly, at his own speed, so the baby lies first on his stomach with arms and legs tucked underneath. The child's breathing pattern is visible from the motion of his back and the Leboyer baby, just two or three minutes old, starts to explore the new world. An arm slides out and touches mother's belly. Back under the baby's body. His legs start to stretch. Another arm comes out. He touches himself. Like the new puppy who stops howling when you put a loud ticking clock in its basket, the Leboyer newborn seems to take comfort from his mother—he's not crying!

Slowly, and with care not to touch the hypersensitive head that's led the way down the birth canal, Leboyer turns the baby onto his side and then, after time to get used to the new posture, on his back for the first time. Smoothly, like a flower blooming, the newborn opens from the fetal position. He's only five minutes old.

The baby's skin is used to warmth, weight, slowness and the rhythm of the uterus. What's new is terrifying. So to make him feel at home Leboyer massages the newborn, his hands imitating the rhythm of the walls of the womb.

Psychiatric textbooks drone on and on about the malevolent effects of separation anxiety. When is that anxiety born? With the initial separation from the mother, of course. So Leboyer aims to take the trauma out of that first separation. After the massage he puts a newborn baby in a bath just a bit warmer than her body. Again the baby meets the maternal waters that carried her, caressed her, made her limbs lighter than in air. In the bath the baby floats as she did in the first stage of pregnancy, when the uterus was still growing faster than she, and her body had freedom.

The world of water must be pure joy to the baby, because she's making little cooing noises. Her eyes are open wide. The stiffness and tension are gone. Her head turns to the left and then right. Her hands open and close. She feels Leboyer's arm. A little leg comes out of the water, goes back in. She opens her lips, sticks out her tongue. She's playing! And she's not yet 10 minutes old. After four or five minutes

'ELLO, MORGENTALER?

" THE OLYMPICS CAN NO MORE HAVE A DEFICIT THAN A MAN CAN HAVE A BABY."
                    JEAN DRAPEAU - JAN. 29, 1973.

Leboyer lifts the baby out of the water, very slowly, and he says the baby doesn't mind this change because she "has something else now. She can play with her hands, with her arms, with her legs. So even the feeling of being heavy again is accepted as pleasant."

When a baby leaves the warm bath that reproduces the sensations of the amniotic sac, it's as if she's being born again, "but if she's going through the experience again she now feels that being born is so pleasant, being out is so pleasant." The experience will stay with her, not as birth trauma but as birth joy.

Leboyer wraps the baby in prewarmed cloth, leaving head and hands unswathed for freedom, and puts her to bed. The child is alone for the first time in her life. Other babies cry ferociously when they're first left alone, but not Leboyer's newborn. This child has gone through changes slowly, has been calmed by loving hands, so she accepts the newness happily. She looks around her. She looks peaceful.

In the 20-minute film that Leboyer made, called *Blissful Birth,* he focuses on babies 24 hours old. Babies born the regular way are either wailing or sleeping, curled up in the fetal position as if, according to Leboyer, "they feel abandoned in a hostile universe and want to negate their birth and go back to the old joy of the womb." Only the Leboyer babies are sleeping on their backs, arms flung open in a relaxed posture.

Apparently that relaxation grows with the babies. Danielle Rapoport, a psychologist who works with the University of Paris and two children's hospitals in Paris, had been conducting a study of Leboyer babies. Of the 1,000 babies he's delivered, she chose as varied as possible a group of 100 children, aged one to four years, to interview and test. Rapoport talked about what she's found so far: "It appears that having been born in the Leboyer nonviolent way really does affect the condition of these children's lives. They learn quickly; their motor skills are very good; they solve problems faster than most children. They're lively and intelligent. And even the relationship of the mothers to these children is more cordial, because these children eat better and cry less than others."

Leboyer, an unassuming elfin little man, can't help grinning from ear to ear: "When those mothers talk about their children, I feel it is too good to be true. All the children born in this nonviolent way—they wake up—they don't cry! They start playing with their body. They make little noises. Then they go back to sleep. They never cry! They laugh; they play; they are always happy. When other children wake up and cry, it is nothing but re-experiencing the anguish they felt at birth; when they wake up alone in the crib, as Freud said, they're reliving the primal pain of being left alone after birth. So they scream with terror."

Though as adults we can't remember our birth, we carry its imprint forever in the dark corners of our minds. And though a birth trauma doesn't produce neurosis, according to Leboyer, it makes people more susceptible to later events that could be troubling. In writing about how birth affects us, in his book *The Feeling Child,* Arthur Janov (also author of *The Primal Scream*) says: "A difficult birth 'teaches' the child that life is a struggle . . . that life is dangerous."

The American Journal of Obstetrics and Gynecology documented the lasting effects of birth trauma in 1972. A group of Indianapolis medical researchers matched the obstetric records of 1,698 babies with their progress at school by age nine; a quarter of all breech-born children had failed at least one grade, and one in five needed academic remedial help.

Writing in *Psychology Today* in 1971, Sarnoff A. Mednick told of a study he carried out on 2,000 Danish men born in 1936. Of 16 men who had committed violent crimes, "15 of them had the most horrible possible conditions at birth." Dr. Mednick, the director of the Institute of Psychology in Copenhagen, also studied schizophrenic and normal children and found 70 percent of the disturbed children in the study had suffered at least one serious complication at birth.

Frédérick Leboyer is 57 years old. He has never married and he has no children. "I had a terrible birth," he says, "postmature and with forceps. It affected my whole life." He's delivered 10,000 babies since starting his obstetrical practice at a private hospital in Paris in 1950. For the first 10 years he was a classical obstetrician: "I really didn't see the babies. I was concerned with them only technically, on a medical level, and as long as the child would cry and scream I would feel that, oh yes, he's perfectly alive. Finished."

Then, 12 years ago Leboyer began to undergo psychoanalysis and soon after, primal therapy, in India. "In analysis I went through the experience of my birth again, and I realized how I had suffered. So I became more interested in the newborn. I started looking at babies and asking myself if they were suffering. I started taking pictures of newborns, and their faces looked exactly like the faces of children in Vietnam who have been burned by napalm. I looked at them, listened to them, tried to see how they were reacting. And I realized it was like torture—birth. So I had to accept that the newborn is not an object, that it really has feelings. I started trying to understand why birth is so painful, and I realized it is only the extreme contrast between before and after that is overwhelming. So all we have to do is give these new sensations slowly. I simply began doing for the baby what we do for the mother: making the experience as pleasant as possible."

Leboyer delivered 1,000 babies the "blissful birth" way and then, in early 1974, he left the private obstetrical clinic in Paris where he's always practised. "I was suffering so much for the babies; at times another obstetrician would deliver a baby in the next delivery room—I could see it from the corner of my eye—and when I was listening to the screaming of the baby, and when I could feel the agony that baby was going through, it was too heartbreaking." So Leboyer stopped delivering babies, not just because he could no longer stand watching this, but also because he didn't want his clinic turned into a sort of obstetrical mecca. He's a shy man who wants to continue living a quiet life, and he didn't want patients flocking to "famous Dr. Leboyer," because for him it's the babies who are important, and no one must steal attention from the newborns. Now he's making another film and writing another book, both on the subject of his birth ritual. And above all he's looking for other doctors to train in his method.

But doctors aren't jumping on the Leboyer bandwagon. There is no scientific proof of his theories, and many European doctors have questioned the technique's medical validity. He ascribes their objections to prejudices of twentieth-century medical training: "During all my medical studies I was given the impression that the newborn is an object. We know that the brain is not mature and the nervous system is not complete when the child is born and thus physiologists say that the newborn cannot think or feel—it's only a digestive tract. Well that's just not true. Psychiatrists know. Psychoanalysts know. But physicians see only the medical level. Of course the rules of sterility are to be respected—but it's not a surgical procedure—it's a natural process."

Of course, when things go wrong, Leboyer uses all his obstetrical training to right them. Emergencies call for standard physical solutions: if the cord is strangling the baby, he cuts it fast; if the child doesn't breathe he's not averse to a spanking.

Nobody knows for sure how much of the environment babies sense, but recent experiments in Sweden have shown that even a fetus responds to noises by increasing its heart rate. That's an indicator of stress, even though the fetus has no idea what stress is. The sense of touch is acute: 20 weeks after conception a fetus can feel touch on its skin.

Frédérick Leboyer isn't the first person to point out that birth is painful. In 1936, Dr. Maria Montessori, the educational pioneer, wrote in her book *The Secret of Childhood*: "When a child is born, everyone is concerned about its mother. She has suffered. But has not the child suffered as well? Care is taken to shield the mother from light and noise. But what about the child who has come from a place where it was shielded from light and sound? It also has need of silence and darkness. . . . Too little attention is paid to the newborn child that has just experienced the most difficult of human crises."

Animals know what newborns need. The majority of monkey species give birth to their young at night. A cat will look for a dark, tranquil place. An animal mother severs the cord slowly with her teeth; licking her young accomplishes much the same thing as Leboyer's massage. Many so-called primitive cultures have touching and bathing rituals with new babies.

You don't need Frédérick Leboyer in person to give your child a blissful birth. As he says: "Anybody can do it. What do I say? Don't talk too loud. Does this require training? Do you need to be a specialist to switch off glaring lights? And be patient. Forget about your watch. Forget about your next appointment and tell yourself that for 10 minutes you will be completely at the disposal of the child. Is this difficult? Any doctor who will not give a newborn 10 minutes should be in another profession. To give a baby a birth that's like waking from a beautiful dream, you need only be humble enough to learn from a newborn."

Joanne Kates is a regular contributor to the *Globe and Mail, Maclean's, Toronto Life*, and *Chatelaine*, among other publications. Her specialty is the subject of women's liberation. "The New 'Nonviolent' Childbirth Method" was first printed in *Chatelaine*, April 1975.

ISABEL LeBOURDAIS

Instant People? Of Course!

A satirical essay which carries conception to its logical conclusion.

Right to life is a noble ideal worthy of everyone's dedication. Indeed, serious reading and much thought must be devoted to the implications for all of us in the view that a human life, a person, begins at the moment of conception. One spokesman (male) has said that Canada had fifty thousand abortions in 1971: "Fifty thousand human beings were killed!" He exaggerated a bit. Statistics Canada recorded 30,949 legal abortions in 1971 and 18,801 in the first six months of 1972. But no one recorded the thousands of illegal abortions. To murder anyone is a terrible thing.

But such early life must not only be saved, it must be given dignity and recognition. Our laws and customs must be adapted to this previously overlooked truth. How can such change be achieved?

We should work to see that all birth certificates are abandoned and conception certificates issued in their place. Also, we should voluntarily cease celebrating birthdays in favour of conception days.

We should demand that income tax deductions be allowed for all unborn children and in order that parents may be assured the full benefit to the end of each year, all women of child-bearing age should be urged to have a pregnancy test on New Year's Eve.

All census-takers or compilers of any kind of population records for any purpose should be required to obtain the results of up-to-date pregnancy tests from every woman of child-bearing age, because in no other way is it possible to guarantee the accuracy of any statement as to the number of persons apparently living in a house or *any* specific area.

A pregnancy test should also be automatic in any other situation where it is important to know how many persons were present at an event or involved in a project. In fact, unless a woman is already known to be pregnant, tests should be mandatory in every situation where it is important to know whether we are dealing with one person or two: passports, for example.

We also know that numbers of fertilized eggs—and these are of course persons—either pass out with menstruation or are victims of spontaneous miscarriages. Surely all churches that believe in life at conception should provide for holy baptism on a round-the-clock, emergency, home-visit basis so that no human being loses this sacred right just because he or she is only a fertilized egg.

19

And surely our traditional obligation to bury the dead requires that funeral services be held even if the dead person is invisible to the naked eye.

All abortions are deliberate premeditated murder, so right-to-lifers should demand that the law be changed to allow no abortions at all. No consideration of a woman's rights is involved since once conception has taken place, she no longer has any. She had sexual intercourse, even if it was rape, so she must bear the consequences. That's really all there is to it. Therefore, all women who have abortions, all doctors or other abortionists, all those who are accessories to the crime must be charged with murder, the woman's health being declared inadmissible as evidence, and her death, even if medically certain, regarded as irrelevant and immaterial.

Even under the present lax law, thousands of illegal abortions take place. While pressing to have the law made absolutely rigid, all right-to-lifers, true to their high motives, should carry on a campaign at every level to have police, hospitals, social agencies and private citizens report every case of someone performing or having an abortion, failure to report such crimes being declared punishable under the Criminal Code.

Murderers must be brought to trial. The excuse of danger to the mother's own life must be eliminated once and for all, since life at conception means another person exists whose right to life cannot be a matter of choice. Nearly fifty thousand legal abortions in a year and a half means we have many more than fifty thousand known murderers.

Is mere imprisonment enough?

A return to capital punishment is advocated by many strong-minded Canadians as a deterrent to murder. If we could ensure that every person who performed, assisted or underwent an abortion were arrested, tried, convicted and hanged, wouldn't that prove the sincerity and unimpeachable moral principles of all those citizens who are bravely taking their stand for a right to life?

Canada would undoubtedly receive a good deal of international attention for such dedication to the superior rights of newly conceived persons. We truly could be proud, even though some newspapers would carry headlines such as: "Pinhead-size persons sacred in Canada," or "Canada now a nation of snoopers." But righteousness always rises above ignorant criticism.

Each point in the program advocated herein is not only logical but is the least that those who believe in the right to life should work for. And as often happens when virtue has its own reward, other unexpected benefits would follow:

Right to lifers would be responsible for solving Canada's unemployment problem!

The moment-of-conception existence of a live person is at present ignored in all laws and procedures except in relation to abortion, but, once accepted, it would affect all records to such an extent as to require millions of pregnancy tests per year, involving the building of new laboratories, the conducting of immediate and extensive research for better techniques, the employment of many thousands of technicians requiring special training that would require hundreds of persons to train them. In addition, all census- or other record-taking would now take so much longer and involve so much more work that far more people would have to be hired to do it. However, the greatest boon to the unemployment situation would be the earth-shaking growth of all departments of the administration of justice.

Canada is already known for having the largest percentage of its population in jail among countries that keep public records—22,000 out of 22 million people. Even if our figure of 50,000 abortions were cut in half, each case would yield two or three murderers and the potential employment figures are staggering. Tracking down, arresting, imprisoning, trying, convicting all abortion criminals would require so many additional police, detectives, court officials, lawyers, judges, prison guards and even hangmen that our entire system would undergo a world-startling employment boom augmented by the building boom in new courts and penitentiaries. And the certainty that unbelievers would follow their own selfish principles instead of those of right to life would keep the employment figures high because of the need for constant vigilance and prosecution.

Isn't it a satisfying thought that every woman who had sexual relations last night without adequate birth control may contain a new person today? And, that that person's life must be protected at all costs?

But there's a blur in the picture . . . the mention of birth control . . . memories of the rather recent past.

Wasn't it only in 1969 that it ceased to be illegal to promote birth control? And weren't the arguments of those who worked so hard to keep it illegal for so long oddly similar to those used by right to lifers today? It was a crime to help anyone prevent conception. Right to life then meant the right of the male sperm to fertilize the female ovum. From the Vatican through the Roman Catholic Church and many other authorities as well, there thundered the dogma that anyone who took measures to prevent that meeting was destroying life. Of course most of those who made sure the Canadian government did not change the laws against birth control practised it themselves, unless their failure to add to the population every ten months was entirely due to good luck.

Now there's a switch. It's no longer murder to interfere with the unfertilized, only the fertilized. Isn't it rather confusing?

Right to life is a noble ideal. Too bad it never seems to be applied to war.

Isabel LeBourdais comes from a literary family which includes her sister Gwethalyn Graham, her father, Frank Erikson Brown, and her grandfather, D. M. LeBourdais. She is best known as the author of *The Trial of Steven Truscott* (1966), and that year she was voted Woman of the Year by the Canadian Press. "Instant People? Of Course!" was first printed in *Chatelaine*, November 1973.

JUNE CALLWOOD

Unfolding as They Should

Four of the teenagers down the block: likable, thoughtful, and in one piece.

Adolescence is a psychiatric disorder only when the victim is not a teenager. In a 31-year-old, for instance, a state of adolescence is called a nervous breakdown. When a man of 45 has adolescence, the condition is described as the male climacteric, or mid-life crisis. In older people, adolescence is identified either as a search for meaning or as self-indulgence, depending upon the eye of the beholder.

Teenagers, however, are not similarly perceived as people in pain. When they become messy, irrational, depressed, testy, narcissistic and stalled, they are not given mood-brighteners or a leave of absence or something cuddly to take to bed. They are advised instead to knock it off and take out the garbage.

The reason teenagers have such a long and wretched adolescence is that they are too young for it. In the first place, they don't have adequate vocabularies to discuss it. If they could be articulate about loneliness or their need for identity or even about what pimples do to their self-image, they could enlist sympathy and support in their affliction.

But their language and insights are inadequate, scarcely better than the wisdom of Grade 6. They behave among adults like prisoners in enemy hands, giving nothing but their name, rank and serial number; torture won't make them tell where the cavalry is hiding.

The truth is, they don't have a cavalry. The only known cure for severe adolescence is a human support system, rooters; plus some acknowledged talents and skills, enough to keep self-esteem out of the infirmary; and a sense of humour, because humour makes misery tolerable.

The age group newly arisen from childhood rarely has discovered that it has any talent or skills at all. Besides, it is surrounded by non-fans. Accordingly, teenagers laugh a lot but seldom have a good time.

Their messages tend to be non-verbal and revolting. To indicate despair, they slouch. When they feel too tight or so loose that discomposure seems to be setting in, they drink, drive too fast, try drugs, steal something or test out the sporty new genitalia. Occasionally they kill someone, most frequently themselves.

They are so alarming to view that most adults would rather not. This is known as the generation gap.

Some families, however, have such a relatively tranquil time that they wonder if something is wrong. There are thousands of parents of teenagers who don't live with their stomach nerves in a knot, and there are thousands of teenagers who are unfolding as they should, sensible, truthful, independent and appreciative.

To prove it, we found four. Maxine Sidran, a researcher, asked around about all-right teenagers: not the brain banks who do calculus to entertain themselves or the gutsy quarterbacks or the concert hall prodigies, but the teenager down the block who gives the general appearance of being in one piece, the likable one, the thoughtful one.

She asked her own friends if they knew a stick-out kid, which led her to Diane Morrison. A Y counsellor recommended Christopher Prendergast. The Big Brothers knew Nat Hall. And the neighbors were high on Scott Crowley. For tactical convenience only, the selections were all made in the Toronto area.

The teenagers themselves turned out to be distinct individuals, each one totally unlike any of the others. But they had two notable qualities in common: a value system that kept them out of trouble, and affectionate respect for their parents.

The parents had more marked similarities. In the first place, they were intact individuals, reliable, responsible, logical, coherent people who can connect with others. The most distinctive feature in them all was steadiness. Without exception, they said what they meant and they meant what they said.

Further, in every family there was consistency and structure. The four teenagers had known from birth what the rules of the house were, and why; and also that they were not subject to whims. Discipline was administered rarely. Something in the household harmony and expectations seemed to work against maverick moods. When discipline was used – and all parents employed a mixture of grounding plus "a talk" – there was clear provocation; parental behavior

therefore was not inexplicable to a youngster.

In all four households the common clashes of messy rooms, lateness for meals, loutish manners or taking off without permission almost never occurred. The parents were unable to explain why their teenagers were so cooperative; it seemed to happen by itself.

In every family, however, attention was paid. Teenagers could ask for suspension or adjustment of the rules and expect consideration. Parents – even when there was only one – spent time with their children, buckets of it. The housekeeping mothers adjusted their outside activities in order to be at home after school. The mothers and fathers with paid jobs put extra emphasis on the quality of their limited time with their families.

In all four families, the teenagers liked the adults, really liked them. With only minor complaints, they saw them as doing a good job of raising them, and thought of their homes as desirable places to be.

And in every family the adults just happened to have an unshakable conviction that their teenager is a wonderful kid. Not perfect, but without any question wonderful. O happy days.

Christopher Prendergast is 15, which is nowhere. He is too young for almost all important independent activity and too old for almost all supervision. He is waiting the year out in the state of gloomy patience common to those in his predicament. Meanwhile he is getting himself in balance. He is willing to take the consequences of a fearless stating of his views, but the price for losing his temper is too high: he wants to control it better.

The concern that dominates his private life is that he doesn't see in himself any excellence, and excellence is what he wants to possess. He once made a list of his goals: astronaut, neurosurgeon, politician, psychiatrist, psychologist. Lately he's been crossing them off one by one; his present school grades are influencing his options.

He's bright enough, and so mature he's out of kilter with most of his age group, but his marks are only average. He says of himself that he appears to be medium all over. He has no special skills, he's a fair hockey player but no star, and he has only the normal number of unexamined friendships, examined hangups, concerns about his skin, arguments with his mother and loneliness.

"I have a definite fear of a 9-to-5 life," he comments, his big 5-foot-10 frame sprawled on a sofa, one Adidas on the coffee table. "I want to be outstanding, but all the things I want to get into cost money, or else I should have started when I was 5."

That was about when his parents split up. There were five children in the family, the oldest 8 and the youngest a baby. They live with their mother, Starr Prendergast, who waited until the youngest was 4 and then enrolled herself in teachers' college. She teaches Grade 6, and is a breezy, sensible, worried, all-systems-open woman, doing her best with the oldest son, Christopher's brother, who is acting out, and Christopher, who is acting in. It is a demonstration of her practical approach to problems that last year she joined a Y group, Communication for Parents of Adolescents. She needed information and guidance and she was not above asking for it; the bumps that began with puberty had been a jolt.

"My picture of raising kids was that they didn't make waves," she explains with amusement. "They did the right thing, grew up, graduated, and that was

" . . . It was an experiment to see what overpopulation would be like . . . but I can't get them to separate . . . they LIKE it . . . !"

that. My biggest surprise was the change they go through around 12 or 13 when they think they know everything and you know nothing.

"I'm learning a lot. I'm learning they don't fall into a mold. As kids get older parents have to learn to compromise. And that's a shock."

She's no quitter and she *tries*; her children know it. When she's angry she blows her stack and they are free to yell back—and do. And when she's made a mistake, she admits it and suffers their delight. It's a noisy, chaotic, sturdy household, full of warmth, humour and flare-ups. It is, most notably, an honest one.

She says Christopher is the child who most resembles her own style; he looks only mildly skeptical at this. Most of their collisions occur around their mutual proclivity to speak their minds. They used to have fiery encounters but now he deals with her in a style he's developed recently, which is to debate the issue with his considerable powers of cold analysis and then leave the scene before he spoils the effect by getting mad.

His older brother, only 15 months his senior, has a venturesome nature that perhaps has shaped Christopher's more conservative tendencies. Chris is a non-smoker and he's not interested in drugs or alcohol, which are endemic in his age group; he picks his friends among those with similar views.

He's a reliable person. If he is going to be later than he promised, he calls home. He believes in promise-keeping.

For all his concern about being medium and about his temper, he is a rock: you could tie a ship to him. He is amazed that most teenagers worry so much about the opinions of others that they live submerged. "I'm not like that," he says. "I'll say what I think no matter what. I have to live with myself and that's all that matters. I know I have to improve but right now I'm exactly the way I want to be at this age."

He seems to be moody after he's made a mistake. He explains that he's thinking it over, trying to figure how it happened, preparing his responses so it won't happen again. It's the hardest work of all, growing. He goes about the chore the way his mother goes about hers: if it's got to be done, do it.

Starr Prendergast says that no matter how her children turn out she isn't going to *mea culpa* herself to death. "I'm doing my best, I'm setting the best example I know how, and I know what my values are. I hope they take the right direction and make it."

They're both doing their best. It's something to see.

Stan and Dorothy Crowley have been married for 24 years. One child is 20, a woman in college. There are two other girls, one 11 and one 9. And there is Scott, who is 14 and is beginning to believe in his own miracle.

He's been an apprehensive child, uncomfortable with outsiders, unhappy at being compelled to go to Cubs, easily hurt by slurs about his colour. Lately he's been developing some hide and some sureness. Sarcasm, for instance, sometimes works against bigots, but if he has to fight, he can. Also he's finding Scouts a pleasure. His sisters don't bug him as much as they used to. Being 14 feels good, feels like things are going to be all right.

The Crowleys' philosophy of child-raising emphasizes activity. Scott, for instance, takes piano lessons and must practise for one hour every day, like it or not; and he never likes it. He's joined a canoe club, takes odd jobs (such as delivering catalogues) in order to pay for a 10-speed bike, volunteered last August to help at the Olympiad for disabled athletes, plays football, chess, baseball.

In addition to school and homework, which give him no trouble, he's spending a lot of time with his father. On Saturday mornings they go together to the basketball league his father helped launch because there was a recreational vacuum in the community. They bowl together and Scott drives with him to Ontario colleges, where his father is an intercollegiate basketball and football referee.

The Crowleys are motivated towards packing the schedule only in part because they believe a child whose life is taken up with supervised, constructive activities is not likely to be drawn into the self-destructive adrenalin-high pursuits that are alluring to idle, bored youngsters. Their more important objective is to prepare their children for the intricacies of adult life. They feel that school and the suburbs provide a healthy but limited range of muscles for the obstacle race ahead.

"We want him to meet all kinds of people, see all kinds of places," Stan Crowley explains. "A lot of people just have a narrow channel while they're young. When they get out in the big world, it's scary."

Accordingly, the Crowleys subscribe to a variety of periodicals and keep abreast of the less sane world outside their walls. They've driven their children to Washington, D.C., to show them ghettos and to Prince Edward Island to show them green hills.

The hidden agenda is to armour the Crowley children with sufficient poise and accomplishment to weatherproof them against the adversities ahead of them as members of society's most visible minority. The techniques don't come in an instruction kit; they are home-made, individually tailored.

"You can talk about prejudice all your life to your children but it won't prepare them for the moment when it hits," Stan Crowley comments.

It hit Scott and all his sisters around Grades 5 and 6. The unsettling effects of pubescence seem to find an outlet in a vicious pecking at selected targets, the children who are different. Scott came home day after day in shock and pain. His mother said gently, "Stand up for yourself."

Eventually he learned to fight back, first with his fists and now with his quick wit. That recess slaughter of his dignity took the heart out of him for a long time. It is only recently that he has been able to trust his peers enough to have friends among them or to value himself enough to undertake anything independent of loyal family support.

Self-control plays a large part in the Crowley household. Scott is required to show respect not only to all adults but also to his sisters, though the younger two are sometimes a trial. When he's furious, he's obliged to keep it under wraps. He retires to his bedroom where he'd like to slam the door, but doesn't dare. Instead, he punches his bed. Hard.

The Crowleys used to administer spankings when their children were younger but discipline now is verbal, rather heated when Dorothy is offended by her children's behaviour, and likely to be a trenchant resolve-making lecture when Stanley is taking them to task.

The family has never tolerated lazing around, or not coming in at night as soon as the street lights flick on, or forgetting the chores, or being rude, or being messy. All the children are accustomed to the rules; they have been there forever, just as they have always been able to count on their mother to be in her spotless home, or their father to sell insurance to house and dress them handsomely. It is the foundation of their lives—and unshakable.

Scott is a stocky boy, 5-foot-3 and 107 pounds. He's bright, amused, cautious and emerging. He's going to be an astronaut or a pilot. There's no limit to what he's going to do. That's what life at the Crowleys is all about.

Diane Morrison is almost 15 and she's in that suspended stage of growth just before the bobsled hits the chute and nothing can be stopped. She's taken the Donny Osmond pictures off her bedroom wall and replaced them with something neutral—animals. She's announced that she's going to be a vet. She's washing her hair a lot, keeping her crushes and her complexities to herself, biding her time.

She lives in a picture-book family. Look, look, says mother. Here comes father. Here comes Dick. Here comes Jane. See Spot run.

She's Jane. Dick is her brother, David, 18 months older, an assured, articulate, gregarious person. Mother is Ann Morrison, a former nurse, friendly and sensible. Father is Stu Morrison, news editor with a radio station. The part of Spot is played by a black and white short-haired cat named Lovey. They all live in a suburban split-level with ivy growing over the bricks.

But they all are very real. When Stu loses his temper, he yells. When Diane's feelings are hurt, she's morose for hours. And Lovey kills birds.

The household operates with effortless pleasantness. The family has a seamless quality, each member of it enfolded by all the others. It is, however, an illusion, an airy-looking structure that floats on steel pilings. A sense of order was built in long ago; there was routine in the babies' lives, when bedtimes and mealtimes didn't vary much and no meant no, and responsibility in the parents, who shaped their choices around the priority of stability and didn't say no too often.

As a consequence, Ann and Stu Morrison take it for granted that Diane will report home after school promptly or else telephone her whereabouts, that she will be punctual on all occasions, that she will ask permission before making plans, that she will observe the curfew, which usually is 9 o'clock, that her room will be kept reasonably tidy and her bed made.

For her part, Diane is aware that she has space to move. If she wants to go to a school dance there will be a family discussion about it around the dinner table. She'll be consulted about the curfew. When she's feeling grumpy, there is accommodation to her mood. She goes outside with her cat and smooths herself out by weeding her flower patch. Her parents understand that; they wait for her to come around at her own speed and appreciate her when she's made it.

An example of the Morrison style of controlled freedom happened when Diane was in Grade 6. She was attracted to a group of fast-moving, relatively unsupervised classmates who were in the habit of sampling their parents' liquor and beer supplies after school. A teacher drew Ann Morrison aside and said she was worried about the company Diane was keeping.

Ann replied stoutly, "*I'm* not."

It was her hunch that Diane was curious to see how other children lived, children who weren't snuggled under parental wings. The Morrisons conferred and decided to let their daughter explore, within limits: she was forbidden to go into any of her new friends' houses.

Still, it was a nervous winter all around. Once the vice-principal caught Diane smoking in the school. She was so upset by the encounter that she never tried it again. And in the spring she was bored with her crowd. She's in Grade 10 now and many of her friends share her aversion to cigarettes, drugs and alcohol.

She's a tiny person, 4-foot-11½ and 90 pounds. Her father, who was small himself at her age, says it influences personality, makes her chippy, made him chippy. She's defended herself against all comers on this subject: she maintains that it doesn't bother her at all, in fact it's an advantage because "everyone likes short people."

When she was younger she was a bubbling, confident gang leader. That strident scrappy person has withdrawn. The present Diane Morrison is neat, careful, somewhat opaque with people she doesn't trust. She's in a holding pattern right now and betrays the currents within only in an occasional testiness that her father, in particular, finds exasperating.

There is already a family legend about the most spectacular of their clashes. One time she prevailed upon him to play checkers with her, though he detests games. It was an edgy match that she ended abruptly by standing up and deliberately knocking the table over, then fleeing to her room. Her father followed in such a fury that when he attempted to punch the flimsy door open, he put his fist through it.

The Morrisons now find that incident hilarious, and especially the consternation all four felt when it happened. It requires a notable amount of safety and strength for a family to enjoy telling that story and know it is in the context of lifelong love and respect.

Diane Morrison has so much certainty about her own safety that even when she was experiencing weeks of nightmares after watching a film in Grade 2 about a burning house, in her dreams she always escaped. And she always had with her the two objects she cared most about then—an Ookpik and her cat. And her family always escaped. In fact, nothing important burned in her nightmare.

That's safety. That much safeness will last approximately forever, and she knows it.

Nat Hall has covered some uneven ground in his 19 years. His parents separated when he was a baby and he hasn't seen his father since. His mother has held a full-time job since he was born. And while he is intelligent, he failed repeatedly in school and dropped out at 16.

It's a combination of stresses that is more than some young people can bear:
it makes them fragile and desperate. Nat Hall, however, is not a case history, he's a pleasure. He's perceptive, astute, relaxed, genial, open and appreciative: a find.

When he was younger he felt the absence of his father. He didn't seem to know anyone else in the world who didn't have one. His mother contacted the Big Brother movement, which provided him with a pal. They went bowling one day, a Big Brothers outing, and Nat returned to describe how the place was packed with kids. His mother told him, "Nat, every one of those kids has no father. Every one." After that he felt less conspicuous and less anxious, anxious to be ordinary.

He remained a sensitive child, the kind to cringe from a raised voice. He still can't abide being yelled at. When he was in Grade 3 the family moved and he attended a strange school where it was his bad luck to have a teacher given to roaring when angry, occasionally clouting the side of a pupil's head. He never stopped being afraid of her. He failed that year.

He stayed in school for the obligatory eight years more, a trial to teachers who were baffled that he could be so articulate and yet score such appalling marks. He was never tested for a learning disability. He was miserable and discouraged and humiliated for a long time and then he gave up trying. He left in Grade 9.

That's what went wrong for Nat Hall. What went right is his mother, Dixie Hall, and her mother, called Nanny. Dixie Hall set the standards for her son, laying down a routine of chores and considerations derived from what she calls "the old school." When he misbehaved she would sit him down for an earnest talk, explaining why it was wrong and concluding with, "Do you understand?" He sees his grandmother as a contemporary, always staunchly on his side, and unflappable.

He's a lanky 6-foot-3, 155 pounds, deft with his hands, detached and philosophical about his adversities. Despite her disappointment at his school record, Dixie Hall says, "There have been many days when I couldn't be a prouder mom."

She cites as examples Nat's empathy for people in pain. Once when he was about 11 he witnessed a teacher making malicious asides to a black child. The child broke down and wept. Nat got up, found the head of the school and reported it. "That took a lot of courage," Dixie Hall says. "That's what Nat is like."

Nat comments drily, "There are a lot of stupid people like that in the world. It didn't really make any difference."

"Yes it did," his mother flares. "Every bit helps." He grins at her fondly. They are both right.

Dixie Hall is a fighter. She has worked almost all her adult life and despite a skimpy salary in the beginning, she was frugal enough to be able to buy the house she shares with her mother and son. She's now an office manager and Nat works in a garage.

He says he lives at home because it's cheaper, but that isn't it. The fact is he cares deeply for his mother and grandmother. If they're 10 minutes late coming back from a cottage weekend, he starts to feel alarm. He gets his car ready to begin looking for them. They've had their differences, and still do, but because they genuinely like each other it always gets sorted out.

The Big Brother movement matched Nat perfectly with a college professor who has become one of his closest friends. He patterns himself on people like that, men he admires. He's known some good ones.

Some of his peers have tried everything: drugs, brawls, crime, booze, macho sex. Something holds him back, he's not sure what. "I get a feeling in my stomach that says no," he explains.

No one pushes him around on that account. He tells someone leaning on his car to quit it. The other says, "Yeah, you want to make something of it?" and Nat says simply, "No." He stands loose and quiet and after a moment there's no one leaning on the car.

The car is how Nat Hall got back his pride. During those mortifying years in a classroom, Nat was working weekends and saving his money to buy it. It still represents his peace of mind. He is always puttering with it, making it perfect. He would love to tear the engine down himself but he would need to consult a book to do it, so he won't. He still can't face a situation even remotely like school.

That's his only problem now, getting back his confidence. He's working on it and some day he'll fix it.

He can fix anything. Ask Dixie. Ask anyone.

June Callwood began her writing career as a reporter for the Brantford *Expositor* in 1940. Her twelve books include *Canadian Women and the Law* (1973) and *The Law Is Not for Women* (1976). "Unfolding as They Should" was first published in *The Canadian*, October 2, 1976.

EDWARD SHORTER

"Twosies" Marriage

The family circle is diminishing— only two can play.

We all know about the Divorce Revolution. But the current crisis in the Canadian family is much more than just a lot of bored swingers who finally convince themselves that staying together for the sake of the kids, the mortgage, or the parents is no longer valid in the with-it 1970s. The fact is that even couples who stay together are starting to think differently about their marriages, from couples, say, in the 1950s.

The reason is sex.

Sexual gratification has taken on an importance it never before had. It is becoming the basis of marriage, and for many couples, this is like throwing a box of dynamite onto the middle of the bed. Some couples can live with this, others can't.

The sexual revolution that began about 10 years ago has shaken every cranny of Canadian society. We're all familiar with the results. Family life is popping at the seams. Children are staying out later at night and, if you call them on it, there's an increasing chance they'll leave home. The daughter of the family across the street has just moved into a commune with her boyfriend. And two of the men down at the office split up with their wives sometime last year.

One divorced young woman I talked to recently said she felt she had had to make an appointment with her husband to have sex with him. It had to be scheduled for one 15-minute(!) slot a week because they were both so busy, work left them so tired, they had so little time to talk to each other.

"You felt you were drifting apart?"

"No," she said. "I just wasn't getting enough sex."

She wasn't some kind of sex maniac. She was just typical of a whole generation of women (and men, too) who are giving sexual pleasure a higher priority in life than even the stability of the marriage itself. This is the news in the crisis of the contemporary family.

Let us try to understand some of the main forces that have been tearing the Canadian family apart.

Item: Divorce in Canada has climbed by over 300 percent since 1968.

Item: "Immorality" charges against juveniles have almost doubled over the last decade.

Item: Illegitimacy has soared from a piddling 4 percent in 1955 to 9 percent in 1972.

All these statistics point, in their dry undramatic way, to a major shift in our intimate lives. We are traveling from the warm, sheltering nest that family life in the 1950s represented (or, at least, that most middle-class families thought it did) to the isolated couple – sexually entwined, mutually adoring, but cut off from children, neighbourhood and kin.

The last 10 years have seen the wholesale erosion of a form of family life that has existed undisturbed in Canada and the United States for about 100 years.

The first signs of the grand transformation are showing up in the monthly statistical publications of Canada, the U.S. and every other Western nation. Opening my morning mail I've been astounded to learn by how much the divorce rate, or the number of female-headed households, or use of the Pill has accelerated by the time each issue of Statistics Monthly arrives. I've been dumbfounded to see an 18-percent increase from 1972 to 1973 in divorce in Alberta, for example, or a 9-percent increase in abortions in British Columbia, or a 50-percent decline in the birthrate in Quebec. Figures like these are unprecedented in our time.

The couple, primarily a sexual unit, is replacing the nuclear family.

Remember those reducing-pill ads where a lithe young thing steps out of an unzipped fatso body to proclaim her 200-pound weight loss? That's what's happening right now: a hand-holding couple are climbing out of the empty emotional shell that much of North American family life has become.

Consider what was bound up in the 1950s-style nest. There was the couple, of course, happily pecking each other on the cheek as hubby drives off to work. But the kids are in the picture as well, cherished as infants, then loved as they grow up. And they bounce up and down in the backseat during weekend outings, and go along to put flowers on grandma's grave, and sulkily accept being "grounded." Grandchildren arrive as soon as possible after the kids are married (the girl at age 21, the lad at 23), and then how happy everyone is to convene on Sunday afternoons for fried chicken.

This 1950s' nest demanded some sacrifices. The woman, of course, had to stay home, nudging along the kids till they left for college or got jobs with the hydro, and ironing hubby's shirts and hankies.

For the nest to thrive, the kids had to make a point of coming home at dinnertime, of eating Mom's macaroni casserole, and not challenging Dad over questions like "The Communist Menace" or "Why Capitalism is Best." They had to reward with smiles and dutiful kisses a mother who had sacrificed her own ideas of career or self-fulfillment that her children might thrive.

But in the 1950s and early '60s, people were willing to make sacrifices like this because they liked the nest. Then all of a sudden they stopped liking it. And no one knows why. The couple remains but the rest of the nest has gone.

Riding with the nuclear family used to be like taking a train trip, the journey would begin with marriage, in the sense that people wouldn't normally have sex before, at least not until they were firmly engaged. The trip would continue for a long time after the sexual passions of the honeymoon had faded, lasting while the children went on through high school, university or got married.

And the trip would be smooth. The train wouldn't jump the tracks. In the 1950s, divorce was a quite unlikely possibility.

Today the trip is disrupted, starting at the very beginning, with premarital sex. A recent *Redbook* magazine survey showed that over 90 percent of young U.S. women have intercourse before marriage. A good many, it's true, do so only with their future husbands, but a good many have different partners. The women start having sex, on average, around age 15. And there's a 40 percent

chance they'll have had more than one partner by the time they hit 15 (to go by another study).

Since there is no similar data for Canada, we can't say precisely what premarital practices prevail here. But there are indications we are not all that different from the Americans.

One survey of a Toronto high school revealed that a third of all the girls and one half of all the boys had had sex at least once. Keep in mind that these kids are still positively monkish compared to American high school youth.

A dramatic change in sex before marriage has taken place among university students, especially women. According to a recent survey, the number of female virgins at the University of Toronto declined from 62 percent in 1971 to 44 percent in 1974. It's clear that women have been the ones most affected by the "sexual revolution" because the number of male virgins dropped by only 4 percent (from 45 to 41).

For Canadian society as a whole, the main index we have of premarital sex is illegitimacy. It's the teenagers who are still staggeringly naïve about contraception, and the tremendous increase in illegitimacy is largely their work. So, more young people have premarital sex more regularly, and they start earlier in life.

They're also setting up house much more often before marriage than they used to. American data show that by 1974 the number of young men living with "an unrelated member of the opposite sex" was twice the 1970 figure—and there had been an enormous rise from 1960 to 1970.

There are two larger points about this increased sexual activity: First, if two loving individuals are sufficient to set up housekeeping, who needs marriage? All the intimacy, the living together, the enduring sexual ties are now possible outside of matrimony. The family is losing its monopoly on sex.

Second, as courtship becomes so completely sexualized, the partners carry right into marriage itself the notion that the point of being together is sexual fulfillment. If you don't get off on your partner, why would you want to be together at all?

The end destination of the family's journey is changing, too. The 1950s nest radiated warmth until the kids departed at age 21, finally leaving the couple in solitude, some 30 years or so after they had first married. Nowadays the children are taking off much sooner, both physically and emotionally.

I'm not talking so much about joining hippie communes as about a new kind of emotional distance between parents and adolescent children. It's not that the kids hate the parents. The famous "generation gap" suggests the idea of hostility, youth turning à la Patty Hearst against their corrupt seniors. But the generation gap never existed.

What we have instead is indifference, not perhaps to the parents as people, but to their moral, cultural and political views. This amounts less to a "crisis" between the generations than a stand off, a shoulder-shrugging, a blank stare, a walling-off of contact and concern by the adolescent toward the middle-aged. A whole generation of young people from 12 to 20 are withdrawing emotionally from their elders, and finding comfort in the arms – or at the elbows – of their companions and peers. They are spiritually, if not physically, leaving home.

Back in the 1950s a number of studies showed how children acquired their political ideas from their parents; the kids of Republicans were Republicans, Liberals were Liberals, etc.

Now, according to a recent survey by two American academics, the kids get their political ideas from their own friends and the mass media. They may not end up disagreeing seriously with Mom and Dad, but the parents just don't have very much influence in forming their thinking.

Another factor diminishing parents' control is the decline of inheritance. The number of estates passed on to children at the parents' death has decreased.

This is not because parents are growing impoverished, but because they're spending it before they die, on condominiums in Aspen and world cruises and golf carts in sunny retirement villages. There's something left for the kids, of course – a house, some silver perhaps – but not enough for them to get excited about, or fear disinheritance.

Maybe the parents are spending it, because the whole idea of the family as an institution stretching across generations of time is weakening. Or perhaps they're disenchanted with the adolescents as ingrates. Or maybe it's because more and more of us work as employees for large corporations and bureaucracies: we get good salaries but manage to burn through every penny – and thus accumulate little. Whatever the cause, the consequence of the disappearance of the estate is to help jerk loose the adolescents from the parents.

One last sign of parental control is the willingness of teenagers to listen to parental advice about dating. Dating is terribly important, in family terms, because ultimately it determines how the family will be perpetuated, indeed whether the whole group will survive.

What's really interesting is the extent to which teenagers are ruling out any parental voice in their social life.

A survey of 145 Toronto university undergraduates asked: "If you wanted to date somebody of another religious faith, would you listen to your parents' objections?" Nine out of 10 undergraduates said they wouldn't listen at all. Only among Jews was there much interest in parental opinion, and even here, one third said they'd let their hearts be their guides.

Juvenile crimes, too, reflect the disappearance of parental control. In Ontario, rapes perpetrated by juveniles climbed from 4 to 34 in 1973; breaking-and-entering doubled; common assault and "robbery and extortion" tripled. Juvenile delinquencies in general increased from 19,000 in 1964 to 44,000 in 1973.

Many of these offences are related to patterns of family life, in that the kids wouldn't do them if they were home with their parents. The crimes reflect judgements about morality and the rules of the game in society that are totally at variance with the rules the parents tried to teach them. But between 1964 and these dry criminal statistics lie the drug revolution, the counterculture, T-shirts with four-letter words written on them, and benevolent provincial governments that grant welfare to teenagers who leave home.

These kids are going off for good. We aren't going to see them again, or at least not until they marry and start having children when, as a whole pile of studies show, they'll become good friends with us.

For many families, however, these problems never present themselves. The train jumps off the track in mid-journey. The couple divorce.

In 1964 Canada had 9,000 divorces. In 1974 there were 45,000 — a fantastic leap. The chances are now close to one in three that young people marrying today will divorce.

There are various reasons. After World War II, people started marrying at a younger age, and statistically, there's a better chance that people who marry young will divorce. More women are working now than before, and know they can make it on their own if they have to.

But the main reason is the new role of sex within marriage. The late 1960s and '70s have seen erotic gratification win out over all other motives in human relationships. The reason you find a partner is not to relieve your loneliness, or to merge your father's leather-goods store with a competitor's, or simply because "society" pressures single women to couple. It's to achieve sexual excitement. Men once went to prostitutes, and women stewed in chastity. Now neither is willing to accept anything other than "a fulfilling relationship."

Make no mistake: "relationship" means sex. To be happy in life, you've got to get off, find an attractive partner, build a stunning body, have a noisy orgasm.

Taking these attitudes into marriage is like holding a karate match in a china shop. Sexual attraction, by its very nature, is fickle and irrational. Here today, gone tomorrow. Today we "love" someone, by which we mean we are compatible with them in bed. Tomorrow the sexual attraction ends. We can't respond anymore. No one knows why. But the romance fades, and the marriage is over.

The unconstrained orgasm has become, if not the purpose of cohabitation, at least its most coveted adornment. The Happy Hooker best-sells her secrets. *Everything You Always Wanted To Know About Sex* answers the questions we were always afraid to ask Dr. Norman Vincent Peale.

In this atmosphere you'd have to be crazy to settle for anything less than total, permanent sexual fulfillment. And if your partner of the moment can't supply it, then so long . . . .

Perhaps this is a bit extreme. But there's no doubt divorce rates have been climbing for marriages for all durations, whether of three years or 23 years. And there's no doubt that sexual discontent is a major factor in many breakups.

The seeking-out of adulterous relationships is one final sign that a marriage is misfiring sexually. It used to be that one women in 10 had had an extramarital affair by age 25; now, according to the *Redbook* poll, it's one in four.

Partly, the *Playboy* mentality has encouraged a lot of men to think themselves unhappy with their wives in bed. But the really revolutionary factor is the wives' sexual discontent with their husbands. For a long time women were resigned to lifeless, mechanical, indifferent sex if they could preserve the nest. "My husband was not the kind of man who really likes women," one woman reported in a survey. "He would do his thing on top of me, and then just roll off and go to sleep." She realized what really good sex could be when she met a man at summer school, then left her husband (but did not live happily ever after).

Another man we talked with said he had been completely happy with his sex life: by and large he controlled his wife in bed, but couldn't understand why intercourse was becoming less and less frequent. A headache or something. He was absolutely dumbstruck when she left him for another man. "I guess she wasn't getting off on me."

We asked a group of people, married around 1929, what had attracted them to their partners. A few replied money or social standing, but most said mutual attraction, or interesting personality, or some other meeting-of-souls formulation. We asked a similar group of university students today what they would look for in future partners. And I was astonished how many—men and women alike—responded "physical attractiveness," "good bodies," or some other phrase indicating how central they felt sex to be in a relationship.

Even for those already married, the quality of sexual experience in marriage has been changing. To go by a recent American survey, couples now have sex more than they used to: up from 1.9 to 2.6

times a week, for example, for couples in their twenties. They have become far more adventuresome, indulging in oral-genital or anal sex. And the percentage of women who report that they regularly have orgasms has increased.

Clearly the sexual aspect of marriage is intensifying. But precisely this intensity makes many uneasy. They ask if they're performing up to snuff, or whether they're being gypped by their partners. When things start to go badly in bed, the end is in sight.

As long as sex works, the partners are delighted with their loving relationship. They revel in Eros, squirreled away in their little apartments. Neither relatives, nor friends, nor neighbours are welcome in the emotional intimacy of this private world. They are not a family, merely two people united by a common sensual interest. It is the triumph of the couple.

Of course, emotions are still, and will continue, to be much involved in the couple-marriage—the whole domain of feeling and sentiment, of mutually compatible minds and spirits and interests.

But increasingly the bed becomes the forum for all this mutual affection and tenderness, the magnifying glass through which all the diverse sources of emotional energy are focused into one white-hot burning dot. When that dot dims or flickers out, the couple stamps their marriage "failed."

They don't realize how they've been victimized by the spirit of the times, by a cultural revolution that has raised in them all the expectation of classic beauty, undying potency, unflagging desire, and eternal happiness. And so, the spirit of the times carries them apart—lonely individuals brooding resentfully at their erotic failure—just as capriciously as it united them in the first place.

"Individuals": the marriage counselors learn how fine it is to be one at social-work school. But mix the desire to do your own thing with the restless sexual urges that our culture has released and you get marriages as stable as the British pound.

Some couples have simply drunk too deeply at the well-springs of individualism. They never flag in the search for maximum personal gratification and, when the promised sensual treats fall short of what the *Joy Of Sex* offers, so little mutual affection holds them together that they part.

I find the one-hour drive into Toronto, where I work, from Barrie, Ont., a depressing experience. It starts when you see that first grey wall of highrise just the other side of the Eaton's warehouse. It becomes worse as you head along Highway 401 towards the interchange with the Don Valley Expressway: the yellow six-storey apartment buildings with their gritty windows looking out on that endless rush of cars. Those were maybe mistakes of an earlier age, you could say, built just after the war when housing was tight.

But there's no doubt that the *pièce de résistance* in this drive—the giant cluster of tall new apartment buildings just where you hit the Don Valley—was built by people who wanted to live there, in couples. Because that's what those buildings are, partly swingers' pads, partly struggling young accountants', partly newly-marrieds'. They don't live with (or near) Mom and Dad. They mostly don't have kids. And the kids they do have will leave sooner than they think.

Looking down on the 401 and the Don Valley are thousands and thousands of couples, happy, in love, sufficient unto themselves, and contentedly cut off from larger circles of community life. What you see in those windows as you drive by is the reflection of the future.

Edward Shorter teaches Women's Studies and the History of the Family in the History Department of the University of Toronto. His book, *The Making of the Modern Family,* was published in 1975, and he is currently working on a history of gynecology and obstetrics. " 'Twosies' Marriage" was first published in *Chatelaine,* November 1976.

LIZ PRIMEAU

The Naked Truth

In which the writer exposes herself to sundry nudists and finds them wanting.

I was brought up in a puritan family where even standing naked in the shower was considered bold. When I was 11, I burst into the bathroom one morning and discovered my father—who had forgotten to lock the door—soaking in a hot tub. In a split second I looked away, but my father's naked, hairy, *accessorized* image was etched forever in my mind.

After he died and we were a family of women, locked doors and private ablutions remained a part of our lives. Pajamas were always worn. Modesty, asleep or awake, was never a stated rule, it was simply understood. The whitest parts of one's body were one's own secret.

I've gone beyond most of that. I haven't had a bath in years and it's much nicer to sleep in the nude. I'd grown to consider myself loosened up a bit, if not entirely free, until one day last summer I drove through the gates of a nudist camp.

Nudism, it had always seemed to me, was just another kooky cult. But then a couple of years ago I discovered that a number of acquaintances, people I'd never suspect, were turning to nudism as a new, liberated lifestyle. Life at a nudist camp was honest, they said. When people take off their clothes, they get rid of a lot of false ideas with them.

So when the invitation to be an observer at a nude beauty contest arrived, I was ready. Except for a no-camera rule,

there were no strings attached: I didn't have to take my clothes off and I could wander the grounds as much as I liked in the interests of learning the truth about nudism. I resolved to get into the spirit of things.

My resolve weakened as I drove past the gates and entered the welcome hut. The man behind the desk was wearing an Expos cap, and Adidas running shoes; he rose and panic overtook me. I looked him straight in the eye and shook his hand. "Welcome to Les Olympiades du Nu," he said, smiling and handing me a guest badge. "Did you find a parking spot?" I stammered no and he came out from behind the desk to direct me to one. As he walked past me his bare stomach brushed my bare arm.

I parked the car and took a few deep breaths. All around me couples and children were strolling towards the disco music coming from the outdoor theatre. Some of them were wearing clothes. That gave me heart and I ventured out of the car and followed the crowd to the beauty contest.

The benches were rough wooden slabs set on concrete blocks. I wondered briefly about splinters before the music went down and the MC appeared on stage. He was wearing a white tuxedo and a leer. "Welcome to the second segment of Les Olympiades du Nu," he shouted into the microphone, "one of the

37

more interesting ones for all you fellows out there .... heh heh .... Judges, poise your pencils, it's the CHEST AND SHOULDERS COMPETITION!!!"

The music went up and then down. "Here's Karen again, our pretty little dancer from south of the border." He breathed it intimately, the microphone close to his lips. "Folks, can't you just tell she's a dancer by the sway in her hips?" Karen offered him a fixed smile and pirouetted stiffly before the judges. The audience whistled and stomped; the judges marked their ballots. Well, so much for the beauty contest. What was *life* like in the nudist camp? I skirted the crowded volleyball court and took the scenic walk to a small waterfall, past trailers with white picket fences and petunias and barbecues. An elderly man in sunglasses snored in a green canvas chaise longue; his wife was hanging out laundry, an apron, with a pocket for clothespins, around her waist.

The path narrowed and zigzagged higher. There was no longer space for trailers, just tents almost invisible among the trees. At the waterfall, a group of teenagers lay naked on the rocks like lizards in the sun, boys and girls together. Twenty feet from them, I divested myself of my T-shirt. I sat for a while and unhooked my bra. No one even glanced my way but I felt like I was doing a striptease at the corner of Bloor and Yonge.

One step at a time. I put my T-shirt back on. I left the waterfall. Halfway down the hill a cocktail party had convened. A portable radio was blaring and people were standing around, drinks in hand, making polite nude conversation. I remembered telling someone once that I was terrified of cocktail parties and she'd said, "There's a trick to it. Just imagine they're all standing there in the nude." I hope she reads this.

After supper I met Bill Flesher. He was fully dressed; even nudists get goose bumps. Bill and his wife Fran run a nudist camp in California, one that holds nude sky diving exhibitions as well as nude beauty contests. They'd been invited to send a girl to this contest but decided instead to come up and check it out. Every year they send at least one girl to the Miss Nude World pageant at the Four Seasons Nature Resort near Hamilton, Ontario, but it's established. Bill doesn't take chances with new ones. "We like to protect our girls," he said. "Nude beauty contests have to be run with dignity, you know."

"But Bill," I said. "Why beauty contests at all? All those terrible jokes from the MC . . . all those visiting voyeurs . . . ."

Bill tried to look patient. "Nudism is like everything else," he said. "Before people can accept it they have to know about it. So we hold beauty contests to attract the public." He fixed me with his brown eyes. "Nudism is a clean mind in a healthy body. Great for kids growing up—they *know* what the opposite sex looks like. Nudists appreciate a beautiful body but they aren't hung up on it. They aren't lunatics, they're liberated people."

My questions were getting to Bill and he was looking a little exasperated. "I have three suggestions for you. First, read some of our literature. I'll give you a magazine that I've just published. Second, experience total nudism. Call up Hans and Lisa Stein at the Four Seasons and ask to spend a day or two there. They have a real classy operation, an indoor pool, sauna and a whirlpool. A good class of people go there. Third, go to see the film that was made at our ranch this year. It should be released this fall and it shows nudism like it is."

Bill pressed his magazine into my hand. Inside were earnest essays: "A Teenager Speaks on Nudism"; "Nudism and Conscience." Delicate questions were deftly answered: "Do men become visibly embarrassed during their first visit to a nudist camp?'' *No, nudist camps are not sexually stimulating.* "What about menstruation?'' *Wear shorts.* Between the essays and the questions, the pages were bursting with cheesecake. There were provocative poses of comely lasses on motorcycles and horses, or perched poolside. Hardly *Playboy,* but definitely hard-sell nudism. "It'll be a collector's item,'' Bill said.

One Saturday a few weeks later I stood on the steps outside the locker room at the Four Seasons, with a very carefully arranged towel over my shoulder. The sun was bright and hot and I felt . . . *naked.* I forced myself to walk, very casually, to the farthest end of the lagoon. I fell on my towel, stomach down. The sun felt good. I rolled over. The sun still felt good. I stood up – *my God, there was a strange man approaching.* "Nice day,'' he nodded aloofly as he passed by. I nodded gratefully and took a few tentative steps without the towel. I was making progress.

Maybe becoming a nudist *was* a liberating experience. There were certainly lots of un-selfconscious people at the Four Seasons, bouncing in the buff on the tennis court, lolling naked in the sun, drinking nude at the bar. "We have 450 memberships here,'' Lisa Stein had told me. "That includes family memberships and singles, about 1,000 people not including children. In this country there are 52 clubs listed, with a total of, I'd say, 50,000 members. And that doesn't include unregistered, private clubs. I've heard there are 10 of them around Montreal alone. Nudist clubs have increased by at least 90 percent in the last 10 years.''

Even if their numbers are growing, nudists haven't come far enough out of the closet to be accurately counted. Roland Senecal, at the head office of the American Sunbathers Association in Orlando, Florida, said their first Canadian affiliate organized in the West in the late 1950s and there are now 16 clubs in Canada registered with the ASA. Total members? Well, he said, maybe 10,000, adding that he knows of 13 private clubs in the East that are not listed with the ASA, as well as an unknown quantity with the Canadian Nudist Federation, a branch of the International Naturist Federation in Europe.

An hour or so later, still standing far enough from people to be a blur, I was beginning to relax. It was time to test myself with strangers. I decided on the pool, the only place where nudity is an absolute rule.

"You float very well. Why don't you try swimming?'' He was sitting on the tiled edge and he wasn't looking me in the eye. "Do you come here often?''

"I'm just trying this out to see if I like it.'' I was relieved to have someone to talk to but flipped over on my stomach fast. "Do *you* come here often?''

"My wife and I are here almost every weekend.'' He nodded at a woman sitting alone at a nearby table. "It's the only place we can be ourselves. This is not something you can do in your back yard – the neighbours may object. Even our children don't entirely approve.''

"What is it about nudism you like so much?''

"It's healthy,'' he said. "It's natural. You get a good tan and you meet nice people.'' He smiled and leaned closer. "But I guess the best thing is no one can judge you by your clothes. I could be a pauper or a millionaire and you'd never know the difference.''

I glanced at his towel – it was thick and expensive looking. At the same time I noticed his wife glaring at me. It was time to dry off. I lay down on my towel on the grass, slitted my eyes and shamelessly compared bodies. There were no obese nudists here, but nobody was perfect either. Voices droned in the warm sunshine: "Miami is expensive and boring. Next year we're trying Cuba." "The Buick starts perfectly . . . it's the *Datsun* . . . ." "My brother-in-law tried that stuff and it turned his hair yellow!" "When the kids are all in school, I'm going back to work. I don't care what Mike says about his income tax." Nudism may be liberating, but sometimes it's like attending an Elks' convention.

The ad appeared in the paper a few months later. FOURTH REVEALING WEEK!" it said. "SEE EVERYTHING YOU HEAR ABOUT NUDIST CAMPS!" Nude female silhouette, legs astride, arms raised: proud animal sex. "ACTUALLY FILMED IN CALIFORNIA'S LARGEST AND MOST EXOTIC NUDIST CLUB!" This must be the film Bill Flesher had told me about, but there was something wrong. It was showing in a theatre that runs films about passionate suburban housewives and promiscuous stewardesses.

The house lights were still on when I slid furtively into a seat. The audience was sparse, mainly men alone. Beside me a young couple necked. The film will never win any awards, but it was nicely photographed. The narrator spoke glowingly about the freedom and beauty of the nude way of life. And there was Bill! And Fran! Dancing nude at the masquerade ball. That must be their daughter . . . and their son . . . there was the nude skydiving. . . .

"What a rip-off," snarled a voice behind me. "Three bucks plus to watch a bunch of families get together in the nude. Let's get out of here. There's some real stuff down the street."

Liz Primeau is a senior editor at *Toronto Life*. She has written articles about Howie Meeker, women and the RCMP, and travel. "The Naked Truth" first appeared in *Weekend*, May 28, 1977.

PAUL GRESCOE

One Kind of Loving

In her life and her novels, Jane Rule is a reasoned and reasonable voice for lesbianism.

Jane Rule was 15, a student in a girls' school, when she learned what a lesbian was. She was reading *The Well of Loneliness* by Radclyffe Hall, a classic novel of lesbian love, when she realized that she was ensnared like the book's protagonist—both of them women locked within 6-foot, slim-hipped, broad-shouldered shells. Jane had always considered her Amazon size and her baritone voice odd but acceptable. Now she was terrified at the prospect of life as an invert, a deviant, a monstrous genetic joke. The words of *The Well of Loneliness* would remain with her, the fear expressed by the main character, the woman named Stephen Gordon: "I shall never be a great writer because of my maimed and insufferable body." Within a year Jane had had her first lesbian affair.

Jane Rule is 30 years older now and no longer as afraid. Her life as a lesbian has brought her happiness, in a loving, sexual relationship that has lasted two decades, and from the beginning her career as a writer in Canada has attracted international respect. The Manchester *Guardian* said of her first novel, *The Desert of the Heart*: "Miss Rule's illumination of this difficult emotional area is very convincing and her writing has a gift for poetically accurate metaphors." In reviewing her latest, *Lesbian Images,* her only non-fiction book, *Ms.* magazine

described her as "the novelist who brought civilizing sense to the heartbreak-and-booze tradition in modern lesbian fiction." Her admirers have included British guidance counsellors, whose journal considered *Lesbian Images* refreshing and inoffensive even for adolescent girls; and 83-year-old Faith Baldwin, the best-selling American author of such relentlessly heterosexual romances as *The Heart Has Wings,* who applauds the compassion and narrative sweep of Rule's fiction.

Within Canada her reception has mirrored the progress of the country's collective psyche, from the repressed early 1960s, through the sexual overkill later in the decade, to the somewhat saner balance of the 1970s—as Canadians make tenuous attempts at accepting homosexuality, male and female, as one configuration of the human condition.

When *The Desert of the Heart* appeared in 1964, a Vancouver *Province* critic tut-tutted, in a review typical of the time: "I learned a lot more about lesbians than I care to know." By 1970 the pendulum had swung so wildly the other way that a Saskatoon farm paper, *The Western Producer,* could write approvingly of her second lesbian-populated novel, *This Is Not for You:* "The author intertwines these unusual characters in this intriguing novel."

Within two weeks, in 1975, a couple of

newspaper reviews revealed how the focus of critical concern has shifted from a concentration on Rule's sexual bias to a consideration of her role as an established Canadian writer. Both reviews were by fellow novelists, neither of whom felt compelled to discuss matters of morality or taste. Marian Engel wrote that *Lesbian Images* brilliantly and critically tells the truth about one kind of loving, and Margaret Laurence, in considering Rule's short-story collection, *Theme for Diverse Instruments,* called her one of the best writers in Canada. Even author Adele Wiseman, who criticized *Lesbian Images* as propaganda that insulted her intelligence, allowed that "Ms. Rule is a virtuosa who sets herself difficult tasks and brings formidable powers of craft and intellect to bear in their execution."

It's her intelligence, reasoned and reasonable, as much as her craftsmanship that makes Jane Rule one of the most acceptable, accessible voices lesbianism has ever had in North America. She is neither shrill nor (in her fiction) propagandizing. Her lesbian creations are no more noble, no less troubled than the heterosexuals who also inhabit her novels. In fact the lesbian narrator of *This Is Not for You* is such a passionless, clenched-tooth character that her creator compares the time she spent writing that book to a prison sentence. Her happiest heroine—in her third and best novel,

"The usual rules, girls? Ace, queen, king, jack . . ."

Against the Season — is a surprisingly well-adjusted unwed mother who likes men.

Her prose is clean and supple and brims with casually located aphorisms that go off like land mines: "What is most tiresome about the dead is having to keep up both sides of the conversation." "Love is the terrible secret people are suspected of unless they're married, then one always suspects they don't." And her detail seems dead on: Agate, the unwed mother, plays Scrabble amid her labour pains — something my wife did before delivering our firstborn. In another place, Rule compares reading too much Colette, the romantic French writer, to having an orgy of rancid maple sugar. Exactly.

A confession: I came to Rule's work so sexually straight that I'd never knowingly spent more than a few moments in conversation with lesbians. Homosexuals yes, lesbians no. My imagination was lettered with the leavings of pop psychology, the sexual distortions of paperback novels and an impoverished vocabulary of street slang like "butch" and "dike." This marks me as unsophisticated, I'm afraid, but no more so than most Canadians. Yet (and this is why I'm confessing) I wasn't affronted, unsettled — or even very titillated — by the tone of her fiction. In her three novels I noticed one four-letter word.

Nearly all her characters, whether hetero-, homo- or bisexual, are richly drawn. Considering her own sex, I can understand if she sometimes invents more interesting females; you don't hear critics complaining that Mordecai Richler writes better about men. She's no chauvinist, though: an initially naïve male character in *Against the Season* grows, in her sympathetic hands, into something of a hero.

This is her strength. Her people are never cartoon figures, never actors in a stock company trotted onto the stage of her novels to play stereotyped parts. Perhaps that's because Jane Rule herself has never been a caricature of a lesbian.

She didn't spring from an emotionally mangled family, for instance. No violent father, no shrinking-violet mother. So happy have her parents been that they could have been lifted from the finale of one of Faith Baldwin's novels. Her mother trained as a soprano but quit to marry Arthur Rule, a salesman with a national building-supply company in the United States. His work kept the Rules on the run, re-settling in new cities around the country. In compensation, Jane's early years had the healthy continuity of family summers on her grandmother's California redwood ranch.

Jane felt cherished. She learned to quilt, she collected animal miniatures, she cared for her sickly younger sister. She was a tomboy too, hunting jackrabbits with a ranch hand, fishing with her father. "I didn't want to be a boy, ever," she wrote later, yet she was always more verbally aggressive than her older brother — a vital trait for a girl forbidden to fight, but forever parachuting into new communities, forced to fend off the taunts of hostile kids. Retreating into friendships with adults, she became estranged from her contemporaries and ignorant about ordinary social relationships. "For years," she recalls, "I read Ann Landers because I had no idea what the world thought."

No signs of her eventual career surfaced during puberty. She avoided books, read at a Grade 3 level in Grade 8. Any writing she did was hampered by her left-handedness, which teachers kept trying to change until she was 12, when her father bought her a typewriter and said: "Tell them all to go to hell and use both hands."

Enrolled in private girls' schools, first in Berkeley, then in Palo Alto, California, Jane finally felt in place, no longer afraid to be big and awkward, active in sports, bright in studies. Her ambition was to be a doctor, but she began composing outraged articles for the student newspaper. One, written when she was 15—lambasting the administration for hiring a charm-school instructor to teach the girls how to walk—got her expelled.

The same year, she looked into *The Well of Loneliness* and saw her own reflection. Alarmed, confused, asking sympathetic adults about her latent lesbianism, Jane was told that she was simply passing through a normal, harmless phase. However, she should make sure that her first sexual experience was with a male.

It wasn't. "The first love affair I had was with a woman who was married and had children," she told me. "All three of her children are my godchildren. I knew her before her first child was born." In the introduction to *Lesbian Images,* she writes: "I am not sorry that the guilt I carried about my first sexual experiences was tempered with real love rather than with correct heterosexuality. Nor do I regret that there was nothing of conventional pairing in that first relationship, which required of me, instead of jealous exclusiveness, real generosity and love for someone else's husband and children. It confirmed for me very early the value of loving, the awareness of sex as one of the languages for loving rather than either an identity or an act of possession."

She was then less lesbian than bisexual—"but it got so confusing," she says. Any man she attracted seemed to repel her: "The kind of man who wants to build a dynasty and sees in your long, strong back his sons." Just such a man, who dated her when she was 18, is still convinced that she'll come back to him one day. In her early 20s she lived with another man whom she loved—but wasn't in love with. "I lived with him for a couple of months. Drastic, silly, un-

reasonable months. I think it was temporary despair, insecurity—and a fondness for the person."

Though she has never hungered for normal marriage and motherhood, she likes children and worked with them throughout her young adulthood. At 15 she left the public high school she'd transferred to—minus her diploma because she didn't satisfy the gym requirements—and went to work as a secretary in the purchasing department at Stanford University in Palo Alto (her parents had moved to Nevada). Dissatisfied, developing a delayed interest in literature, she entered Mills College in Oakland, California and earned an honours degree in English. While there she taught twice a week at a school for mentally and physically handicapped teenagers. One of the school's successes was a 16-year-old mute and supposedly illiterate boy who learned to use an electric typewriter and suddenly announced to the startled staff, in a typewritten message, that he could read. "He cried," Jane says. "We all cried."

After Mills she went to London, England, to write her first novel, do occasional graduate studies at University College and work as a part-time volunteer with children at a private orphanage.

Back in the U.S. she found a job teaching science and English at a good girls' school in Concord, Mass. And there she met a slight, handsome woman whom she would later call "the companion of all my work." Helen Sonthoff, another English teacher, was married, childless, "and it was very clear very early on that we were very important to each other," Jane Rule says emphatically. She was 23, Helen was 38.

Two years later, in 1956, Rule came to Vancouver to help a male friend move and decided to remain amid the sea and the mountains. Sonthoff arrived a couple of months later, on holiday, and stayed. They bought a house and began living together in a relationship that, now that I think of it, is seven years older than my own with my wife.

By then Rule had decided writing was her being. She'd already apprenticed her way through dozens of unpublished short stories and two unpublishable novels. "The first novel was everything I knew. Then I added 50 pages because it wasn't long enough. It was terrible — poetic, symbolic, all very murky with deep feeling." *Who Are Penitent* had a lesbian theme and Rule didn't even bother to look for a publisher. For her second novel, quite heterosexual, she couldn't find a publisher.

To keep up the house payments, she worked as an adviser to foreign university students at a social centre, and in 1958 joined the University of British Columbia's English department, where Sonthoff was already teaching. And she kept writing. She even sold short stories to *Redbook* magazine. They were short stories about young married couples with station wagons and conventional sexual habits; when her agent asked how she could write about them with such understanding, Rule replied: "I shop at Safeway."

She started work on *The Desert of the Heart.* To absorb the flavor of its Reno setting, she spent six nights there as a "change apron" in Harold's Club, breaking bills for the gamblers, and made more money — up to $50 a night — than she has ever made since. On her fourth night the floor boss told her: "You keep going like this, young woman, and you'll be a dealer."

Rule, wandering the club with thumbs in pockets and elbows akimbo to ward off pickpockets, watched with shrewd eyes and later drenched *The Desert of the Heart* in this sort of detail: "The young man had to guard his machines from tourists who did not understand that, in the etiquette of gambling, to put hands on another man's machine was a greater offence than to put hands on his wife."

The group of women working in the club, she says, was among the most intelligent she'd ever met, two of them models for characters in the book: young Ann, a sometime cartoonist who works as a change girl with the older Silver, a hulking bisexual woman with whom she has a casual affair. Enter Evelyn, a middle-aged English prof in Reno for a divorce. She falls in love with Ann, who calls herself "a freelance lover," and they walk out of divorce court together into the sun, determined to try to live happily ever after.

That was too much even for *The Lesbian Feminist,* a New York newsletter, which remarked: "The novel's ending [is] too neat, reminiscent in its rather melodramatic, Reno courtroom setting of the very soap-opera-*Redbook*-magazine mentality Evelyn criticizes in her landlady."

Lesbians lucky in love were hard to place. Twenty-two publishers in the U.S. rejected the book before Macmillan Company of Canada agreed to a joint publication with a British firm in 1964, and an American company published it a year later (it has just been reissued in hardcover in the U.S.).

When she knew the novel was appearing, Jane approached her parents with the manuscript. Though she and Helen had been discreetly honest about their relationship, she'd never discussed her lifestyle with her mother and father. No, they told her, the subject of the book would not bother them. "I think you are very courageous," her father said. Never has either parent tried to pressure Jane to marry or have a family (both her brother and sister have kids).

Perhaps the most dumbfounding fact of Jane Rule's life has been its virtual lack of tension. For at least a dozen years she has been publicly identified as a lesbian yet she has tasted little of the contempt she feared. After *The Desert of the Heart's* publication a UBC faculty member did challenge her reappointment as a lecturer because he said he suspected she was a lesbian, but he was voted down. The book also spawned scores of desperate telephone calls to its author from across the continent, from lesbians who found it a positive oasis of understanding.

Jane Rule has tried to resist the tightrope role of spokeswoman for such a diverse movement. Several years ago, when she used her living room as the site of a 12-week seminar on lesbian lifestyles, she learned how divided and defensive a group of lesbians can be. "There were well over 50 women," she says, "and nobody qualified as a lesbian. If you were a monogamous couple into raising dogs out in the country, you had no political consciousness and therefore you weren't a true lesbian. If you were living in a commune and doing demonstrations, you were just political and using lesbianism as a tag, just exploiting it. If you had a woman lover but were also married, the fact that you had something to do with a man meant you weren't a lesbian. If you had a child – no way. It was one of the saddest things I've ever seen in my life. And the only thing I could figure out was that each one of those persons had felt so beleaguered that her own choice had to be the only one."

As the seminar progressed, Rule sat in what she calls her Archie Bunker chair, made a reactionary speech and insisted on formally refereeing the meetings. "It was *my* house," she says, "and I was left every week to clean up the psychic blood that had been spilled."

Just as she sidesteps unnecessary strain in her life, she avoids tension in her fiction – which is my major criticism of her work. There's an evenness, a monotone to her plots. Even in a dramatic scene, as when a minor character in *The Desert of the Heart* slashes her wrists, Rule immediately telegraphs to the reader not to worry, the woman will be all right, don't get excited. "I don't like being defined by tension," she explains. "There's plenty of plot in life that distracts you from really seeing what's going on. That need for tension in order to concentrate your attention on something is what I resist in living."

When I met Jane Rule and Helen Sonthoff two years ago at their home on lush Galiano Island, between Vancouver and Vancouver Island, I was struck by the sheer harmony of their existence. They live in a cedar Pan-Abode with Scandinavian furniture, *New Yorkers* on the tables, John Korner, Jack Shadbolt and Gordon Smith paintings on the walls, homemade wine in the cellar, and the only sign of militant womanhood is the upraised fist of Women's Lib adorning the back of the toilet seat. I felt more peace there than in the homes of many married couples.

When I returned recently, their life was fuller but now it was fraught with a new tension. *Lesbian Images* had been heartily received, was well into its paperback sales, and another of Jane's novels, *The Young in One Another's Arms,* was to be published in March. Helen at 60 was retired from UBC where she had lately been a member of the university senate. They had sold their Vancouver house to live full-time on the island. But last spring Jane suffered a sudden attack of arthritis that left her bedridden for days, and now she was forced to wear a neck brace to support deteriorating discs in both her neck and back. She worried about whether she could maintain her writing schedule of up to five hours a day, seven days a week.

They met me at the floatplane dock on a glistening fall day, Jane in a corduroy jacket and slacks, her full face punctuated with squarish glasses and bracketed by short hair, standing taller than the smiling, silver-haired Helen.

We talked about *Lesbian Images*, which in its accounts of a dozen lesbian writers (including Radclyffe Hall and the bisexual Colette) refuses to accept lesbianism as either a sin or a sickness. The book is devastating in its criticism of psychoanalysts—"misguided, misinformed and morally biased"—so I was surprised to hear that its author had been seeing a Freudian psychiatrist. "I don't think I would have gone to a 'psychiatrist'—in quotes," she told me. "I went to her as a friend." The woman psychiatrist helped her to a revelation: why was she working at two full jobs at once, teaching creative writing and lecturing at UBC, as well as writing? She, along with Helen Sonthoff, is now retired from the university.

As we talked about how the public climate has changed, softened in its response to lesbianism—"*Lesbian Images* would not have been published 10 years ago," she said—I realized that she might have helped alter that climate.

I remembered the day I met her a couple of years before. We'd sat over scotch and as the afternoon ebbed, I no longer looked at her as A Lesbian, nor as a woman in a man-sized body. I was reacting to her purely as a *person*, with emotions and desires independent of sex, and I understood (in a circumlocution of logic helped along by the scotch) that this is why the lesbian characters Jane Rule creates are so sympathetic: they are, most of all, human beings.

Born in Winnipeg in 1939, **Paul Grescoe** has been a western-based writer-editor for *Maclean's* and *The Canadian* as well as a regular freelance contributor to *Saturday Night, TV Guide,* and *Canadian Business.* He is now editorial director of both *Alaskafest,* a magazine produced in Seattle for Alaska Airlines, and *Vancouver Magazine,* of which he is part-owner. "One Kind of Loving" was first printed in *The Canadian,* December 4, 1976.

JOHN PARTRIDGE

McMaking It

From sweeping floors to Hamburger University, the steps of a successful McDonald's licensee.

He is an aggressive retailer with a strong personality who creates a niche for himself and his McDonald's within the community. The job requires a great deal of hard work . . . . But for those who put forth the effort, the financial returns and personal sense of accomplishment will be extremely gratifying – Ray Kroc, founder and chairman of McDonald's Corp., on the successful licensee.

It's 7 a.m. as Rick Hession eases the 1976 Thunderbird onto Highway 401 at Kingston. He drives fast but confidently, lounging back into the seat, one hand on the wheel. He's 32 years old, six feet tall, 175 pounds. He has medium-length blond hair and boy-next-door good looks.

Hession is the owner-operator of two McDonald's restaurants, one in Kingston, the other in Brockville, 50 miles east, where we are heading for an 8 a.m. crew meeting – a combination performance review, training and goal-setting session.

I'm here to spend the weekend with Hession, to work in one of his stores in order to find out what he went through – and why – to get to where he is today, a licensee of possibly the most successful fast-food chain ever.

The Big Mac belt buckle Hession wears proclaims his loyalty; the leased T-Bird and its array of pricey options

proclaim his business success. And he is both loyal and successful in ways cynics have long considered old-fashioned. To them, he'd likely come across as an overgrown boy scout imbued with such antique virtues as a belief in fair play, team spirit and the work ethic. Even to the less cynical, Hession's apparently unquestioning acceptance of every aspect of the McDonald's system at first seems just too ingenuous.

Item: "I'm so thrilled to be a McDonald's licensee that if I hadn't been able to raise the money for a franchise, I'd be working for the corporation."

Item: "Being involved with McDonald's is a little like a religious experience. You really do feel exhilarated by what you see going on around you."

Certainly it would be easy to dismiss such comments as self-serving eulogies calculated to enhance Hession's stock in the franchise sweepstakes at McDonald's head office, particularly when further conversations reveal he's highly ambitious. But it wouldn't be fair. Hession's loyalty and enthusiasm are real, vouched for even by his competition. And they're not unusual in the McDonald's fold.

The degree of success he has achieved, on the other hand, is unusual even by McDonald's standards. In 1974, its second year of operation, his Kingston store set a system-wide record for the

largest sales increase in one year—up 81% to more than $1 million. This, added to his high-profile involvement in community sports and charitable work (which the company preaches so loudly that only a brave man would ignore them), won for him the much-coveted Ronald McDonald Award—named after the corporation's clown mascot—as top Canadian licensee.

Hession is, in short, very much a golden boy of the Golden Arches. He's also a dedicated achiever who'd likely make a go of any business to which he turned his hand. Certainly he appeared earmarked for success at Facelle Co., Toronto, where, after graduating with a B.A., he rose in seven years from rookie salesman to product manager. He left Facelle because, he says, a lot of corporate infighting was going on. He preferred to devote his energies to battling in the marketplace. He wanted control of the action. He had some misgivings, though. "I was 26 years old, but I looked 22. Who the hell was going to put their business in my hands?" Instead he decided to buy someone else's idea—a franchise.

He explored many operations, talked to franchisees of various systems, including McDonald's—which he at first rejected fearing labour costs would be prohibitive. Closer investigation, however, convinced him this was not the case (they run at about 20% of gross sales)

and, when he saw an ad for McDonald's licences, he took the bait.

It took Hession six months to put together the $125,000 financial package—$75,000 up front—then needed for a franchise. (These days, it's well over $200,000, with total cash requirements nudging $100,000.) He sold off almost all he owned, including house and cottage, and while he trained with McDonald's, he and his two children were supported by his wife, from whom he has since separated.

He's reticent about the separation and contends that the strain and long hours involved in getting that first franchise on track had no real bearing on it. (Rumblings persist within the system—despite official denials—that McDonald's has a poor record where divorce is concerned.) But he does allow that it was back-breaking labour. "I worked 100 hours a week the first year. I sat down once and added it up because I couldn't figure out why I was looking so rotten."

Now, four years later, his work week is down to about 65 hours. He reckons about 40 of those are divided between his two restaurants and general administration, leaving the other 25 for the community and promotional work he genuinely enjoys. As well as being on the Kingston Hospital Board and a director of the local Boys' & Girls' Club, Hession works with retarded-adult groups and is a fund-raiser for muscular dystrophy. He sponsors annual bantam hockey and baseball tournaments, a senior A hardball team and a team in the local businessmen's hockey league called the McDonaldland Fighting Cookies. "I told the guys," he grins, "that if a bunch of big, bruising jocks like them would play for a team with a name like that, then I'd sponsor it."

Although his two stores provide a good living, Hession would like more. In fact, he'll open another in Kingston shortly. "I think I could probably handle as many as I could get," he says, adding that he's met McDonald's licensees in the U.S. with as many as 38 restaurants. "I'd rather get more stores than have to think about what to do with the money. I don't think ploughing the profits back into bonds or mortgages would be anywhere near as satisfying as putting it into new stores. Nor would any of them return as much on the investment from what I can see." At which point we witness another of life's daily melodramas—an unwary speeder hauled over to the highway shoulder by a policeman in an unmarked car. Hession chuckles: "I think that's dirty. Everybody deserves a fair shake."

I doubt anyone got an entirely fair shake at Hession's restaurant while I was on the shake machine. It wasn't pumping in the syrup or drawing the mix from the machine that caused me problems. It was the Multimixer—the machine that produced the first meeting between Ray Kroc and the brothers McDonald, which in turn begat the empire of twoallbeef pattiesspecialsaucelettucecheesepickles onionsonasesameseedbun. (Consult your children for pronunciation and metre.)

The function of the Multimixer is to blend the shake mix and syrup and whip them to the desired consistency—known in the trade as "secondary overrun." Removing the shake from the spindle re-quires a very deft touch. Doing it too slowly leaves a wasteful amount of mix on the spindle. Doing it too quickly, which I did, produces an even more wasteful phenomenon—wall-to-wall shake. By the time assistant manager Larry Speagle tactfully suggested I might like to brush up on my sweeping skills, I had transformed the formerly spotless shake station and my shirtfront into multi-flavoured disaster areas.

This, I suspect, had some bearing on the comment on my PLOE (Prospective Licensed Operator Evaluation) form that I had picked up things only "fairly well." The remark was certainly no reflection on the teaching skills of Ann, the 16-year-old whiz-kid under whose tender tutelage I had laboured.

Ann was probably as close as humanly possible to McDonald's ideal of the perfect crewperson—smiling, polite, sincere, fast, intensely loyal and attractive to boot. Her first function was to introduce me to the "window." This is where orders are placed, the counter beyond which never-ending lines of voracious people form.

At first I played shadow to Ann as she waltzed her way through the Six Steps: smile at the customer; take the order and repeat it back; prepare the order; present it (arches on the side of the bag facing the customer); take payment; thank the customer. All the while, she gently questioned. Did I understand which bag to use for which orders? In which sequence the items should be placed in the bag? Why Big Macs mustn't be stacked on their sides? (Because the contents might ooze out, which would never do.)

Then I tried. I longed to say: "Hey, people, I don't really work here, I'm just researching a story . . . ." But I knew they wouldn't give a damn. They just wanted food—fast. Time passed. I began to get the hang of it, even survived a couple of minor contretemps over my formerly untried change-making capabilities. I developed an enormous admiration for the "smile, smile, smile" morale of the front-line troops, marveling at their consummate patience in dealing with the grandparents of this world who insist their grandchildren be allowed to order individually no matter how many people are behind them in the line.

I also noted the awesome responsibility of the "production caller." He's the one who decides how many of each item are to be cooked at any given time. He bases his calls on everything from the previous day's cash sheets to the weather and the number of cars driving into the parking lot. Our production caller was all of 18.

Ann next guided me through the mysteries of the fry station, then turned me over to another whiz-kid crewperson at the condiments table. Here, tray after tray of buns came whizzing out of the toasters, all requiring a squirt, squirt, squirt with the sauce, a plop, plop, plop with the cheese, then a lightning two-handed number with the lettuce and the pickles. Phew. So much for day one.

Day two began at 6 a.m. First I helped set up the store for business. From then on I frenetically cooked rack after rack of pies and fish fillets, chopped lettuce and Spanish onions and, in between, swept, mopped and buffed up counters and equipment. ("If you've got time to lean, you've got time to clean.") Stiff and exhausted, I packed up at 4 p.m.—to read with some surprise on my evaluation form that I had not been exposed to "a real pressure situation."

"What you learn here is the right way, not what you're doing in your stores . . . ." Training instructor Rick West is setting out ground rules for the week-long BOC (basic operations course) at the—wait for it—Canadian Institute of Hamburgerology. The BOC is the second phase of McDonald's program for trainee store managers. It's generally preceded and followed by four-week

stints of in-store training and it ends with an exam.

Physically, the institute consists of a large seminar room in McDonald's Canadian head office in Toronto. It's equipped with sophisticated rear-screen projection facilities. There are 19 pupils in the class. Eighteen are trainee managers and assistant managers. They range in age from late teens to late 30s. Five are women. A few are veterans of several years in crew ranks, but most have been "on board," as they say at McDonald's, for less than eight weeks.

The nineteenth pupil is a slightly bemused writer who is struggling to come to grips with a curriculum which includes such esoterica as basic refrigeration, shortening-filtering and lot-and-lobby.

West launches into an autobiographical spiel that dwells largely on the goals he has set for himself and has achieved. Eighteen students then follow suit, with West constantly prodding for more positivity, more confidence, more goals, goals, goals. By the end of the exercise everyone has declared that he/she will be a full-fledged manager before the year is out. It must be infectious; even I am psyched out of my usual taciturnity to burble quite brightly about what I'm doing here.

I'm reminded of Rick Hession during one of the videotape presentations. "As Ray Kroc has said many times," the voice-over intones, "McDonald's is a religion and we are all true believers."

Maybe not quite all. It later becomes clear that at least a couple of the students will be liable for "a recommendation as to termination or rescheduling." This isn't so much because of the 75% pass mark on the daily written tests as because they do not participate enough. That is a cardinal sin.

The rest are blameless angels in this regard—as gung-ho a group as you could wish for, even to the point of rushing out to the nearest McDonald's for lunch and critically comparing it to their own. And keen-eyed—particularly when called upon to evaluate their colleagues' performances. On one occasion, after four students turn in a magnificent pantomime of how to prepare regular hamburgers, a fellow-trainee coolly notes that they forgot the onions on the first six patties. Fearsome.

But whether we were being taught the complexities of the Multiplex carbonated drink dispenser (a "posthead mixing system") or how to troubleshoot toasters, one vital reason for McDonald's success made itself clear at every turn: the company manages to make that old saw "take care of the pennies and the pounds will take care of themselves" a highly motivating force.

Time and time again, Rick West presented us with what I christened—in true McDonald's style—the PLYE or profit-loss-yield-equation. For instance, according to the powers that be, the optimum yield per gallon of soft-drink syrup should be $19.75 in sales. But, West told us, last month the overall average for the 20 Toronto-area stores was only $18.50. "So let's say the average Toronto store uses 240 gallons of syrup per month. That's 4,800 for 20 stores, multiplied by $1.25 in losses per gallon. That's $6,000 per month, or, in a few months, enough to start building another store."

His exposition was greeted with an audible intake of breath, repeated every time the PLYE was calculated. For, as all good managers know, McLogic says more stores mean more money and more opportunities for employee promotion. And there's a specified yield for every product found in a McDonald's—from 15.4 shakes per gallon of mix, down to the fact that one 12-ounce package of reconstituted onion should suffice to season 507 hamburger patties. You even know how much mileage you should get from a specified amount of floor cleanser. And the oft-repeated homily is that if you exceed optimum yields you are ripping off the customer, whereas if you fall below you will not realize the "fair and equitable profit" to which you are entitled.

To understand what McDonald's people mean when they talk about "fair and equitable profit," you should first study the growth the company has undergone in its 21 years of existence.

In 1955, the company's two stores produced sales of $235,000. In 1966, the year McDonald's went public, its 862 stores (691 of them licensed) produced total sales of $219 million, for a net income of $4.9 million. In 1975, 3,706 stores (2,546 of them licensed) rang up total sales of $2,478 million, for a net income of $86.9 million.

But what of the licensees? What do they get in return for their sizeable investment plus the 11.5% of monthly net gross sales—total sales less any provincial sales taxes—they turn over to the company in service fees and rentals, plus the minimum 4% they are obliged to spend on advertising? On top of that, a licence is good for 20 years and one address only and the company owns the land and the buildings. Also, there are rigorous standards of QS&C (quality, service and cleanliness) they must maintain in order not to jeopardize their licences. Even Rick Hession says McDonald's "holds all the cards," though he believes that's the way it should be—his reasoning being that one bad apple can spoil the whole barrel.

Even so, things don't look too rough, particularly for Canadian licensees. Canadian president George Cohon says the average pre-tax profit of a well-run store is 10%-15% of total sales. Last year, total Canadian sales averaged $860,000 per store, outstripping the U.S. average by $130,000.

Among the reasons cited for this lead

over the U.S.: there's less competition for the fast-food dollar in Canada; Canadians have more leisure time; Canadians may have been preconditioned to McDonald's by their travels in the U.S. and by spillover advertising before the Golden Arches crossed the border in 1967. (Interesting timing, when you think about the cultural implications.)

But there's also a fair amount for the licensee above the bottom line. Centralized buying for almost all items, for example: the company says the volume contracts it negotiates for Canadian stores (almost 200 of them and still counting) produce savings to the operator of "approximately 4% of his gross." (It also says the average cost of food and other supplies is about 39% of gross sales.)

It's also difficult to dispute the company claim that "all the advantages of brand identification, uniformity of appearance, menu and service are inherent with McDonald's."

Then there are the vast libraries of multimedia sales, training, marketing and maintenance aids distilled from the collective experiences of nearly 4,000 stores. (It would take an Olympic weightlifter to budge the complete set of McDonald's manuals.) And there's training at the Canadian Institute of Hamburgerology and other regional training centres. (Tuition is free, but licensees must pay for the students' room and board.)

Finally, there's Hamburger University, which is located on the outskirts of Chicago . . .

For a moment, I thought Hamburger University's assistant dean Roy Lewis was being serious when he asked the assembled students to return their pencils on completion of the test because "we do have to get a yield of 2.67 students per pencil." I felt better when loud guffaws greeted the remark. But I also noticed that everyone complied with the request.

For a prospective licensee, there's no escaping the rigors of an AOC (advanced operations course) at Hamburger University. It's taken only when he has completed the minimum requirement of 300 hours' work in a store.

With its Ivy League nomenclature—from "dean" and "faculty" to the "Bachelor of Hamburgerology" degree it confers upon its graduates— Hamburger U. epitomizes the successful mixture of pizazz and pretentiousness which McDonald's has brought to the hamburger business. It is, however, smaller than the name suggests—two gymnasium-sized classrooms, two student lounges, administrative offices and TV and photographic studios where training films are produced. But its modern architecture is impressive. And its trappings of academe undoubtedly do something for the self-esteem of both staff and students, relatively few of whom are graduates of conventional universities.

The AOC lasts 11 days. It covers much the same ground as the BOC but in far greater detail. Equipment classes are graced with the presence of the real thing, whereas in the BOC we'd used slides and filmstrips.

Apart from a sprinkling of new licensees, most of the 131 students in class 218—HU has graduated about 11,000 BHs since it was founded in 1968—have around five years' experience in the system. Does all that McDonald's *esprit de corps* evaporate a little in five years? Not much, I'd say; the class was almost as gung-ho a group as my fellow BOCers in Toronto. Witness, for instance, the ear-splitting din produced during a class on transactional analysis when roleplaying "managers" attempted to find the right ego state in which to deal with roleplaying "complaining customers."

Transactional analysis in the hamburger business? Grown men and women sitting in a classroom discussing motivation through recognition in terms of "warm fuzzies" (positive strokes) and "cold pricklies" (negative strokes)? Yes, and the same grown men and women obediently listen as they are told that, if they don't live up to the "just about perfection" McDonald's advertises, they are in effect lying to customers "who really want to believe, especially after Watergate."

It's easy to laugh at. But it works. And in context—at HU, CIH, or on the floor of Rick Hession's store—it all seems perfectly natural. More than that, it's downright infectious; as most McDonald's people say, it's as much fun as it is hard work. "If it wasn't," Roy Lewis tells me, "I think a lot of us would quit."

And yet something keeps niggling away at me. It's not the philosophical leap I would have to take to devote the kind of effort and energy (110%, George Cohon says) to the hamburger business which, in spite of all McDonald's has done for it, still somehow lacks a certain cachet. No, I could swallow my pretensions—probably for a lot less than 10%-15% of $860,000.

But it is a little hard to reconcile the apparent rigidity of the system with the emphasis Cohon, for one, places on his licensees as "independent businessmen." Would I really be independent in a system where even opting to put the onions on a hamburger before instead of after the pickles is classed as a "market decision"?

I raise the subject with Rick Hession as we head back along the 401 to Kingston. After all, one of the reasons he gave for wanting his own business was that corporate life lacked flexibility.

"Some guys do fight the system," he says. "But to me that's idiotic because they never do as well as the guy who operates by the book. I know I'm not going to invent many better systems than the first 4,000 stores have when it comes to how to run hamburgers and buns or cook pies and fries. So when someone else simply lays it on me, that's fine. It gives me the time to get into the areas that I really want to work in—recruiting and motivating staff, promotion and community work."

But maybe Hession also resolves the issue in a more subliminal way—by what a former Kingston journalist describes as "the irony of treating his McDonald's as if it were so special as to be one of a kind."

Something Hession said to me at our first meeting in Toronto suggests this may be the key. When I asked him for the name of a good place to stay in Kingston, he immediately suggested an independent motel near the restaurant. "Unless," he added, "you'd prefer to stay in one of those chain hotels."

John Partridge is managing editor of the *Financial Post Magazine*. He maintains a part-time career as a member of the bluegrass band, Cody. "McMaking It" first appeared in the *Financial Post Magazine*, October 9, 1976.

DOUG FETHERLING

A Few Uninterrupted Words about Stuttering

It wouldn't bother me as much if you didn't let it bother you.

I am in the wings watching a stand-up comedian on television. He is telling a joke about a man who stutters. The man stutters so badly, in fact, that he has an unnatural fear of elevators – the old-fashioned elevators in which you have to tell the operator the floor you want. In the story, the man has an appointment on the fifth floor of a 25-storey building, and for hours beforehand he repeats to himself the words, "Five, please. Number 5." But when he finally gets to the building he discovers what he knew all along: that he can't get the words out. The attendant thinks him either rude, deaf or aloof – probably some combination of the three – and finally decides that his passenger wishes the penthouse. The man gets off at the 25th floor and walks down 20 flights.

The studio audience found the joke funny (you had to be there) and so did I, but with a difference. I found myself laughing less at the premise than at its familiarity. I too stutter, though far less now than formerly, and spent years fleeing down stairwells, hating myself for my disability. I had forgotten that particular dilemma simply because I'm better now and, besides, elevators these days have buttons. The joke, however, brought to mind similar problems every stutterer will recognize but few others ever consider.

Telephones, for instance. Before dial phones, when one had to deal with an operator, I was practically incapable of making outgoing calls. The operator allowed the customer only a couple of seconds to get out the number – "Atlantic 8000, please" – and two seconds was seldom enough time. Even now, on those days when the old speech impediment wells up, I occasionally have difficulty. Someone I'm calling will say hello and expect an immediate response. If more than a few seconds go by, many people (women especially) will hang up, mistaking me for an obscene caller or heavy breather. By now, however, most friends and associates know better. On those infrequent days, they wait patiently, three, four, even five seconds, inspecting their fingernails until I begin. The same people inform me that, once I start, they have difficulty shutting me up. Would that it had always been so.

Stuttering (a word I prefer to stammering, which is too genteel) is a difficult subject to discuss. For one thing, it's funny. Showbusiness figures, Porky Pig not the least of them, have made it so. Vaudeville comedians such as Rosco Aikes and Joe Cook made their reputations through pretending to stutter. For all that, though, people react differently to stuttering in real life. Stuttering makes the average person uneasy and sometimes impatient. He will struggle to suppress, not delight, but nervous laughter. Given that, it is a difficult subject to write about seriously, though it's serious enough to those who are afflicted.

Part of the problem faced by people who stutter is that the impediment embarrasses them as much as it does their interlocutors, though somewhat differently. No one would argue that stuttering is one of Canada's major social problems. In the dictionary of diseases and disorders it occupies a tiny place. Blindness and deafness, to name only two, are, of course, much worse. That fact, however, doesn't make life easier for the people who, while they're luckier than some, are less fortunate than most. Stuttering is a constant, nagging complaint and it interferes with practically every activity involving other people. Speech pathologists at the Clarke Institute of Psychiatry in Toronto estimate that about 1 percent of the population stutters at some time in their life. The number of adult stutterers is much smaller. It's made to seem smaller still by the way such people have tended, until recently, to shy away from frank discussion. Now both Toronto and Montreal have chapters of the Council of Adult Stutterers, a group affiliated with similar organizations in the U.S. Most stutterers, however, prefer to forget about their problem in the vain hope that others will not notice it. Stuttering is one of the last taboos.

People who stutter severely tend to make jokes about themselves, in an only sometimes unconscious attempt to forestall jokes from others. But that is as close as many come to discussing the subject. They seldom come out of the closet lest they be accused of being in questionable taste or of vying for sympathy. The no-

tion of bad taste is, to my mind, one of the great obstacles in overcoming, if not the disability itself, then the fear that prohibits such adults from dealing with it. It is from that stance, with a view toward spreading the information and adding some bits of personal recollection, that I write.

Like many people I stuttered badly as a child. Unlike most of them, I did not "outgrow it." The idea that the child will outgrow the affliction is the doctor's usual way of reassuring anxious parents. In truth, stuttering, whether in children or adults, seems to have no one cause and, hence, no one cure. In the 18th century it was thought that people stuttered simply because they couldn't remember what they wanted to say. One advertisement from a British newspaper of that period prescribes "pots of ointment from Osburn's toy shop in Fleet Street, also good for *preventing* loss of memory." Later and more commonly, it was supposed that people stuttered simply because they were dim-witted. It is surprising (and infuriating) how widespread that view is today. The belief accounts for the way in which the word "dumb" has come to mean "stupid," instead of simply "mute."

Generally, though, stuttering is taken to be a neurotic manifestation of some psychological disturbance suffered as an infant or small child. This view practically eclipsed all others after Freud came along. It was particularly linked to "primary stutterers," those in whom the disability is first noticed between the ages of 2 and 4, and who often recover. Theoreticians attribute stuttering to various such disturbances; most such talk is speculation. In some cases, stuttering is probably tied to "minimal brain damage"—some minute nodule, otherwise unimportant, somewhere in that part of the brain about which, despite recent advances, not much is really known. (It is significant, for example, that a disproportionately high number of stutterers – but not me – are left-handed.)

That answer, however, does not explain the fact that stuttering is relatively uncommon in females generally and that serious cases are downright rare in adult women. Neither does it say anything much for possible genetic explanations – the fact that, if a parent or older sibling stutters your chances of stuttering are three or four times what they would be otherwise. Nor does it explain a few positive points: that stutterers are far below the rest of the population in suicide and heart disease. Still, the purely psychological view dominates, especially among laymen. That itself is one of the difficulties. To stutterers, at least this one, amateur dinner party psychoanalysts have always been a greater, more constant hazard than the store clerks, bank tellers and service station attendants with whom one daily struggles to do business.

This simplistic answer, while doubtless applicable in many cases, does little to help the sufferer. It only makes the listeners who believe in its simplicity comfortable with their sophistry. It leads others to think immediately that you were reared on the set of a real-life Tennessee Williams play or else that you are a sensitive little flower, given to melancholy, moodiness and sensitivity that is anguished in the extreme. This excessively Byronic notion has been the common one in literature. Writers dealing with the problem usually do so only to show that a character is a romantic misfit. In *Long Day's Journey into Night,* for example, Eugene O'Neill has someone explain away his stuttering by saying that it "is the natural eloquence of us fog people." Nonsense.

The simple fact is that people tend to treat stutterers, if not as emotional basket cases, then as freaks or deviants to be either pitied or indulged, even romanticized. The interpretation in each case says more of the straight person than of the stutterer himself. I learned this in elementary school where, because I couldn't read aloud or recite the daily prayer, I was labelled retarded and either kept from moving to the next grade despite my marks or sent off to special classes for problem cases. I remember trying to point out to teachers their faulty reasoning, only to have my tongue get sore at the roots, as it often was in those days. In the end, I only seemed to confirm their mistaken suspicions.

Later, the effects were to me more pronounced. By stuttering I have foiled job interviews and similar important meetings and nearly blown many others. For years my social life was confined within the boundaries the handicap imposed. And while I cannot state that the impediment has ever got me fired from a job (not that I can prove) it certainly once contributed to that result. At one point in my childhood, I remember, I was considering going to a job printer and having cards made reading I AM A MUTE. I felt that silence would be better than the struggle and at least the silence could be explained deviously. At the time (I was about 11) it seemed like a solution, if not a cure – the elusive cure stutterers often search for.

As a child, my effect upon speech therapists, to whom I was forever being referred by social agencies, was to make them nervous wrecks, while I sat there inwardly calm – but outwardly stuttering and sputtering. Nor did I find much useful in the various treatments recommended in the popular press and referred to in literature. The myth about Demosthenes, who cured himself by practising with pebbles in his mouth and went on to become a great orator, struck me as preposterous. So did such suggestions as learning another language – a feat that, when I attempted it for other reasons, enabled me to stutter in two languages instead of one.

57

...THEREFORE, AS THE RATIO OF STUTTERING PER PERSON IS HIGHER IN MONTREAL THAN ANY OTHER CANADIAN CITY, MY THESIS POINTS OUT THE OVERWHELMING SOCIOLOGICAL DILEMMA YOU HAVE HERE.

J'AI OBSERVÉ QUE LES GENS DE MONTRÉAL BEGAIENT PLUS QUE PARTOUT AILLEURS AU CANADA. J'EN DÉDUIS DONC, SOCIOLOGIQUEMENT, QUE LES MONTRÉALAIS...

STUTTERING, HELL!... IT'S JUST ALL OF US ANGLOS TRYING TO SPEAK FRENCH.

...ESSAIENT DE PARLER EN FRANÇAIS, BOUT DE CRISSE!

In time I came upon biographies and memoirs in which all sorts of unlikely persons of some renown and accomplishment were revealed as former stutterers. While interesting, these did not indicate any clear pattern. For example, Nietzsche stuttered, but then who knows what went on in the mind of that curious philosopher? Michael Arlen the Younger, the American critic, and Joseph E. Atkinson, one of the legendary figures in the history of Canadian journalism, both stuttered well past adolescence. Henry Luce, the founder of *Time* magazine, continued to do so all his life. So did Arnold Bennett, whose tormented speech probably helps account for the fact that he left behind so many letters and journals, without which English literature would be the poorer. The poet Maxwell Bodenheim stuttered because of some injury to his palate, but the ailment seems only consistent with his other woes—he was also lame, tubercular, syphilitic and poor. Somerset Maugham, who suffered all his life, once said that, had it not been for his impediment, he would have become prime minister of Britain. The person to whom he made the statement, Winston Churchill, quickly turned and left the room in disgust.

I mention only a few writers and editors because I am most familiar with them. Revelations of past impediments are strewn through the life stories of all manner of famous people, especially actors, actresses and broadcasters. The difficulty with such books, of course, is that they never quite explain how the person in question managed to overcome the problem. The reason for the omission, naturally, is that there is no valid explanation or magic formula. Many people put more faith than I do in analysis. I have never tried it and now feel no need of it since (allowing for exceptional days) my problem has been reduced to a thoughtful hesitation. Others say that breath control is the key. Still others, noting the obvious fact that no one ever stutters while singing, believe all that is needed is an audible rhythm as background. Some people report success with a small hearing-aid-like device that emits a subtle but steady rhythm in the stutterer's ear.

My own experience is that the problem simply lessens and stabilizes when one overcomes, not some primal trauma, but the long, discontinuous series of traumas the impediment itself brings on. One must strive to make his stutter, in the words of the Irish writer Patrick Campbell, "little more than a diverting characteristic." The better part of doing so, it seems to me, is being self-confident in dealings with people who talk normally. People who are ill-at-ease. People who must at all costs be kept from thinking that your stutter bars you from public life. People who put you down for your stutter when they really want to put you down for your class, background and so on. The major difficulty with which I continue to struggle is that of people who act as though the stutter is in poor taste or is a communicable disease.

This little article, for which I'm being paid $600, will probably cost me many thousands of dollars in work over the years. The common feeling is that, because one has stuttered, he will do so again, without notice and *deliberately,* and so shouldn't be invited to deliver lectures or appear on television or occupy positions of trust. Others like me, or like the worse-off former me, know that that isn't so. It is for them that I stick out my neck (and not my tongue): to show that the ailment gets better as one becomes more in touch with oneself but that the effects of it—be warned—live on in other people.

Doug Fetherling writes regularly for the *Canadian Forum* and *Saturday Night.* His books include *Hugh Garner* (1973), *The Five Lives of Ben Hecht* (1977), and several volumes of poetry. "A Few Uninterrupted Words about Stuttering" was first printed in *The Canadian,* April 2, 1977.

PAUL GRESCOE

Intimations
of Mortality

Irritability, insomnia, loss of self-confidence,
depression, mental lapses—and impotence.

Helmut Ruebsaat was 39, a married man with four children and a flourishing practice as a family doctor in Castlegar. He was also desperate. Castlegar is a small town in southeastern British Columbia and at the time, 1959, Ruebsaat was one of three doctors around. His patients knew what his car looked like, who his friends were and where his favorite fishing hole was—he couldn't escape them. Meanwhile, his marriage was eroding as he and his wife realized their increasing incompatibility. Pressured, he turned to his Anglican religion for comfort and eventually decided to become a doctor-priest, a medical missionary in a foreign country. But his bishop turned him down, suggesting gently that Ruebsaat was merely trying to flee a failing marriage.

That was Helmut Ruebsaat's mid-life crisis.

When he was 40, he moved to Vancouver with his family, resigned to remaining a general practitioner but determined to pursue a quieter career and perhaps repair his marriage. His practice was more contained in the city, his religious faith was less consuming, but the relationship with his wife ebbed even further. After a brief separation, they were reconciled, yet as the years passed

it became obvious that their marriage wouldn't make it. Something else was becoming obvious to Dr. Ruebsaat. By his mid-40s his body was starting to wind down with age, getting fatter, less fit. He had sweats and hot flashes. His temper flared too often. He doubted his own abilities. His sex life suffered. And a psychiatrist said he was in a state of depression.

That was Helmut Ruebsaat's climacteric.

Now, at 56, he is through the worst of it—remarried, a father again, more even-tempered, no longer depressed—but some symptoms of the climacteric, like the sudden sweats, continue. Four years ago a Vancouver writer named Raymond Hull (who'd collaborated with Dr. Laurence Peter on a bestseller, *The Peter Principle*) called Dr. Ruebsaat and asked him if he believed in the male climacteric. The doctor did.

"The term was frowned upon by the medical profession so I didn't call it that," Ruebsaat recalls now. "Many doctors treat people for it but don't call it that because it's offensive to most males—menopause or climacteric or change of life, any of them. Men consider this a womanish, sissifying disorder that insults their male ego. But I became aware that I had actually been treating a lot of people in that crisis without having really sat down and analyzed exactly what was happening. You do it more as part of your daily practice, intuitively, and I hadn't read any scientific studies about it."

He and Hull researched the subject and last year Hawthorn Books of New York published their study for laymen, *The Male Climacteric*. In it they write: "Many men—usually somewhere between the ages of 45 and 60—undergo major physical and emotional changes that produce severe disruptions of their health, their careers and their private lives." The book is a detailed discussion of the causes, effects and treatment of the climacteric, written in almost painfully unadorned prose and with a glossary of medical terms to help the dullest reader. New York socio-journalist Gail Sheehy, in her book *Passages: Predictable Crises of Adult Life*, calls the Ruebsaat work "the first full-length treatment of this subject" and borrowed liberally from it in her chapter on the crises of the middle-aged man.

It's hardly the first-ever treatment of the climacteric, unfamiliar as that term is to most people (the usual pronunciation, incidentally, is cli*mac*teric). As early as the 1940s and '50s, medical journals were publishing articles on the climacteric as a critical age for men. Then, in the 1960s, it faded as a concern while the image of the "male mid-life crisis" replaced it in the popular press.

There's a significant distinction between the two terms. The mid-life crisis involves a man's identity: who he is now and what he might do with the rest of his life. Forty is usually considered the approximate age such self-examination occurs in the male. I had a 40-ish dentist who was unhappy with his long-ago choice of career. "What right," he once complained, "what right did that 18-year-old have to decide that I was going to be a dentist?"

The climacteric comes later in life. Though the name originates in the Greek word *klimakter*, meaning a ladder's rung, meaning a turning point, meaning perhaps the mid-life crisis, it has come to signify something different in current medical jargon. As a word, it's an umbrella under which a host of symptoms sit—psychosomatic, psychological, physical and sexual problems that combine to create a syndrome called "the climacteric." The syndrome was summed up neatly in the book *A Letter to My Wife* by John Koffend, a *Time* writer who eventually fled to Pago Pago, Samoa. Impotent, insomniac, depressed, Koffend writes at one point: "I feel I must knock myself out with Valium: I can't stand my thoughts in the dark. I'm getting old, I'm 53, my hair is mostly grey, the exercises are harder to do now and I don't do them as frequently. I loathe my work (that's not quite true), I hate myself, and I really can't see any way out."

Doctors generally don't like the phrase "male menopause" because it suggests the end of a monthly cycle (the Greek *menos* means month). Well, there's some evidence to indicate that a man may have his own cycle, an emotional one, which may occur on an average of every five weeks instead of a woman's four. Research done at the University of Pennsylvania has shown that men have constant, predictable cycles in which they move from a period of elation to a mood of worry and then back to elation. Raymond Hull, Dr. Ruebsaat's co-author, describes the start of a cycle he experienced: "The symptoms began on the afternoon of Saturday, September 5: alternate hot and cold spells, depression, brief feelings of going crazy, and gain of weight, apparently caused by water retention, because I did not eat more than usual. The symptoms reached their height on Monday and had almost disappeared by the afternoon of Wednesday. During this time I felt unable to think clearly or act decisively. I could do no useful writing, although I did some reading. I did not feel much like meeting or talking to people."

And Dr. Betty Steiner of Toronto's Clarke Institute of Psychiatry makes a definite equation between the male climacteric and the female menopause. They have the same biological foundation, she says, though the hormone loss in a woman happens much earlier and often more suddenly. But men have similar problems to women in their menopause, including hypochondria, hypertension and migraines.

Dr. Ruebsaat prefers to call the male syndrome the climacteric. In his book he spells out the symptoms in diligent detail and in conversation he told me how common some of the physical conditions are. Urinary irregularities: "60 to 65 percent of the men at that age have some urinary problems. They may not recognize them because they come on so gradually." Fluid retention, or swelling: "That's not a very great factor." Hot flashes: "If men admit to them. They usually call it something else. Probably sweats rather than hot flashes. Very common in middle-aged men." Heart symptoms: "Especially in men who don't take care of themselves physically. More than 30 percent of men have them." Peptic ulcers: "Fairly high, about the same range as heart symptoms, maybe a little less. And perhaps not ulcers as such, but stomach ailments: spastic colon, swallowing difficulties."

Perhaps the classic symptom of the climacteric is impotence. In a paper called *The Crisis of Middle Age,* Dr. Steiner points out how impotence can move from a one-act farce to a full-blown tragedy. A man may drink too much one night and, feeling amorous, fumble his attempt to make love to his wife, failing even to have an erection. "His wife may try to reassure him that it is not important, but the man's masculinity, his primitive basic need, is threatened. The next time intercourse is attempted, both

the husband and wife are concerned that impotence should not occur again. The partners become anxious and are now spectators rather than participants in the act, with the result that impotence may recur and a vicious circle is established." Dr. Steiner says the man may develop a Don Juan complex, retreating into affairs with other women. Or he may start suffering the tired businessman's syndrome, pleading fatigue to his wife – "Not tonight, dear."

In the introduction to *The Male Climacteric,* Raymond Hull records an example of his own impotence. A woman friend visited him at his country cottage, taking along her nightgown and toothbrush. That night, after a pleasant dinner, they retired – to separate bedrooms. Hull was deeply disturbed that the woman didn't arouse him, and he was embarrassed to discuss it with her. She went home the next day, leaving behind the nightgown, which Hull sheepishly mailed back to her.

The climacteric's other mental and emotional symptoms may include irritability, insomnia, loss of self-confidence, moodiness, depression and a lessening of a man's mental abilities, his powers of memory and concentration. These mental lapses, Dr. Ruebsaat writes, may happen in part because of fluctuations in hormones, those chemical messengers in the blood that stimulate activity in the body's cells.

He believes that hormones, in many cases, are the cause of a man's impotence and loss of libido. The doctor distinguishes between the two, incidentally: "There's a lot of men with a lot of libido who can't get it up, and the other way around too: there's a lot of men who get erections but couldn't care less." Ruebsaat writes that for 85 percent of men aged 45 to 60, any change in their hormone level is hardly noticeable. But the rest do experience a sudden dip in their hormone level. He admits, however, that this isn't necessarily a factor of middle age: much younger men can suffer from the same problem.

Still, he told me that he treats some of his own patients with hormones – and that's where he and many other Canadian doctors disagree. Dr. Gregory Brown is a professor of psychiatry at the University of Toronto and head of the neuroendocrine research section at the Clarke Institute where he studies the influence of hormonal substances on the nervous system. Dr. Brown believes in the concept of the male climacteric. But he argues that the hormonal changes in a man seldom appear before the age of 60 and that any decline in the level of testosterone, the major male hormone, is most noticeable in the 70s. "The climacteric doesn't usually start until the late 50s," says Dr. Brown, "and it's gradual." He sees little need to treat younger men with hormones. "It's ridiculous," he says.

Dr. Ruebsaat – who insists that the climacteric can start in the early 40s – has another argument for hormone therapy, one he didn't mention in his book. It's based on fairly new research, he says, that shows that while a middle-aged man's hormone level might not change much, his aging tissues respond less to the hormones he has – so he might need higher hormonal levels to respond normally. (Parenthetically, he mentions that sexual intercourse appears to increase the hormone level in the blood. "Not the sexual desire or the anticipation or the fantasizing but the actual act. So that one could conjecture that with slackening off of sexual activity, there might also be a slackening off of this stimulus to further hormone production. So, employing the old saying, 'If you don't use it, you lose it.' ")

In arguing that older men might need more hormones to respond normally, Dr. Ruebsaat refers to a 1974 study by Dr. Roy Witherington, chief of urology at the Medical College of the Georgia School of Medicine, and by Dr. Robert Greenblatt, the school's head of endocrinology, a Canadian who studied at McGill. In a paper called *The Controversial Male Climacteric,* they conclude: "It appears that the male climacteric is an elusive but real entity that may benefit from adequate hormonal therapy. A skilful blend of psychologic support and testosterone administration can bring about increased

"...BUT MOM, I LIKE WATCHING DAD READ THE PAPER! ... IT'S HIS MOODS AND EXPRESSIONS, THE NUANCES ARE INCREDIBLE ... THE AMAZEMENT, THE FRANK BE-WILDERMENT, THE FELT HORROR THE BRIEF FLASHES OF INSIGHT, THE RARE RELIEF OF A SLIM HOPE REALIZED ... IT'S BETTER THAN TV..."

sexual vigour and a significant lessening of the symptoms common to many men who are approaching middle age."

Men *approaching* middle age? That would seem to support Dr. Ruebsaat's theory that hormone problems can arise in some men at a much earlier age than experts like Dr. Brown believe normal. But when I spoke to Dr. Witherington, he suggested that he and his colleague didn't really mean exactly what they had written. He agreed that few men younger than 60 have any hormone problems—either in the amount of hormones they have or in the way their tissues respond to hormones. He also said that most of their middle-aged male patients haven't had true hormonal deficiencies. "Hormone therapy probably works as much for its anabolic effect—for its protein-building effect—and it would work on anyone at any age." Perhaps 20 percent of their patients with sexual troubles don't respond to hormone therapy, he says, because their problems are psychological.

Other doctors, however, believe the finding of American sex researchers Masters and Johnson, that fully 98 percent of all sexual problems are psychological in origin. The danger in overselling the idea of hormone therapy, says Dr. Brown of the Clarke Institute, is that hormonal changes in a man are such a minor cause compared with the social and psychological ones.

Even Dr. Ruebsaat doesn't like to give his patients hormones unless absolutely necessary—and unless combined with other treatment. He tells the story of a contractor who works from his home and couldn't turn down new business. The man wanted higher doses of hormones to cure his impotence, but Dr. Ruebsaat told him he had to change his lifestyle too: "Get an answering service. Go to bed early. Give sex a priority in your life rather than doing it after the 11 o'clock news." The contractor, with the help of

his wife, is trying to reshape his life and it seems to be helping, his doctor says.

Doctors are hesitant about administering male hormones because they tend to cause high blood pressure or fluid retention in patients who are already prone to such conditions. And occasionally an increase of hemoglobin gives them ruddy faces. However, the most worrisome hormone-induced condition is cancer. "If a man already has [latent] prostate cancer, I wouldn't give him hormones," Dr. Ruebsaat says. "That would probably provoke the growth of it. But it will never *create* the cancer."

Besides hormone therapy, *The Male Climacteric* has a battery of advice for the man who suspects he has the syndrome. The first suggestion is to fill in the book's charts, which list a range of symptoms from "rarity of erection" to "self-delusion." The reader reports how long he has had any of the conditions, their severity, their cycle, whether they're getting worse. The book warns: "Don't fall victim to the medical student's disease (*morbus clinicus*) and experience nearly all the symptoms you've read about."

If a man feels climacteric, Dr. Ruebsaat advises him to see his doctor, taking the completed charts with him. Again, a warning: "You may find that your doctor does not accept the existence of a male climacteric at all. Some don't . . . . Don't worry: it does not matter what label is put on your condition."

That raises an interesting point. Why bother with the term "climacteric" when a doctor could treat a patient's individual symptoms without labelling them with the whole syndrome? There's an obvious comparison: why bother using the word "menopause" for a bunch of symptoms of the female change of life? Dr. Ruebsaat considers "the male climacteric" a convenient catch-phrase to use as a general diagnosis, and one that prompts a doctor to treat the whole man instead of his separate, ailing parts.

For instance, if a middle-aged man complains of impotence, his condition might be considered as one symptom of the climacteric. In that case, Dr. Ruebsaat says, "we should treat the organic changes that can be treated, we should try to prevent further deterioration of his system by giving this man a lifestyle and nutrition style and a balance of rest, recreation and work that this man has never had before. And we are compelled to see both him and his sexual partner—which we don't usually do. We are compelled to give him a complete physical—which we don't always do when we treat his symptom. We are compelled to find out whether the man is in a job situation that is destructive to his health."

Impotence is only one symptom that might demand this whole-man treatment. The man could come in complaining of an ulcer. "And if we just treat the symptom of an ulcer or an angina pectoris or a prostate problem, he ends up getting an electrocardiogram done, getting his prostate ripped out and getting a few pills thrown at him—and then we leave him in his misery." By using the broad diagnosis of the climacteric, a doctor might get a man talking about other problems he'd normally never discuss.

General practitioners don't always have adequate backgrounds to deal with sexual problems—in the past, few medical schools spent much time on the subject—and they don't always have the time to counsel a man who may be climacteric. Dr. Ruebsaat himself has trimmed both his patient load, accepting few new patients into his practice, and the time he spends in the office, working only four days a week. He's taking his own advice, being married more to his wife and family than to his work.

His brow is permanently corrugated with worry creases, but he looks fit for a 56-year-old. When I saw him, he was tanned and relaxed, having just returned from a camping trip in Hawaii. He seems to have achieved some peace in his second marriage, to a woman 12 years his junior.

His living room wall is hung with his own oils. His other hobbies are more physical: swimming, scuba diving, skiing and cycling. To reduce the tensions of middle age, he has taken up Transcendental Meditation. Slightly overweight, he blames his seven extra pounds on his background. He came to Canada from Germany in 1951 and, as he says, "I'm still trying to shuck off some of my European delicatessen habits." He follows a high-fibre, low-cholesterol diet—no white bread, for instance, and no ice cream.

What the doctor is doing is what he advises the reader of his book to do. To put it simply, he says the middle-aged man should take it easy, take care of himself and take stock of his life. "He must recognize and change the attitudes and situations that are producing stress in his life. This may require the adoption of new moral, social and economic values; it may require the discarding of perfectionist or excessively competitive work methods; it may even necessitate a change of job or a move to an entirely new environment." A man may need the advice of a psychiatrist, Dr. Ruebsaat says, but the most important treatment will come from within as he helps himself through those critical years of the climacteric.

Paul Grescoe specializes in subjects of social concern, and he has been a staff writer for the Toronto *Telegram's* Showcase section and for the Hamilton *Spectator*. In 1978—in attempt to master their own mid-life crises—he and his editor-wife, Audrey, left Vancouver with their two children and moved to Alberta to found two city magazines. "Intimations of Mortality" first appeared in *The Canadian*, September 18, 1976.

ELAINE DEWAR

In Search of the Mind's Eye

In the weird world of ESP, seeing is not believing.

The car wheeled up to the curb at precisely 12 noon Central Standard Time, October 31, 1976. Russell Targ, a six-foot-five physicist with thick sandy hair and Coke-bottle thick glasses, stepped out from behind the wheel. As he walked away from the car, he started his tape recorder. "It's a bright, sunshiny day. In front of me is a huge, silvery building with a white dome gleaming in the sun. It's a circular building with metal sides. It looks like a flying saucer. The target is the 80,000-seat Louisiana Superdome stadium."

Two thousand miles away in Menlo Park, California, a young astrophysicist sat in a small laboratory in the Stanford Research Institute, a pad of paper on his knee. At precisely 12 noon Central Standard Time, knowing only that Targ was somewhere in that time zone, he began to describe what Russell Targ was looking at. His impressions were disturbing. He "saw" a "large circular building with a white dome" that looked like "a flying saucer in the middle of a city." He made a rough drawing of it.

The astrophysicist's drawing of the Superdome and Russell Targ's photograph of it now hang in Targ's lab at the Stanford Research Institute, trophies from a five-year voyage through the looking-glass world of psychic phenomena. They are tangible evidence of an ability that Targ and his research partner Harold Puthoff believe we all share. They call this phenomenon remote viewing.

Remote viewing is the transfer of information from one person to another across cities, across continents. Targ and Puthoff claim we can hook our minds to someone else's and—in some unknown way—see what they see, feel what they feel, hear what they hear. Remote viewing, they say, is the breakthrough in psychic research we've all been waiting for.

Most of us have a schizophrenic attitude towards psychic phenomena. We are fascinated and repelled by the idea of mind-to-mind linkages. We may have experienced a brief, mysterious connection with someone else at some time in our lives, or we have friends who swear they "knew" the precise moment Aunt Harriet passed on in Timbuctoo. While many of us believe that psychic phenomena exist we understand that believing is not the same as knowing. We wait, our experiences on hold, hoping scientists will settle the question for us.

Because of the tremendous implica-

"Don't laugh! He used to be a nuclear physicist."

to weed out many of the cranks and freaks claiming supernatural powers who pour into their labs for testing. Parapsychologists by necessity have also armed themselves with sophisticated double-blind tests to guard against the dreamers in their own ranks, and with complex statistics to bring order out of random psychic occurrences. By 1969 parapsychology as a discipline had learned enough from past mistakes to make it in the big-time of American science. Margaret Mead talked the American Academy for the Advancement of Science into including the Parapsychological Association in its membership.

But just as parapsychologists were winning acceptance by practising a good defence, physicists were taking the offence. In the 1960s physicists noticed that watching an experiment sometimes played a role in its outcome – that human consciousness seemed to influence behaviour of matter at the nuclear level. At the same time new research had painted a picture of a sub-atomic world in which each nuclear particle seemed to affect the behaviour of every other particle; some particles even seemed to move backwards in time. In the bizarre context of the nuclear zoo, psychic phenomena no longer seemed ridiculous, impossible or even far-fetched.

In the last eight years physicists like Nobel laureate Brian Josephson have been nosing about parapsychology conferences and dragging "psychics" into their labs for tests. First-rank physicists like David Bohm and John Hasted of Birkbeck College, London, Gerry Feinberg of Columbia University, and Henry Stapp of Lawrence Berkeley Laboratories have turned their considerable resources and powers of observation to psychic stuff. In 1973 the British journal *New Scientist* took a poll of its readers who are primarily scientists and technicians. Eighty percent thought para-

tions of psychic phenomena, scientists have attacked the question with particular rigour. You don't tear down one way of looking at things and substitute another unless you know you're dealing with something real. Psychic phenomena must be demonstrated in the lab with textbook precision before anyone will take them seriously.

The scientific method is based on two principles. First, to find out how something works you must be able to observe it under controlled conditions. Second, it is not enough to observe something: you must develop a hypothesis, a tentative theory that makes sense of it, that connects it to a body of existing knowledge. The less violence the phenomenon does to accepted theories, the easier it is to convince others you have something meaningful.

Since the 1880s when British physicist Sir William Crookes first tried to coax the paranormal into his laboratory, parapsychologists (people who study psychic phenomena) have been furrowing their brows over the problem of controlled observation.

In all that time progress has been made in only one area. While parapsychologists have not been able to control psychic phenomena, they have learned

67

psychologists were the wrong people to study psychic phenomena. Many even volunteered that "paraphysics" was a more useful way to describe this burgeoning field. Although the lure of psychic phenomena glitters for some physicists, it takes extraordinary courage to join the chase. Psychic research teeters on the brink of the scientific world. While the frontiers are filled with brass rings for the grabbing, one mis-step and reputations that took years to build come crashing to the ground.

Targ's and Puthoff's reputations are as solid as granite, or were before they headed full-time into psychic research. They work for one of the most prestigious research houses in the world, the Stanford Research Institute. The SRI is awash with funds from the American government and military. Since its formation in 1946 SRI researchers have poked their noses into a welter of pressing concerns: classified studies of nuclear-weapon death counts, the 18-minute tape gap Richard Nixon was curious about, and the possibilities of LSD for use in chemical warfare, to name a few.

The SRI stamp on remote viewing gives it a veneer of respectability. Then there's the business of where Targ and Puthoff publish. In 1974 their first report appeared in *Nature* magazine, one of Britain's finest science journals. In 1976 they published in the *Proceedings of the Institute of the Electrical and Electronics Engineers* (the IEEE), a journal read religiously by 150,000 professional engineers and physicists around the world. The IEEE has also published three successful replications of their work with remote viewing, one of them by Dr. Charles Tart, head of the Parapsychological Association.

Their résumés are even better. Russell Targ is 42 and has a B.Sc. from Queen's College in New York. He did two years of graduate work in physics at Columbia University, then joined the Sperry Gyroscope company in Long Island to do research on microwaves and plasma physics. In 1962 Targ moved west to Palo Alto and went to work for Sylvania, a company in General Telephone's orbit, where he invented a high-power gas laser now used in fusion research.

Hal Puthoff, 41, has a Ph.D. in electrical engineering from Stanford University. He worked for the Naval Security Group in Washington and then for the National Security Agency. As a researcher on a computer project known as LIGHTNING he won a commendation for outstanding performance from the U.S. defence department. He holds laser patents and has supervised Ph.D. candidates at Stanford. His list of publications in a cut-throat field is impressive – 28 papers and a textbook on the fundamentals of quantum electronics. His book is used in American graduate schools. When he moved to SRI in 1972 to do more research on lasers he was at the peak of his career.

Targ has been involved in psychic research since he was a teenager. By 1972 he'd developed an ESP-testing machine and had wangled funding from the National Aeronautics and Space Administration (NASA) to try it out. Until 1971 Puthoff was blissfully unaware of the whole field. His interest was sparked by a book called *Psychic Discoveries Behind the Iron Curtain*. He recognized the names of some of the Soviet researchers who had also done good work in quantum electronics. He was intrigued enough to design his own experiment to test a wild theory about communication among plants. He'd already moved to SRI when his proposal caught the attention of a New York "psychic" named Ingo Swann.

Swann claimed he could mentally influence mechanical devices, raise the temperature of thermistors without touching them, and leave his body to travel on the "astral" plane. Swann wrote to Puthoff and asked to be tested. Almost as a lark, Puthoff agreed.

Early in 1972 Swann flew out to Palo Alto. Puthoff arranged a test of his psychokinetic powers on a super-sensitive shielded compass called a magnetometer. Swann walked into the lab, deflected the magnetometer without touching it and to Puthoff's horror and delight described what the machine looked like on the inside. Accurately.

Puthoff was hooked. "Suddenly I had this magnetometer data which I thought was potentially one of the most important things I'd ever heard of in science. I mean the *possibilities*. All I could see was that there was a whole lifetime of physics here in an unknown area." But how was he going to break the news to SRI that their bright new boy wanted to trip the light fantastic with a flakey psychic? While mulling that over he met Russell Targ and astronaut Edgar Mitchell at a Stanford University conference. Targ and Mitchell thought his magnetometer data was terrific. Targ suggested a partnership: he needed a place to do his ESP testing work for NASA. So Targ, Puthoff and Mitchell marched into SRI and laid out a package. Here was this fascinating information: a man's mind could influence a machine. Here was Edgar Mitchell, astronaut, telling everybody that psychic research was important. And Targ had money. The SRI management took a deep breath and said, if you can do a good scientific job, why not?

It was Swann who put them on the trail of remote viewing. He was bored with the ordinary ESP tests, the cards, the dice, the snakey leads and wires on the EEG machines. He asked Targ and Puthoff to bring a set of map co-ordinates to the lab: he promised to describe the places to which they corresponded. Targ and Puthoff humored him on a coffee break and Swann did just fine. They dragged some top secret co-ordinates out of the military. Swann described details of an installation that didn't appear on any maps, items of more than a general topographical interest. He scared hell out of the military.

Those experiments and the work they did with Israeli conjurer and metal bender Uri Geller in 1972 convinced Targ and Puthoff they had something hot. Geller had not been able to bend keys and spoons under controlled laboratory conditions, but he had divined what lay inside a set of closed film cans and had reproduced drawings hidden in various parts of the lab.

A blue ribbon panel, to use Puthoff's phrase, convened at SRI to set up an experimental program. Reputations were at stake: the protocols in these experiments had to be so precise that no one, experimenter or subject, could cheat subconsciously or otherwise. An SRI division director selected 100 targets in the Palo Alto area to remote view. The targets were kept in individual, numbered envelopes in the division manager's safe. Only he had the combination and only he knew the targets. To do an experiment Puthoff went to the manager's office, and with a device called a random number generator, he picked a target. He then left the building (guarded by a knot of other researchers) and drove to the location.

All the targets were less than 30 minutes by car from SRI. Exactly 30 minutes after Puthoff left the institute, Targ started asking the subjects where Puthoff might be and what he might be looking at. The subjects spilled their impressions into a tape recorder and drew images of the target. When Puthoff came back to the lab 45 minutes later, the subjects were taken out to see the site. Each subject did a series of experiments: some did nine, some four. Targ and Puthoff gave the unedited tape transcripts and the drawings to a group of independent judges who had to match the transcripts and drawings to the targets. The series were evaluated statistically to see if the subjects were doing better than chance would allow. The results were spectacular.

Targ and Puthoff reported on one subject in *Nature* in 1974. In 1976 they reported on the results of a group of experiments with six subjects, three of whom had never participated in psychic tests before. Two of them identified the targets. One had seven direct hits out of a possible eight, another had five out of nine. All but one of the subjects scored heavily above chance. They were able to describe details of pedestrian overpasses, tennis courts, swimming pools, formal gardens, city hall squares, drill presses, Xerox machines, computer terminals.

One subject, a southern California photographer named Hella Hammid who is a friend of Russell Targ, did well on these "real time" experiments and then accurately predicted where Puthoff was going to go and what he was going to see 15 minutes *before* he punched the random number generator to get his target. She did that four times in a row.

"The first day," she says, "I closed my eyes and there was this one thing that kept persisting, a red, barn-like structure. And then I had a strong feeling that this was like a stage set, it wasn't real. It was very clear." Twenty minutes later she drove out to the target to meet Puthoff. He was at a miniature golf course. At the spot where he'd been standing while she was recording her images there was a small, red schoolhouse with a peaked roof. "It shook me up. I'd just done something that wasn't in my book. And yet I knew it wasn't just my imagination. I mean there were witnesses there."

The precognitive tests Hammid did have been successfully replicated with others by a professor of psychology at Mundelein College in Chicago. But that doesn't make the results palatable, even to Hella Hammid. "It was mind-boggling to be able to describe something when he didn't even know where he was going yet," she says. "It was ridiculous, not possible, right?"

But it's not ridiculous to Targ and Puthoff. They brought out a quickie book last January entitled *Mind-Reach* to spread the word outside the scientific community. By the time it was published they'd tested 50 different subjects. Remote viewing, they said, worked every time. Their conclusions were not exactly conservative: our description of what human beings are capable of, they said, has to change. Our description of how the universe works, they said, is shallow. From now on our vision of ourselves and our world must include psychic functioning.

The only conclusion their critics draw is that there is something seriously *wrong* with Targ and Puthoff. University of Oregon psychologist Ray Hyman declared their work "unbelievably sloppy" after spending one day with them when they were working with Uri Geller. Hyman now says that Targ and Puthoff are "schizophrenic" and that he'll never believe anything that comes from their lab. *Time* magazine went after them twice, in 1973 and late 1974, branding them as blind Gellerites even though they published nothing on Geller until late in 1975 and went out of their way to say Geller had not been able to bend metal under controlled conditions in their lab. *Time* also raised the spectre of a Scientology conspiracy at SRI since Hal Puthoff was a known Scientologist, as were some of his subjects. Scientologists believe in psychic functioning.

And yet if anyone is involved in a conspiracy it's Targ's and Puthoff's critics. Most belong to the American Humanist Association which has been flailing away at them through its magazine *The Humanist*, edited by State University of New York philosopher Paul Kurtz. Last year Kurtz helped form a sub-group of the AHA to "evaluate the claims of the paranormal." The group, called CSICOP, publish a biannual journal called the *Zetetic* (the skeptic) which roasts those who dare to make paranormal claims. In its pages Ray Hyman recently questioned the statistical procedures used by SRI and pointed out that judges may have heard through "the SRI grapevine" what the targets were and how subjects were doing on individual days. To Hyman and Kurtz remote viewing is so much garbage. But Martin Gardner, member of the AHA, on the board of the *Zetetic,* and one of CSICOP's leading lights, raises the *ad hominem* to new heights. A regular contributor ot *Scientific American,* Gardner wrote a particularly nasty review of *Mind-Reach* for the *New York Review of Books* last March. He called Targ and Puthoff a pair of "bumbling keystone cops, fervently believing, violating over and over again the simplest canons of sound experimental design." He hinted darkly at *Time's* Scientology conspiracy and then ridiculed the forward to their book, written by Richard Bach, author of *Jonathan Livingston Seagull,* suggesting a conspiracy to gull us all.

Targ and Puthoff have been fending off the critics' complaints for the past half hour. They are slumped in the leather chairs in their lab, trying to relax, which should not be hard to do since this room is more like a den than a physics laboratory. There is a deep leather sofa, a coffee table, a basket with plastic flowers, a couple of large tables. The hard blue California sky pounds at the window; the atmosphere inside prickles with resentment.

Targ writhes impatiently. No, the judges didn't hear things through the "grapevine." Some of them disapproved of the project. If there had been any leaks they would have run screaming to management. No, there's nothing wrong with the statistics: they've gone over them with a fine-tooth comb. "Martin Gardner's punishment for a failure in reality-testing," Targ snaps, cheeks flaming, "is that he just might be the last person in the world to discover that psychic functioning exists."

Puthoff, on the other hand, takes criticism in stride. He has cool, he has tenacity. He has the used-car salesman's ability to slough off the foulest smears on his integrity. Questions about the Scientology conspiracy are gently pushed aside. He leans back in his chair, runs his plump fingers through thick black hair and smiles boyishly. "I haven't done anything in Scientology for four years. I really thought Martin Gardner's *Jonathan Livingston Seagull* conspiracy was more charming," he drawls.

"Anyway," says Targ, "I think there were more Jews involved in the experiments than Scientologists. Why don't they assume a Jewish conspiracy?"

The critics, according to Targ, are naïve fools. "If I make a laser and burn a hole through a fire brick with it, there's really nothing to argue about. Remote viewing is like that—the data speaks for itself. If you don't believe it, go out and do it. We believe we are going to change the consensual reality from psychic functioning being impossible to being ordinary. That's what our prediction is."

But Targ and Puthoff aren't waiting for the consensus to settle in its own good time on the side of remote viewing. They've launched a crusade. "We're principally concerned with creating an environment for this research," says Targ.

That's why they've gone wildly public in the last few months, transforming themselves into travelling salesmen of ESP. They've criss-crossed the continent, flogging their book, appearing on TV talk shows, presenting their latest findings at the annual meeting of the IEEE, writing proposals for new projects, writing memos to management on how the critics have got it all wrong again, slipping experiments into their schedule whenever there's a free moment. A reporter from CBS and the journalist from *Weekend* are towed through the lab in tandem. The tour includes a screening of a film made about Targ and Puthoff by NBC. *The National Enquirer* calls once a year.

Selling remote viewing to the public is easy. But Targ and Puthoff must also corral physicists into taking remote viewing seriously. Neither Targ nor Puthoff is a theorist yet they are searching almost desperately for a theory into which remote viewing can be squashed. Targ fervently believes other physicists will follow his lead because they are used to handling bizarre phenomena. "Psychic functioning isn't horrifying to physicists. It's just new data."

Targ may be too optimistic. Making sense of remote viewing is a gargantuan problem. Not only is information somehow transferred from brain to brain, it is also transferred from the future to the present. Targ and Puthoff hope to borrow from the world of electronics to get a handle on what they call the "real time" transfer. For the moment they can ignore the how questions (how brains receive and transmit images) and instead work by trial and error on increasing the quality of the information. But that still leaves the sticky part: what is going on when someone like Hella Hammid describes an event before the event has happened?

Out of the atomic nucleus pours an infinity of possibilities. Nuclear particles, says Puthoff, act as though they are connected to each other even though they are separated by relatively vast distances. There are solutions to physics equations which suggest there are connections in time as well as space. The normal order of cause and effect, the stately progression of events from now to tomorrow, dissolves. Targ and Puthoff's new world is a smirking chaos – anything is possible. But how do they know that the description of the weird things going on in the nucleus apply to the big world, *our* world?

"That's why we're talking to this theorist, O. Costa de Beauregard," says Puthoff. "He feels he can make the connection between the nuclear world and ours and substantiate it." He grins confidently.

O. Costa de Beauregard works for the prestigious Poincaré Institute in France. Targ and Puthoff sing his praises. He has clout. He may write the frontispiece for the French edition of *Mind-Reach*. He also may have the missing link, the theoretical bridge over which Puthoff and Targ can dance into scientific history.

Puthoff, Targ and their colleagues have been squeezing theory out of de Beauregard for the last two days. By the time Puthoff drags him along to speak to the Institute for the Study of Human Consciousness in Berkeley, de Beauregard has been pumped dry. He has also caught a cold. He creaks his hellos in a rasping whisper.

The folding chairs are filled with an odd assortment of physics graduate students from the nearby Berkeley campus, a scattering of psychologists, parapsychologists and other interested parties. Elizabeth Rauscher, a 34-year-old theoretician from Lawrence Berkeley Laboratories (one of the most respected physics labs in the world) is sitting in the front row. She is working out her own theory of remote viewing for Targ and Puthoff and envisions an eight-dimensional universe in which it might find a niche. Philippe Eberhard, head of the experimental high energy physics division at Lawrence Berkeley, is also here. If Puthoff can't convince this sympathetic audience that the theories he's working on are fruitful, he has a fistful of trouble.

Puthoff is California-sleek in white pants, open-necked shirt and camel jacket. He holds a copy of *Mind-Reach* aloft. "For those of you who want more detail," he grins, "this is a commercial. It's got an introduction by Margaret Mead and a foreward by Richard Bach who wrote *Jonathan Livingston Seagull.*"

"Humphhhhhhh," says the audience.

He strides to a blackboard. "Basically, we think we're very far from understanding how remote viewing works. We're being pushed into esoteric avenues. Right now we're investigating an extra-dimensional model that Elizabeth Rauscher is working on. The idea is that three spaces and one time are not enough to explain it. There's complex space and time."

He brushes a clump of hair out of his eyes, his diamond ring flashes and he begins to write Rauscher's equations on the board. He stops, steps back. Something is wrong. "In three spaces," he says, rubbing out one line and scratching in another, "the distance between New York and Berkeley is 3,000 miles. On the other hand, if you add three more spaces and one more time, so that you're working with complex space and time, the distance might be close to zero. You, or your consciousness, might be right next door."

"And you might not," snickers a man in the back row.

"Oh come on," snaps a grey-haired gentleman. "I can't buy that."

Elizabeth Rauscher leaps to her own defence. "We're not saying this gives an answer to *why* remote viewing exists," she says. "We just want to see if it can fit into the normal body of physics. We use complex geometries in physics now."

Puthoff lets her sink like a stone. "I agree with you," he says to the grey-haired gentleman. "It's very far out. So we ask our theoretical physicists to grind out experiments to test it. In the meantime we have another theory we're working on."

He invites de Beauregard to take the floor. De Beauregard rises and turns to face the audience. His lips move. No sound comes forth. He sinks back in his chair and waves at Puthoff to proceed.

"In the equations in physics," says Puthoff, "there are generally two solutions. One set is usually thrown out because there is no data to match it. But our data may change that. Normally, we have a view of things in which causes *precede* effects. For example, you have a rock in your hand and you throw it into a pool of water. The water is disturbed, waves ripple out and the rock sinks to the bottom of the pool. Now in general it can be shown that randomness increases in the universe. But the other solutions to equations already lying around suggest something different. Symmetrical but different. In place of causality we have finality."

He scrawls PHYSICS on the left side of the board, and writes CAUSALITY under it. He writes ANTI-PHYSICS on the right side and FINALITY underneath that.

"If you made a movie of the man throwing the rock into the water and you rolled the film backwards you'd see the rock flying up and landing in the man's hand. If you rolled the film backwards you'd say 'Wow, psychokinesis.' "

"Or you'd say somebody rolled the film backwards," growls a heckler.

Puthoff smiles grimly. De Beauregard's face is a looming red beacon. He jumps up, tugs at Puthoff's elbow and mutters frantically in his ear.

"What he said," translates Puthoff, "was that if you think about experiments over here, under Anti-physics, you have

73

to reverse everything."

"Gee," sighs a pony-tailed fellow in the corner. "Kinda like Merlin."

"The event rushes out of the future and into the past. It's key factor to point out that in the universe we have symmetry by law and a symmetry by fact. The things we are able to observe fall into the physics category. The law of finality reverses everything."

"That may be possible in terms of elementary equations," says Philippe Eberhard, obviously exasperated. "But there's still the problem of entropy and friction. It's easy to empty a bag of flour on the floor, but try to do it the other way around."

De Beauregard grabs the chalk from Puthoff, scurries to the board and scrawls DECREASING ENTROPY. He turns triumphantly. But Eberhard has heard enough. "Mention me as the most skeptical person here," he says on his way to the door.

A few minutes later, the meeting dies in desultory applause. Despite the hard sell, nobody's buying.

Elaine Dewar was the senior entertainment editor at *Maclean's* until 1976. She has contributed to *Weekend,* the *Globe and Mail,* and *Maclean's.* "In Search of the Mind's Eye" was first printed in *Weekend,* July 30, 1977.

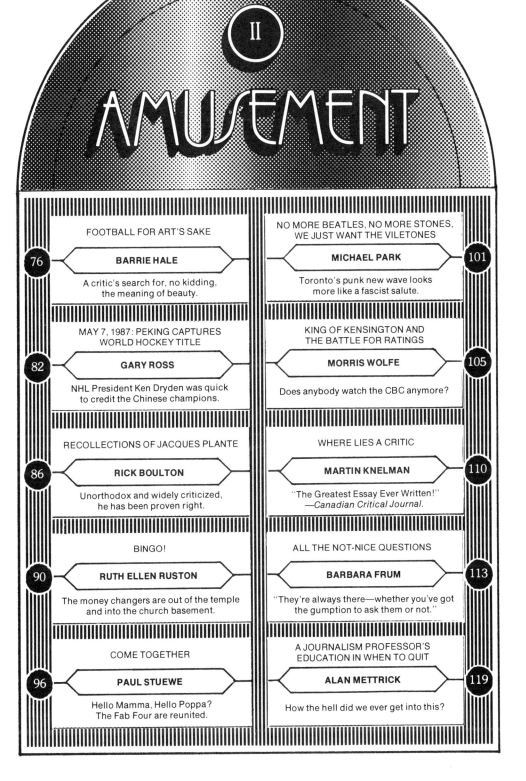

II

AMUSEMENT

FOOTBALL FOR ART'S SAKE

76 — **BARRIE HALE**

A critic's search for, no kidding,
the meaning of beauty.

**MAY 7, 1987: PEKING CAPTURES
WORLD HOCKEY TITLE**

82 — **GARY ROSS**

NHL President Ken Dryden was quick
to credit the Chinese champions.

RECOLLECTIONS OF JACQUES PLANTE

86 — **RICK BOULTON**

Unorthodox and widely criticized,
he has been proven right.

BINGO!

90 — **RUTH ELLEN RUSTON**

The money changers are out of the temple
and into the church basement.

COME TOGETHER

96 — **PAUL STUEWE**

Hello Mamma, Hello Poppa?
The Fab Four are reunited.

**NO MORE BEATLES, NO MORE STONES,
WE JUST WANT THE VILETONES**

MICHAEL PARK — 101

Toronto's punk new wave looks
more like a fascist salute.

**KING OF KENSINGTON AND
THE BATTLE FOR RATINGS**

MORRIS WOLFE — 105

Does anybody watch the CBC anymore?

WHERE LIES A CRITIC

MARTIN KNELMAN — 110

"The Greatest Essay Ever Written!"
—*Canadian Critical Journal.*

ALL THE NOT-NICE QUESTIONS

BARBARA FRUM — 113

"They're always there—whether you've got
the gumption to ask them or not."

**A JOURNALISM PROFESSOR'S
EDUCATION IN WHEN TO QUIT**

ALAN METTRICK — 119

How the hell did we ever get into this?

BARRIE HALE

Football for Art's Sake

A critic's search for, no kidding, the meaning of beauty

One afternoon about 10 years ago, when I was writing about art for the Showcase section of the old Toronto *Telegram,* I was tinkering with a particularly finicky bit of criticism and getting nowhere—the breast-beating among the Showcase staff being even shriller than usual that day. Eventually, in search of peace, I took my problem to the other side of the newsroom, to a typewriter in the sports department. I was just getting into it, spinning a truly devastating analogy, when the sports editor walked in, took one look at me sitting in the middle of his world, and snorted: "I've heard of some wild personnel changes in my time, but this is ridiculous."

What he was trying to get across, in his rough, unlettered way, was that it was unthinkable that any clown who spent as much time as I did looking at *pictures,* writing about so-called artists his kid could paint better than (yeah, yeah, yeah), would know anything about *sports.* Take football—wouldn't know an end-around from his elbow. And there I was in his office. What if word got around? (I could have told him: Listen, I used to *play* the game, Charlie. But he would have just laughed at me.)

It happened to me lots. I would be exactly where I wanted to be, with five, six

other guys leaning against some bar squinting up at the *Game of the Week*—watching, say, Kenny Stabler scramble to pass on third-and-long for Oakland, throwing on the dead run with that peculiar, graceful-awkward left-handed delivery of his, a perfect, beautiful strike to Branch. Thirty-eight yards, first down Oakland. Beautiful. It would somehow come up that I wrote for a newspaper, which was terrific, and then it would come out that I wrote about art—yeah, painting and sculpture, stuff like that—which was considerably worse than suffering the heartbreak of eczema, seborrhea and psoriasis. I don't mean to say that everybody would get up and move away, but there were times when I felt strongly that the guys closest to me would have been more comfortable if I had just, you know, *swished* on out of there and left them alone.

It still happens, with considerable frequency, in the world I normally live in. Long ago, for example, I gave up trying to explain to people at, say, the opening of a one-man exhibition at some gallery that the reason I had to leave so quickly was that I had to get to a TV set and watch this *game.* Game? Yeah, you know, *football* . . . oh, indeed? As I say, I don't bring it up much anymore; if they want to equate football with a certain coarseness of taste, that's their problem. And their loss. My desk, this weekend, is strewn with invitations to exhibitions at a dozen art galleries, as it is at this time every year – the new art season is underway and I have many things to do; also on the desk, however, is Street and Smith's *Official Pro Football Yearbook,* which tells me that this weekend approximately 350 football players in whose fortunes I am particularly interested will be hammering away at each other somewhere. Moreover, the Toronto Argonauts, who must do me as a hometown team these days, are this very afternoon playing the Tiger-Cats in Hamilton. Behind me, the people I am closest to are moving around in the house, wondering what I'm going to do. They halfway know already, and I am preparing to take that look on their faces when I tell them. As often as it has happened to me I am still not used to it, the way the faces of people go all funny when I turn away from so many other things and toward, once again, football, only football.

There are some games that I simply must see, be a part of because I really care about the Pittsburg Steelers, the Oakland Raiders, the Los Angeles Rams and maybe most of all, the Minnesota Vikings. Oakland, partly because I was born there, but only partly. Some of being a fan – a word that is probably a corruption of "fanatic," whose Latin root means, among other things, "inspired by divinity" and which rhymes, imperfectly, with "addict" – has to do with things like that: a sense of place, even if it is not really your place anymore and is three time zones and more than three decades away now. Long before a football franchise was even thought of in Oakland, it was the Rams, simply because they were the Rams; when I was a kid I fell in love with their helmet design. (It was never San Franciso. I tried hard for a few seasons, but I could never get

close to that team, possibly because of the silly name. The *Forty-Niners,* for God's sake; all that dumb grasping after grandeur and tradition that state is capable of, recalling the great day some bubblehead stumbled over a gold nugget on Mr. Sutter's property and set off the Gold Rush – some roots those are.)

Minnesota is dear to me not only because their quarterback is Fran Tarkenton, 15 years a pro and still scrambling around like a Georgia college boy, but because Joe Kapp *used* to be their quarterback. Also because of the Minnesota line, and not just from the day when they got famous by stomping their way to dominance of the Black-and-Blue Division, but from way back when the Vikings first got their franchise and their new coach, Norm Van Brocklin, assessed the capabilities of the first Minnesota linemen: "They're small," he said, "but they're slow." Bud Grant is the Minnesota coach now, of course, Grant the Ice King, one of the few few football coaches I have ever really liked, maybe because of his stoicism, maybe because he is where he is today because he learned what it was all about on our own bleak, cold Prairies. I like Pittsburgh, too, because of their defence, and because it is so improbable that anything nice could ever happen in a city like Pittsburgh. Similarly, I don't really like Regina, but I stand in awe, always have; could those guys play so superbly so much of the time simply because they have had to overcome the dreadful circumstance of actually *living* in Regina?

It also works in reverse: I will go a long step out of my way to watch somebody, anybody, tromp on the Dallas Cowboys. And sometimes a single player will do it. I don't particularly care one way or the other about the New York Jets, but I hold Joe Namath, still working miracles while he hobbles around on knees held together with chicken wire and Silly Putty, in something too close to reverence, I suppose, given the emphatically profane character of the man. But the point is, finally, that it is impossible, not virtually impossible or just about impossible but out-and-out beyond the conceivable, to properly watch a football game without caring, really caring, about who wins or, sometimes just as important, who loses. And I am, I think, a true fan—surly and scornful in defeat, cruel and ungracious in victory.

If so far this has been mostly an American testament, it is largely because I grew up in Vancouver, a city, then and now, only grudgingly Canadian and, especially then, not much of a football town; the models were elsewhere and elsewhere meant the coast. Nothing east of the Rockies; all those people cooking flapjacks on the streets of Toronto during that famous Grey Cup of 1948 had no-

thing to do with us. The high school I went to did not even have a football team; for contact sport, like the inmates of various other institutions of the day that placed such emphasis on the fact that we lived in *British* Columbia, we had English rugby, which is, of course, football's precursor, and a game of fluid incident and constant motion that is nearly as tiresome to play as it is to watch. Nobody much watched, as I recall. Some of us took our ambitions to a new inner-city football league, and I made tackle.

I would make more of the fact that I was a starter at tackle and played both ways most of the time, except that on our team there were only three of us—me, and there were bigger *halfbacks* in that league, and a tall, rawboned kid who would have looked more at home on a

" . . . nobody's speaking to him anymore . . . he's a poor sport . . . the only person in the office who doesn't think the Argos will go all the way this year . . . "

pitcher's mound about the time Ring Lardner was inventing baseball, and the third guy, who was the perfect football build, thick-necked, terrific-legged, heavy muscle all over, except that he had apparently stopped growing along about his 11th birthday. Most of our backfield came intact to the team from a tough downtown high school, and hungover to each Sunday game, still in their party clothes from the night before. Our quarterback was eerily clean-cut even for the 1950s; he *looked* like a football hero, and, on the odd occasions when the rest of the team let him, he played like one.

Two moments stand out in my season with that team. The first was our first practice in full strip, which meant, in that league, when the equipment finally arrived, which meant the last practice before the first game. The line coach tried out various helmets on me, and when he found one he thought would do, put me down in blocking stance, told me to put my head down and charge a nearby tree. Big tree. "You're kidding," I told him, asked him, but he just stood there and looked at me. I charged the tree. "Feel okay?" he asked. "Yeah, coach, sure, fine," I said. The other occurred during a game when the league leaders were trashing us all over a gravelly field in North Vancouver. They ran their fullback over my side of the line as a matter of course, but this time their end ran off someplace, their tackle blocked to the inside, and when this guy got to the hole there I was, surprise, surprise. He didn't pause, he ran right up the front of me like a big squirrel. I grabbed his legs and down we went. They couldn't believe it, so they ran it again; the end disappeared, the tackle blocked in, the fullback came, crash.

"You got hit pretty good out there a couple times," the line coach said to me at half time. "Couple nice tackles." He was stone crazy, of course, but I suppose that is a requirement of coaches. We finished that season with an immaculately mediocre record, third in a league of five teams.

By the time the B.C. Lions came along in 1954, I was fully prepared to be a fan of the kind of team they turned out to be. They won one of 16 league games their first season, and they won that one, I well remember, because a fog bank crept into Empire Stadium from Burrard Inlet late in the second half; it encroached as far as the Calgary 10-yard line, the Lions ran their fullback around end into it, and by the time anybody found him again he was across the Calgary goal line with the ball still in his hands. The next few years, as I made my way out of high school, into and finally through university, things did not get a great deal better for the Lions. Their best season in those days was nine wins and seven losses in 1959—not much to build a love affair on; but it was during those years that I became, irretrievably, a fan.

You may wonder, many people have, how, out of this trashcan of pretence, mediocrity, deprivation and violent farce that was the football of my youth, comes the obsession of my advancing middle age. I am not a jock, as I think I've made clear; I never really was, even though I played, and if you don't believe me ask a *real* jock. To this day, I think of most football coaches, and just about anybody with a crewcut, as being people who properly belong in Marine Corps green with their names in white over their breast pockets like the serial numbers stenciled on the side of a truck. Nor am I a jock-watcher, or hanger-on; most of the people who do the play-by-play of the TV games, for example, I listen to just to keep my anger honed, to *keep up for the game,* as it were. There are exceptions, notably Alex Karras since he joined ABC Monday Night Football. Howard Cosell, to take the other end of the stick, is exactly my idea of the kind of clown I don't want anywhere near me when I'm sitting in the stands watching a game live. Cosell would no doubt say that he is only trying to get at the essence of the poetry-in-action that is professional football as we know it today. He would be close to the truth there, but the thing is, Howard has only *verse* in his soul; the poetry *is* the action.

I am not at all unaware that the whole thing may be regarded as a particularly dubious form of para-military exercise—the point is readily conceded in a sport that has called some of its quarterbacks generals and its defensive backs and linemen soldiers, whose very uniforms are the quintessence of strutting belligerence and some of whose most important events take place in a structure known as the Coliseum. But I don't watch football because I am missing a war, and I don't think many of us do. The violence of the physical contact is basic to the obsession; the sheer physical striving, man against man, that is the basis of all competitive sport, is at its purest and most fundamental in football. And yet it is as formal and complex, in the rules by which it governs the expression of its contentious striving, as chess, which, as we know it (there ya go, Howard) is a product of the Age of Reason. Such ingredients provide the wherewithal for aesthetic achievement, and football, with each play discrete in its beginning and end from the plays that precede and follow it, provides a more abundant ground for the appreciation of such achievement than any other team sport I can think of. (A fully adequate verbal expression of the ideal marriage of form and content has yet to be uttered; it is probably inexpressible, anyway. Better tongues than yours have worked at it for thousands of years, Howard, so shut up.)

I can sense the chokes and gasps out there as the word leaves my typewriter . . . *beauty?* Am I trying to say that all those animals out there stomping on each other, all those clowns in the stands jumping up and down and screaming, are in pursuit of *beauty?* Yes indeed. It is no less than that that has kept our hands groping at the TV set these many long, lean autumns, bereft of any other satisfaction in the enterprise—a winning season, for example—no less than beauty that has even got us out of the house when the only sensible thing to do was pour another drink and turn up the thermostat, to go and sit in the cold for three hours and watch a real game, live.

Most of the autumns *are* lean, for most of us. Only two teams out of nine get to the Grey Cup, only two out of 26 to the Super Bowl, and most of us don't live there. The last really satisfying year for me was 1964, when the B.C. Lions, the Joe Kapp-Willie Fleming-Bob Swift B.C. Lions, came to Toronto fully mature and beat the Tiger-Cats 34-24. *Ten years* I had waited for that game. Beauty? Yeah, sure, plenty of that; for one thing, I will die unconvinced that Willie Fleming (who still holds the best yards-per carry average, 7.1, of the CFL's all-time Top 10 rushers) ever made an unbeautiful move in his life. But beauty, I will admit, was only part of it, or at least I will allow that it was a beauty forged in ambition and contentiousness, like most of the rest of our lives. I wanted the Lions to win, vengefully, because I was from there, I had paid my dues long enough, it was *my turn*; and I wanted them to win with all the violent physicality and urgent striving expended by every player actually on the field—I must have lost five pounds that afternoon, thrashing around my living room in front of the TV set, spending myself in an orgy of empathy.

I tied off the loose ends of a lot of my youth that day, but I remained a fan, sort of an itinerant fan, I suppose, shopping the TV section every weekend for the proper team to cast my lot with. I live in Toronto now, a city that has the kind of football team I am used to—by early September they were three games behind the league leaders and struggling ever downward, but one Sunday afternoon early this season, on a day that was way too cold even for autumn in Toronto, I joined nearly 40,000 other people to watch them lose a game by three points in the final couple of minutes . . . something they had already done too much of. I went in hope of winning, sure; as long as there are 12 guys on your side of the field there is always a chance of that . . . but in Toronto right now that can hardly be *the* reason. There are times when the behavior of their defensive line is a joy to behold, that's part of it, and sacking the opposing quarterback does have a delicious beauty all its own; they also have a back named Doyle Orange who, however forlorn the cause, can be counted on for a couple of runs from scrimmage that satisfy every canon of beauty, and a few more that are at least pretty—another good reason, the best, maybe. But the back, that afternoon, belonged to *them,* Montreal, in this case, a guy named Johnny Rodgers. On one occasion Andrusyshyn kicked a punt directly to him; the ball described its classic arc against the sky, the field stretched level and clean before him, the intervals between the advancing tacklers shifted dramatically every tenth of a second; he gathered in the ball, began to pump his legs strongly, faked with his helmet, his hips, dipped his shoulders this way and that, and the first tacklers were gone. The lane down the sidelines opened for a moment and he ran down it, 56 yards for a touchdown. It was beautiful. So was the Montreal blocking. It was beautiful, but he is *theirs* ; the next time, I hope somebody—Corrigall, maybe—*kills* him, you know what I mean?

Barrie Hale has covered the art scene for a variety of Canadian and international publications. Columnist, critic, and editor, Hale's work regularly appears in *artscanada, Arts Magazine* (New York), *Saturday Night,* and *Maclean's.* "Football for Art's Sake" was first published in *The Canadian,* November 1, 1975.

GARY ROSS

May 7, 1987: Peking Captures World Hockey Title

NHL President Ken Dryden was quick to credit the Chinese champions.

STOCKHOLM—Before the largest audience ever to watch a sporting event, Peking edged the NHL-champion Vancouver Canucks last night to give China its first world hockey championship. The Number One District People's Team, facing elimination for the third game in a row, handed the Canadians a 3-1 loss before a crowd of 55,950 and an estimated 450 million television viewers.

"A lot of work went into this tournament," said Hockey Canada president Alan Eagleson. "I think we've proven that hockey is an international sport—this game was broadcast live in 18 countries. Commercially it was a success. But it burns me up to see a series this important ruined by bad officiating. The NHL will have to re-think its participation next year if the system of choosing officials isn't looked at pretty carefully. The Canucks should have won it all. They got a raw deal out there, let's face it."

"I'm proud of the team," said Canucks' owner Bobby Orr. "A lot of people thought the North Stars should

have been here, but I think we proved that beating them was no fluke. We ran into some bad calls, otherwise who knows? It seems like every time we play outside North America we run into this."

The game was controversial from start to finish. With the first period barely underway, Lin Fun's clearing pass deflected of the referee's skate into the centre ice area. No one was more surprised than Kevin McCarthy, who found himself with a clear path to the goal. He was hauled down from behind by Fun, but play carried on.

Vancouver coach Bobby Clarke protested so vehemently that referee Vladimir Popov assessed the Canucks a bench minor. The game was delayed for several minutes as Clarke threatened to pull his team off the ice.

Shortly after play resumed, Rick Blight had a golden opportunity to give Canada the lead. The veteran right winger picked up his own rebound and had an empty net to shoot at. As he has done so often in the series, C. K. Yang came up with a brilliant save.

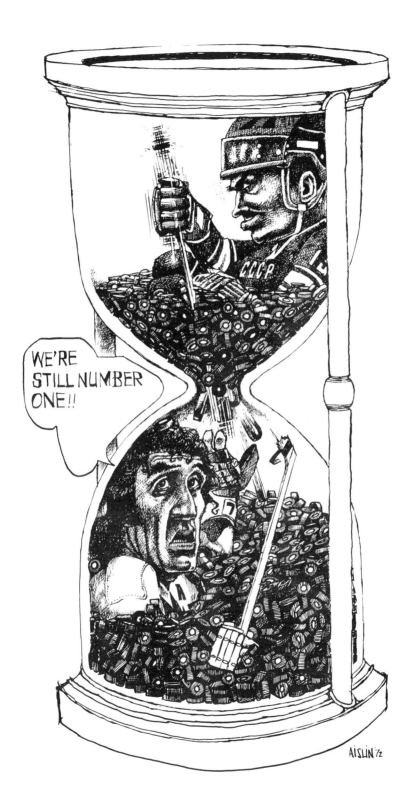

The Canucks scored late in the period, but the goal was called back. After bobbling Mike Gartner's slapshot, Yang dropped to his knees to cover up. The puck squirted loose and Bruce Boudreau, parked on the doorstep, poked it home. Though the red light went on, Popov ruled that the whistle had blown.

The Canucks took a 1-0 lead on Terry Lindsay's solo effort at 2:18 of the second period. Peking came back to tie it up less than a minute later, when Wing Wong took advantage of a miscue in front of the net and beat Pat Riggin for his fifth goal of the series.

Riggin was again outstanding in goal, stopping 16 shots in the second period, including key saves on Peng Chan and You Lee. At the other end of the ice, the Canucks' only near-miss came late in the period with Peking a man short. Vancouver captain Denis Potvin's drive from the point hit the post. Mark Napier was unable to control the rebound with Yang out of position.

The Chinese came out flying in the third period, forcing the Canucks to take three penalties in a row. Only the heroics of Riggin kept them in the game. At one point he stopped four successive shots from point blank range.

The Canucks, playing their 18th game in 24 days, had no answer for the persistent forechecking and precision passing of the Chinese. Wong's line in particular dominated play whenever it was on the ice. Vancouver was called for icing six times before the teams changed ends midway through the period.

At the 12-minute mark, Potvin was carried off on a stretcher after tumbling head-first into the goal post. ''It looked like he sort of lost his balance,'' said Riggin. ''Lum was cutting in on the net, but Denis got back. I didn't really see what happened because I was watching the play. He was going full speed, though, and I could tell he hit the post pretty hard. He went completely limp. At first

his eyes were open, but he didn't know where he was.'' Potvin was taken to hospital with undetermined injuries.

Potvin's misfortune seemed to spark the Canucks. When Chiao Ng went off for hooking at 14:06, the Vancouver power play functioned as well as it has all series. But it was Yang's turn to perform miracles. He robbed Mike Gartner from in close and made a fine skate save on Napier's screened drive from the point.

Then the power play backfired. Wong intercepted Napier's centring pass just before Ng stepped out of the penalty box, and the Canucks were caught with one man back. Wong made no mistake, drawing Kevin McCarthy out of position before sliding the pass to Ng.

Riggin moved well out of the net expecting a shot, but Ng elected to deke and had little trouble tucking the puck behind the Vancouver netminder. It was the first time Peking had been ahead in the series.

The Canadian players argued to no avail that Ng had been offside at the blueline. An incensed Bobby Clarke again threatened to withdraw his team, and only after World Hockey League officials negotiated with Clarke and Hockey Canada president Alan Eagleson did the game resume.

Vancouver went all out in an effort to get the equalizer, but Wang, named the tournament's most valuable player, was equal to the occasion. With a minute left in regulation time, Riggin was pulled in favor of an extra attacker. The Canucks did everything but send the game into overtime. Then, at 19:51, Wong's rink-length shot found the empty net, sealing the game and China's first world hockey title.

Peking coach Tai Dop Cheung called his team's victory gratifying and well-earned. ''We believed we would win,'' Cheung said through an interpreter. ''At no time during the tournament did we lose faith. We were behind in the series against Moscow also. Hockey is a collective sport. Each player contributed equally to the victory.''

Cheung was asked if he had made strategy changes after losing three of the first four games. ''The Canadian team is strong,'' he said. ''We knew to win we must prevent goals. Opportunities arise when a team plays according to plan. Our players knew they must concentrate on defence. The Canadians have many outstanding scorers. To win we must stop them. This was the strategy at all times.''

NHL president Ken Dryden expressed disappointment, but was quick to credit the Chinese. ''There's no question that they've improved considerably,'' said Dryden. ''We saw that at Prague last year. We saw it here in their victories over Moscow and West Berlin. The Peking team skates as well as any team I've seen. If they have a weakness, it's the work of their defencemen in their own end. But what they lack in size, they seem to make up for in mobility. Offensively, they have no weaknesses that I can see. And Yang played superbly tonight, as he has all series. I'd say that he made the difference. I'm personally disappointed, of course, both at the outcome and at the number of disputable calls. But we scored only 12 goals in seven games, and it simply wasn't enough.''

Clarke, who has been critical of the officiating throughout the series, was less charitable in his assessment. ''The guys play their hearts out, and we lose it like this. Nobody expected us to get this far, but the guys came up with a big effort. When we came back to beat Oslo, that gave us a real boost. But how can you win against a team like Peking *and* the referee? I've seen brutal refereeing, but this was a joke. Losing's never easy. But losing this way is really tough. I'm proud of the team. The guys have got nothing to be ashamed of. I'm not saying Peking didn't play a great game, but in 20 years

of hockey I've never seen so many bad calls. No way.''

''Sure I'm upset,'' said defensive coach Tom Bladon. ''We have them on the ropes and they come back to beat us. Maybe we got a little too confident after winning the first two. We has a good first period, but Yang kept them in there. In the second and third we came out flat. I guess they were just hungrier than we were. There were some bad calls, but we missed a lot of scoring opportunities. You've got to take advantage of your opportunities. I don't mean to take anything away from Yang, but we were our own worst enemy. We let up, and you can't let up against a team like Peking. I thought we outplayed them overall. I still think we're a better team. But that's not what the record book will say.''

Gary Ross is a senior editor at *Weekend Magazine.* He has published fiction and poetry in a couple of dozen magazines etc. —*Saturday Night, Malahat Review,* and has written a novel, *Cold Water,* which is now in search of a publisher. "Peking Captures World Hockey Title" was first published in *Weekend,* May 7, 1977.

LOOKIE THERE, HOLY JEEZ, GOSH DARN, YIPEE-OO aye!

AISLIN 77

RICK BOULTON

Recollections of Jacques Plante

Unorthodox and widely criticized,
he has been proven right.

Jacques Plante was hockey's great innovator. He was an honors student of the game, had a brilliant grasp of its dynamics and revolutionized two aspects of goal-keeping: he pioneered the use of the face mask and popularized leaving the net to play stray pucks (when attacking teams fired the puck around the end boards. Plante whirled to intercept it behind his net; today, of course, the play has become standard goal-keeping procedure). In his 24 years as a pro (he retired for good in 1975) Plante became an authority on the habits and traits of opposing forwards. Between games he brooded over his game, fretted about how to polish and improve it. In many aspects of hockey he was ahead of his time.

In the early 1960s, for instance, Plante said that hockey players were under-coached. He wasn't referring to the kids in the peewees—he meant the pros. He asked how one man could know all there is to know about offence, defence, back-checking, passing, playing left wing, playing right defence, playing goal. He advocated a specialist goal-keeping coach and said that NHL coaches should appoint assistants, as they do in baseball and football, to specialize in specific skills. That, of course, is becoming the

trend today: New York's Fred Shero now has three assistants: Mike Nykoluk to coach the forwards, Barry Ashbee to coach the defence, Marcel Pelletier to coach the goalies. And Johnny Bower now serves as the Maple Leaf goalkeeping coach as well as assistant to coach Roger Neilson.

Like any pioneer, Plante endured the criticism that he was unorthodox without cause. He was the first goalie to develop hand signals to warn defencemen about an impending icing call. Because he developed a free-wheeling and now widely copied style of net-minding in which he not only ventured behind his goal but as far out as his own blue line, it was said by some that he played to the crowd. Even today, you can still find people who remember him as a showboat for flashing his hands over his head in an extravagant victory sign the moment the game ended. But by and large the fans loved him—and he usually had the last laugh. After playing in a game at Madison Square Garden in New York, Plante said the nets weren't the right size. People laughed. Then officials measured the nets and found that he was right.

He always complained about his asthma, a chronic ailment that led him to switch from defence to goal-tending

86

when he was six years old and playing hockey in Shawinigan, Que. His reaction to Toronto was so severe that he could cope only by flying in just before the game and flying out right after it. No one then was more startled than Plante when he was traded to Toronto for the 1970-71 season. Reminded that Plante found Toronto's lakeside climate bothersome, Leaf general manager Jim Gregory took the precaution of installing him in an apartment in the city's less-polluted north end (Willowdale). In his days with Montreal, he was allowed to stay at the Westbury Hotel, next door to the Gardens, because he swore he was allergic to the Royal York Hotel, where the rest of the Canadiens stayed.

Plante was different. He used to knit to relieve tension, he was an avid reader of historical biographies (Lenin, Stalin, Churchill), a competent landscape painter in oils and so dedicated a cook that he never set foot in a Toronto restaurant while he was a Maple Leaf. He didn't smoke or drink. On the road he roomed alone. In ten years with the Montreal Canadiens, on uncountable trips to New York, he never once toured the town. If age slowed his reflexes in the last few years of his career (he played until he was 46) his experience more than compensated for it. He was very shrewd. For example, he worked out a deal with the Leafs so that while he played for the team—1970-71 to 1973—he didn't receive a cent in salary. The Leafs are to pay him his salary beginning in 1981.

If Plante does not rank as the number one goal-keeper of all time, it's only because statistics aren't everything. No one had better statistics. His lifetime goals-against average was 2.37 in 837 regular-season NHL games. The Canadiens' Bill Durnan, who retired in 1950, compiled a lifetime goals-against average of 2.35, but he played only a little more than seven NHL seasons. Plante had 82 regular-season shutouts, a number surpassed by Terry Sawchuk's 103 and Glenn Hall's 84, but he still holds the record, 14, for most shutouts in the Stanley Cup playoffs. He won the Vezina Trophy a record seven times, five consecutive years with Montreal beginning in 1956. In 1962, as well as winning the Vezina, his sixth, he won the Hart Trophy as the league's most valuable player—the last goalkeeper to do so. In 1969, playing with the St. Louis Blues, he shared a Vezina (his seventh) with Glenn Hall. He was named to the league's first all-star team four times and the second team four times. He was on six Stanley Cup winning teams, all of them in Montreal.

Plante's 10 years with the Canadiens did not end happily. Although he played brilliantly, his Montreal bosses never became accustomed to his eccentricities. His habit of wandering away from the net gave coach Toe Blake ulcers, and many fans happily anticipated the day when Plante would get caught out of position by an opposing forward (in fact, according to Andy O'Brien's lively book, *The Jacques Plante Story,* Plante was only caught outside his crease six times in his pro career). As strange as it seems, Plante says today that he could never be sure of his job in Montreal; among other things there was some adverse reaction to his introduction of the mask in 1959. His nose had been broken by a shot and cut for seven stitches. Blake had previously opposed his requests that he be allowed to wear his practice mask in the games, but with his nose broken he reached for his mask and walked past Blake wearing it. Blake did not object, and when the Canadiens won the game—they were playing the Rangers in New York—he let the incident pass. Plante had made goal-tending history.

Plant infuriated Blake in other ways, too. One memorable night he declined to take part in the pregame warm-up on grounds of asthma. Blake was furious. "How can you run a team if you're never sure your goalie is going to play?" he asked. Years later, Plante's often noisy ideas on the subject of the two-goalie system helped introduce that concept to the point where it is standard procedure today. Once again, he was ahead of his time.

Plante's unpredictable health bothered Montreal management. Privately, they called him a hypochondriac and noted that he didn't suffer from asthma from the time he was 14 until he joined the Canadiens at age 24. Even when he suffered injuries that were visible on X-rays, Blake was suspicious.

At the end of the 1963 season the Canadiens traded Plante to the New York Rangers. In New York, he developed knee trouble, made mistakes in goal, and his goals-against average climbed. Ranger management began talking about his "phantom knee." Finally, coach Red Sullivan exploded, and Plante found himself playing with Baltimore of the American Hockey League. Eventually he had knee surgery, proving that the Rangers had been wrong in believing that the pain in his knee was in fact a pain in his head. But he quit hockey in 1965, a retirement that would last three years. One of his most distinguished achievements—and happiest memories—occurred during those years when he went into goal, cold, to play for the Junior Canadiens against the touring Russian national team, beating them 2-1 in Montreal.

When he came out of retirement in 1968, Plante was 39 years old. Playing for St. Louis he reconfirmed his belief in himself, the money was good and, combining with Glenn Hall, he played well. From St. Louis he came to the Leafs, where he tutored Bernie Parent. In 1973 the Leafs traded him to Boston. He helped the Bruins finish the season, winning seven of eight games and taking over third place from the Rangers, but he was a flop in the playoffs. He admitted

his nerves were gone. Soon after he announced he was heading for the World Hockey Association, where he managed, coached and played until his retirement in 1975.

Typically, his last days in the NHL were shrouded in controversy: the Bruins somehow failed to send him his share of the play-off money, and he had to ask NHL president Clarence Campbell to collect. He never did get his equipment back from the Bruins, who claimed it was lost. Plante believed the Bruins were mad at him for jumping to the WHA with a year left on his contract. Playing in the WHA, he developed stomach pains that team doctors could never diagnose.

But the most interesting thing about Plante were not his pains but his ideas. For instance, he said that players should talk on the ice—he said he wanted to be told if an opposing player was behind the net—and he himself talked all the time, shouting instructions to his defencemen or warning them when an opposing checker was coming at them from the blind side. If a teammate had the puck behind his net, Plante often indicated to which side he should pass the puck to ensure that it would clear the zone. And as for his roaming tactics, he admitted he sometimes made mistakes, either by anticipating incorrectly the flow of the play or by getting in the way of his defencemen, but he did not leave the goal until he was sure he could gert back. He could afford to wander because he was a superior skater.

Indeed, Plante was technically almost a perfect goal-keeper, a stand-up goalie as opposed to a flopper. He had a mathematician's grasp of angles. He knew, in relation to his position between the goalposts, exactly where he was at all times. His mind was a computer bank of opposition plays and shooting characteristics. He was almost impossible to fool. When his playing days were over he admitted that he even studied which players used black tape on their sticks and which used white; the puck was easier to see if the player had white tape on his stick.

Plante was dedicated in practice, went to bed faithfully at 9.30 p.m., covered 30 miles a day on the stationary bicycle, watched his weight, what he ate, the temperature of the fruit juices he drank. He was especially careful of how and when he used his eyes. A goal-tender's biggest problems, he used to explain, are his eyes and his nerves. To relax he'd read, cook lasagna, knit undershirts, play bridge. He'd leave a stack of records playing while he slept, placing the loudest, liveliest records at the top of the stack so he'd wake up progressively.

As a Maple Leaf, Plante spent most of his spare time answering mail. According to Leaf publicist Stan Obodiac, he received more mail than any player in the team's history, averaging 200 letters a day. Partly, it was a reflection of his personal popularity, and partly it was the result of a television appearance he once made on *Hockey Night in Canada* in which he mentioned he had prepared a tip sheet for young goal-tenders. It contained 15 pointers, such as, "On a breakaway do not rush towards your opponent. Wait for him at the edge of your goal crease." Or, "Sur un echappe, ne fonce pas vers ton adversaire. . . ." Plante's tip-sheets, mimeographed at the Gardens on Gardens' stationery, often included personal notes to the boys (and sometimes girls) who had special questions. He answered every fan letter.

Rick Boulton is editor of *Maple Leaf Magazine*, the feature sports magazine that includes the lineups for each Toronto Maple Leafs home game. He writes regularly on sports issues and personalities. "Recollections of Jacques Plante" first appeared in *Maple Leaf Magazine*, February 1977.

RUTH ELLEN RUSTON

Bingo!

The money changers are out of the temple and into the church basement.

Upstairs the church is waiting for Sunday. Remote, exalted, encased in plaster, icons of the power that moved the Western world through two millennia stare into darkness. The chapel is vacant, its doors locked against worshippers and vandals. Below in the basement hundreds of hands in rhythm sweep the cards after each punctual call. *54 under the G.* Studious as diviners, they follow the pulse, for luck is the vulgar brother of grace. The losers' loss is the temple's gain, keeping it weekly warm and dusted. This does not immediately concern the players; it's simply humanity haven, time passing. And nowhere in evidence is the prophet of love, with a voice of thunder, turning over the tables of the moneychangers.

". . . *make not my Father's house an house of merchandise. And his disciples remembered that it was written, The zeal of thine house hath eaten me up.*" John 2: 16, 17.

What's happening to the churches, God only knows. I'm here to hip you on bingo.

"Ah, really reaching out there," says Reverend Barry Jones at the Montreal Catholic Archdiocese when I call for an appointment, indicating that as a moral issue bingo is in the coffin.

"Aesthetically, I don't like it," he says that afternoon. "People who go to bingo don't necessarily go to church. I'm espe-cially opposed in lower income areas where people may be taking from the grocery money to play. But when the church is in trouble, you put your aesthetics in your back pocket and go with what will save the church."

You'd never ask her the name of her hairdresser. Her facial contours resemble tundra. The home-roll cigarette has replaced teeth as a fitting accoutrement to the mouth. It don't need no fancy fingerwork, it don't make no fuss for ashtrays, it just sets there fuming in her face. Her hands are free to roam the cards—14 of them all laid out like shingles before her. Her eyes operate like digitals. But after one call she lifts her head. Her eyes narrow and sweep the hall. *22 under the I.* The marker lands dead on 22 as she announces *bingo* barely disturbing the cigarette, which makes another perceptible movement as her lips curl into a smile.

A pro. No undue exultation. Winning is why she came here. Her two teenage sons beside her with stacks of cards that almost equal hers, grant her tacit congratulations. The group further down the table gives her dirty looks. They're downy soft and wrinkle-free. Came for the good clean fun of it all. Later, one of the shaggy juveniles wins with a little more noise than his mother and a much broader smile.

"Well, you've been at it long enough," one of the good group grudgingly acknowledges.

"Be better for them to spend some time in church instead," another woman grumbles. This one keeps a glass and gilt statuette of the virgin above her board. No rabbit's feet nor onyx elephants, no heathen idols for her. She settles into the next game with rising fervor, chanting softly after each call, "54, ya bum."

He does not call 54. She does not win. Some other player triumphs. She groans and dumps her tokens on the table.

"This is a very relaxing game," says the lady across from me.

She's a swell-looking lady, a yesteryear mama. We're sandwiched in between the two opposing moralities. I'm trying to keep my eyes off her good luck charms, an enormous diaper pin and what looks like – egad – a bottle of blood.

"You should play more cards," she suggests. "Gets boring with only two." I dutifully purchase more and she opens the cap of the sponge-top bottle and marks my free centre spaces with red ink. Whew.

"The free centre looks like it's marked now. It doesn't distract your eyes." She notices my distracted eyes. "This was my diaper pin when I was a baby," she confides, blushing. This congenial woman has somehow managed for 50-odd years to hold onto the catch that held up her drawers, as a token of trust and hope. And the cards she marks with her spongee bottle are collected each day and redistributed among her competitors, so that other eyes around the room may know that their free space is truly free.

It *is* harder with four cards. My brain insists on savoring each numeral, called or not, before passing down the column. I've barely perused half my cards when the announcer calls *36 under the N,* and I scramble back to the top. The lady opposite is playing 10 cards but when the next number is announced she reaches over to drop a marker on a 36 I had neglected. Her wrist roams the cards in a swift undulation. Mine operates like a rusty gearshift. "Just look at the last digit," she tips me, and if it ends like what he called, then look at the whole number . . . and keep a roll of markers coiled like this in your fist so you can just slap 'em down as you find 'em." At the table across from us, I witness another stylistic variation. Several players fill their cards with the transparent markers before each game, removing the red plastic discs as the numbers are called.

But soon there is no time for such distracted observations. My concentration winds tighter, narrowing to the quadrangle of my playing space. Each muscle of my face seems individually lifted, like a marionette's It is essential to keep the shoulders mobile. This is a feline tension, relaxed but ready. My mentor continues to catch my omissions, filling my card with her upside-down aid.

Nearly, nearly. Nearly a full line.
Bingo!

Oh bummer. That wasn't my voice though it almost felt connected. Wasn't my win. "Ah well," my lady condoles, screwing up her nose, screwing up her nose, "but see, if only he'd called 42 here, or a 17 over there, you would have won." No time for ifs, the hall comes to order promptly for the next round.

Bingo – game, lottery, tradition, obsession. A weapon for women fighting the empty nest syndrome, a place to stash the old folks, a bit of family fun. The world's most popular form of gambling, it has raised more money for charities than any other type of fund raising. Ubiquitously available, inexpensive entertainment.

It's a variation of the old-fashioned Italian parlor game lotto, in turn derived from the nearly 450-year-old Italian National Lottery. It came to prominence in

North America during the Depression when cheap thrills were hard to find. Throughout the war, many of those who also served sat waiting it out in the bingo parlors.

Newspaper columnist Scott Young wrote: "To Canadians, bingo is much more than just a mild game of chance. Indeed, to some who visited Canada's backwaters during the war . . . bingo meant Canada: Long rows of phlegmatic pioneers and their wives and children seated intensely at long wooden tables in village halls across the land, night after night, enjoying the Canadian equivalent of a fling at the gaming tables of Cannes."

In 1970 bingo was removed from the Criminal Code and placed under the jurisdiction of the various provinces. The hot-blooded days of the great bingo wars ended. As the number of players steadily increases, the controversy subsides. No more will the gentlemen of Timmins proclaim that bingo is corrupting their wives and daughters. Church basements are no longer raided as common gaming houses nor priests charged as their keepers, so housewives need not threaten to smash their prize lamps rather than turn them over to the heat. The right to have fun at the tables is finally acknowledged. As long as it's For A Good Cause.

To the public arbiters of morality, bingo is not a game; it's a lottery. There are no accurate records to determine how legislation alters the game but, according to John Scarne, undisputed Don of Gambling and author of *Scarne's New Complete Guide to Gambling*, "When a state legalizes bingo the annual handle usually drops to one-third of the previous illegal handle. Partly due to the fact that the state places so many restrictions on the game's operation that many of the former illegal promoters quit. Business may also drop off if the size of the jackpot prizes permitted are much smaller."

Quebec, the lottery capital of North America, has cracked up some of the stiffest licensing regulations of any province. Last year it issued licences for nearly 33,000 games with a maximum jackpot limit of $3,500 per occasion.

Bingo is the social club for the average Quebec citizen. It emerged at the old-time town fairs and flourished year-round in parish halls. The Catholic church draws its wealth from the working poor. At a time when the major Protestant denominations were supported by managerial and upper classes, the Catholics led the way in using bingo as a fund raising activity, with other charities stampeding at their heels. It isn't the most efficient form of fund raising since approximately two-thirds of the take goes into operating costs, but it's the one people flock to and enjoy. Now, almost all denominations sponsor bingos and less than 50 percent of licences issued go the the Catholic church.

"We're interested in controlling the games, not in making money," says Roland Yelle, administrative secretary of La Régie des Loteries et Courses du Québec. However, bingo yields the Montreal municipal government $1,000,000 annually in tax revenue. For in Montreal where half the province's games are held, as in several other Quebec municipalities, the civic government levies a 10 percent amusement tax on the gross incomes of the games as well as a five-cents-per-person flat rate according to the capacity of the hall, or one percent of the ticket price.

Quite a few governments have arbitrarily declared themselves Good Causes in order to profit from lotteries. But in effect, the Montreal civic government is indirectly taxing the churches, as well as other charities. And some of them don't want to pay.

In the grey subterranean chambers of Montreal's morals and drugs department, I meet Constable Trèfle Beauchamp, Montreal's one-man avenger of bingo wrongs. With the police department's shortage of manpower, Constable Beauchamp is the only policeman working full-time on bingo. There are about 25 games played daily in various areas of the city. They don't raid the halls and make wholesale arrests of the players any more, but Beauchamp does lay about two or three charges a month for tax evasion. Since legalization, all organizations running bingo games must submit detailed financial reports, subject to stringent regulations, but Beauchamp declares that many of them submit false reports. He discusses one case where two men convicted of fraud were ordered to pay $29,000 restitution for evaded taxes and sentenced to 10 days in jail, to be served on weekends. Their sentences were light because their profits had all gone to help the children's organization they worked for. They hadn't pocketed any of it.

Some players cheat with less munificent aims. Beauchamp teaches me how. A fast hand with a felt-tip pen can transform a 3 to an 8, a 4 to 14, etc. Individual squares can be pasted on the card. Several times in the past they've caught ladies with miniature printing presses in their purses, stamping out the numbers as they're called. "With prizes up to $1,000 it's worth it to some people to try it," the constable says. But a complaint must be lodged before charges can be laid and it is the nature of bingo to segregate each player in his own fevered realm, oblivious of the evil schemes of others.

In the chaos preceding legalization, professional gambling organizers would sometimes move in behind charitable fronts, bilking the charities of their profits. The regulations curtail these activities but it is the charities, not their professional employees, that submit financial reports of each bingo to the government. Beauchamp keeps some organizers under careful scrutiny.

Graft seems to pop up with alarming regularity in every form of gambling, for good cause or bad, legal or not.

"Upstairs the churches are empty," says Constable Beauchamp, "but the basements are full."

Many churches are in the cringeworthy position of having to seek their financial salvation from what they stringently recognize as sin. Ordinary income from religious practices, such as collections and ceremonial fees, is not covering operating costs. Within the Montreal Archdiocese only 90 of 256 parishes have no debt. And 28 percent of all parishes have resorted to bingo for fund raising.

Some say we've all gone Godless these days. It could be. The church is down and I don't want to stomp it, but not the least of its concerns is official hypocrisy. With one voice the church still condemns those who take the Name in vain and make love without a licence, while the recourse of individual parishes to bingo is "not recommended, but not forbidden."

Cardinal Villeneuve did forbid it, in 1947, in submission to civil law when Duplessis clamped down legally on bingo in retaliation for the church-sponsored anti-vice campaign. But individual parishes continued their fun and fund raising, disregarding the order. Within the hierarchy, power seeped backwards into many lesser hands and church authority was decentralized. Now, with congregations reduced to a trickle and the archdiocese dependent on the funds of debtor parishes, the moral complexities of gambling are discreetly ignored, or handed over to theologians and accountants.

At 2461 St. James Street West, Ste. Cunégonde Church is closed for financial reasons. Vicar Maurice Campeau, speaking halting English, his second language, says: "The church has been closed five and a half years but we still have a chapel where parishioners worship. At that time some people suggested we play bingo to keep the church open. We decided to close the church because it's a poor *quartier* and most people are on welfare. Secondly, when you play bingo you play for yourself. As soon as you start the game nobody talks. You don't play bingo for fun, you play for money. It's like a fishing lure, flashing, but I know that people who play bingo don't all go to church. And I know what Jesus said to the merchants in the temple.

"I can't judge other parishes. It's their decision. I just know that here it's nonsense to play bingo. We took the good solution and most parishioners follow our directions. You should just see our church, our community. What do you think is a church? I don't talk about people who go to a building."

When morality itself is in the dry dock having its barnacles scraped, when *Psychology Today* exposes the Samaritan act as just another symptom of personality disorder and Jesus himself is suspect of masochism, it's sure refreshing to find some people who take a moral stance in the face of financial loss.

Still, it's hard to think of bingo as intrinsically bad. To most players it's simply a game and games are played in all societies, to annihilate rural boredom and detoxify urban stress. Etymologically, the word "game" originally referred to the leaping of wild animals. Perhaps it's the *good cause* clause that's hard to swallow, as it's played under the mantle of the church; I don't know. I keep wondering if maybe the whole thing isn't an oversight. Sometimes even, or especially, in church, Christ seems so far away. Fortunately the kingdom of heaven is within, because if our only link to the truth were words, we'd be in terrible trouble.

Half-past the puritans, the hedonists are waiting . For them bingo lacks the glamor of radical sleaze. Since it lost its standing as a cause célèbre after legalization, most people who don't play the game like to snicker at it. It's middle class. Worse, lower middle class. Pantywaist roulette for the ladies. "So Canadian," sneers one affluent freak, "so conservative."

Whatsamatter middle class? As if there were all that much of anything else in this country, thank God. Whatsamatter conservative? We should build our own Las Vegas, that seething degenerate fantasy spoiling the southwest United States?

No condescension intended, but I'm not so partial to games myself. I drove my friend to frustrated tears when she tried to teach me gin rummy on a three-day train trip. Why, I wondered, completely baffled, should we spend our time on these meaningless Machiavellian intrigues when we can watch each tree and rock throb by at this easy leisurely pace?

To hell with mah-jongg and backgammon. Deal me out of bridge or euchre. But when the gamelust blows my way, you might find me at Good Morning Bingo, down in Resurrection Hall.

The hall steams up with the sweat of victors and losers and just plain players. A paunchy, unshaven man in a T-shirt invites me to "come see a real bingo fanatic—she goes to eight games a week"—his wife. She's a neat, small woman, her hair tied back in a red kerchief. Under the smoke-obscured arches of the Centre Paul Sauvé, which seats nearly 1,000, she plays each call with an icy intensity. Her husband disinterestedly marks a couple of cards, smoking endlessly and staring at his wife through puffy eyes. They say nothing to each other, even at intermission. After several games he scatters his markers with a violent shove and stalks off to the refreshment stand. The halls are filled with these women who took a chance on a man and likely stuck with their luck throughout their lives and the deterioration of their dreams. Unlike life games, with bingo there is always a winner.

The game has its addicts for sure. A headline in my file reads "Housewife Turns to Crime to Pay off Parlor Expenses." In a celebrated case in England a British naval officer sold secrets to the Soviets to liquidate his wife's bingo debts. One in 10 members of Gamblers Anonymous is bingo-afflicted.

But the bingomaniacs are exceptions. Most players come once or twice weekly to meet friends and bask in the game's genteel tensions. It costs about $4 per person each night. In Quebec, it seems more families come than in Ontario; more men and children, more laughter and chatter. The tables are dotted with crocheted marker-holders in lacy lavender, aqua, and other voluptuous pastels. Aproned attendants hustle cards and Cokes.

On a podium at the front of this quasi-cathedral, the caller, minister of fortune and scapegoat for the wrath of the unlucky, announces each number bilingually through the loud-speaker system. He's an employee of Mr. Bingo, a professional company that runs the games for the centre and other charities. It's hot in the hall and as the night goes on, he looks strained and tired. Air pressure juggles the balls in the machine he attends, spewing out a numbered orb in pulsations.

And then the evening ends. He packs up the machinery as the hordes make their way out to the bus stops, leaving long rows of empty tables, flotsam scattered on the floor, like the residue of a banquet.

Ruth Ellen Ruston is a Hamilton-born freelancer who contributes to the pages of *Weekend, Toronto Life,* and other Canadian publications. A world traveller, one-time bartender, and CBC production assistant, she is now flirting with fiction. "Bingo!" first appeared in *Weekend,* August 14, 1976.

PAUL STUEWE

Come Together

Hello Mamma, Hello Poppa?
The Fab Four are reunited.

FLASH!

Los Angeles (AP-UP-IP) Oct. 5, 1974: David Geffen, president of Asylum Records, today announced that the Beatles will be getting together again for an extended concert tour of North America in the Spring of 1975. Geffen also revealed that the famous British pop group have been signed to Asylum on a multi-billion dollar contract, with a 16-lp album of all new material scheduled for an Xmas release. Although its contents have not yet been finalized, Geffin said that the album (tentatively titled *Do You Still Luv Us? We Bloody Well 'Ope So!*) will definitely include Yoko Ono's new four-hour "minimal opera," *Schrecklichkeit in der Kosmos,* as well as a selection of Derek Taylor's press releases set to four-part harmony and a "no holds barred" interview with Allen Klein. Geffen described the album as "Something no true Beatles fan will want to be without."

27 Roach Gardens
Wahwah, Ontario
October 6, 1974

Dear Mom,

Imagine my surprise when the big announcement hit the air-waves! This is a rock critic's dream come true! Naturally, I immediately contacted the editor of *Schmeatle Magazine* and nailed down a firm commitment for a cover story by Yours Truly! Now I know that you don't like my writing for them—I agree, they are dirty, disgusting and an affront to common decency—but this is my *Big Chance!* Do you think you could send me my old Beatles posters (they're underneath the toilet seat from that Alice Cooper concert) right away? And could you send me some money? Schmeatle still hasn't paid me for that article I did on Iggy Stooge's exorcism six months ago.

Got to run,
Rocky

Clutching his copy of the new Paul McCartney album close to the vest of his three-piece Irish tweed suit, Tommy Tuneful hurried into his tastefully furnished apartment in Executive Towers. He slit the plastic wrapper open with a practised swipe of one manicured thumbnail and delicately placed the record on the turntable of his $2,000 custom-syled component system; then he remembered that he was hungry, so he fixed himself a light snack of Camembert cheese and Peek Frean biscuits before activating his components and settling down in the seductive arms of his waterbed chair. "Ah, bliss," he thought as the mutely throbbing bass line of the opening track began to insinuate itself into his consciousness. . . . .

Tommy felt in his bones that Paul McCartney was a good person, and was sure that he had been the primary creative force in the Beatles. Although rock critics liked to put Paul down for being "simpleminded" and "naive," Tommy knew that they were just a bunch of effete intellectual snobs who envied McCartney his total mastery of rock music. For Tommy had ultimate proof of his greatness: no matter how depressed he was after a day at the insurance office, listening to one of his Paul McCartney albums *always* made him feel better.

Speaking of feeling better, Tommy decided to give his girlfriend Samantha a ring; but her roommate informed him that Samantha had gone to a Sensitivity Training session at the Community Centre, and would not be home until later. "Is there any message?" she asked. "Yes," Tommy replied, "would you be good enough to tell her that the new Paul McCartney album is really *groovy!*"

Washington[AP-UP-IP] Nov. 11, 1974: The firm of John Ehrlichman and H.R. "Bob" Haldeman Ltd. today announced that they will be in charge of promotion and ticket arrangements for the Beatles' forthcoming tour of North America. Although neither has had any previous experience in concert management, both men expressed confidence in their ability to handle the complicated plans for the Beatles entourage. "We're not going to screw up this one," Ehrlichman made perfectly clear, while Haldeman indicated that he would "rollerskate over my own grandmother" if he thought that it was in the Beatles' best interests. Both added that "all previous statements should be considered inoperative at this point in time."

R.R. 1
Armpit, Saskatchewan
November 12, 1974

Dear Mom,
Thanks a lot for sending me that Beatles stuff—I'd forgotten how *cute* they are!

My story for *Schmeatle* is going o.k., although I'm having some problems with what point of view will work out best. *Schmeatle* likes you to pretend that you spent a week in your subject's hip pockets, so I'm reading all of their *Rolling Stone* interviews for background. Just got another assignment from *Schmeatle* to do an article on Lou Reed's tailor—he lives around here somewhere—so be good and don't forget about the money, 'cuz I still haven't gotten paid.
Rocky

Clutching her copy of the new George Harrison album close to the billowing folds of her saffron sari, Doris Dharmabumma hurried into the meditation area of her ashram in Metafarcical Manor. She spoke a brief prayer of sorrow for the violence she was about to commit before violently ripping off the plastic wrapper and reverently placing the record on the turntable of her $39.98 Guru Mahara Ji Quadraphonic Sound System; then she remembered that her material body required replenishment, so she fixed herself a modest repast of dried sunflower seeds and brown rice before turning on the record player and reposing contentedly on her Genuine Tibetan Prayer Mat. "Hare Krishna Krishna Hare . . ." she chanted as the gentle melodies of the opening track began their slow progress around the karmic wheel. . . .

Doris knew in her hearts of hearts that George Harrison was a good person, and was certain that he had been the primary creative force in the Beatles. Although rock critics liked to call George's music "gooey" and "syrupy," Doris knew that they were just jealous of the fact that he existed at a higher level of consciousness than they did. For Doris had ultimate proof of his greatness: no matter how tired she was after a day of yoga practice, listening to one of her George Harrison albums *always* made her spirits soar.

Speaking of soaring spirits, Doris decided to telephone her friend Dubadip, with whom she had a profound (and of course non-carnal) spirtual relationship; but the resident Guru of his ashram informed her that Dubadip was at the moment struggling to reach the Seventh Plane of Holy Delight, and could definitely not be disturbed. "Is there any message?" he inquired. "Yes," said Doris, "please tell him that the new George Harrison album is really *cosmic!*"

New York [AP-UP-IP] Dec. 25, 1974: The firm of John Ehrlichman and H.R. "Bob" Haldeman Ltd. today announced that responsibility for security arrangements for the Beatles' spring tour of North America would be assumed by Hunt, McCord, Liddy & Amigos Enterprises Inc. of San Quentin, California. At a press conference called to introduce Messrs. Hunt et al, a spokesman for Ehrlichman and Haldeman Ltd. (who refused to identify himself but described his statements as "usually reliable") said that they would be keeping a "low profile" in an effort to frustrate the "dirty tricks" which enemies of the Beatles would doubtless attempt to play on them. This was given as the reason why members of the new firm refused to talk to the press about their backgrounds, although when questioned by reporters as to his experience in providing such security, Hunt was heard to snap, "Don't bug me!"

442 Blue Jay Way
Valhalla, British Columbia
December 31, 1974

Dear Mom,

As you will by now have guessed, I won't be home for the holidays. At the last minute *Schmeatle* sent me out here to try to interview Howard Hughes, but he wasn't in. On the positive side, one of the chicks at the commune where I'm crashing spent a whole summer hanging out at Apple headquarters in London, and she's given me a lot of new insights into the Beatles' mystique (although most of them are libellous, I'm afraid). Anyway, hope you're well and don't forget the you-know-what.

Happy New Year,
Rocky

Clutching his copy of the new Ringo Starr album close to the faded threads of his J.C. Penney jean jacket, Harry Hickey scurried into his furnished room at the YMCA. Carefully selecting the appropriate blade of his Swiss Army pocketknife, he removed the plastic wrapper and gently placed the record on the turntable of his AM-FM-Stereo-Short Wave-Police Band-Tape-TV console (which after only 34 more easy payments would be *truly* his); then he remembered that he hadn't eaten for three days, so he rummaged through the dresser drawer and popped a handful of assorted uppers, downers, and animal tranquilizers that he had ripped off when his boss at the warehouse wasn't looking. Then he switched on the console and sprawled out on his bed, gradually closing his eyes in mute ecstasy as the ricky-ticky rhythms of the opening track began to interact with the compulsive twitching of his right forefinger. . . .

Harry was absolutely certain that Ringo Starr was a good person, and knew for a fact that he had been the primary creative force in the Beatles. Although rock critics liked to call Ringo's music "derivative" and "simplistic," Harry knew that they were just a lot of old rejects from the 1960s who couldn't even get it on when a really good boogie band like Uriah Heep came to town. For Harry had ultimate proof of his greatness: no matter how exhausted he was after a day of stacking boxes and sweeping floors, listening to one of his Ringo Starr albums *always* made him feel all warm and tingly inside.

Speaking of feeling all warm and tingly, Harry decided to call up Sue Fungoo, whom he had met a few days before at the Motherloving Massage Parlor; but her roommate informed him that Sue had had to work late because there was a Rotary convention in town, and would probably not come home at all. "Any message?" she asked. "Yeah," Harry said, "tell her that the new Ringo Starr album is really *far out!*"

Pleasantville, N.Y. [AP-UP-IP] Jan. 15, 1975: *Reader's Digest* magazine today confirmed that it has commissioned former U.S. Vice President Spiro Agnew to write a twelve-part series on the Beatles' forthcoming tour of North America, tentatively titled "The Most Unforgettable Rock Group I Ever Met." When contacted at his Baltimore home, Agnew stated that his former attitudes regarding the immorality of rock music had undergone a dramatic change: "I've had a lot of time on my hands lately," he said, "so I've listened to some of my son's Beatles albums and find them quintessentially unobjectionable, and at times even insidiously pleasant." *Reader's Digest* executive Melvin Laird added that "Mr. Agnew's extensive experience in both the political and legal professions makes him particularly well qualified to write about the Beatles."

44 Screech Alley
Come-by-Chance, Newfoundland
January 16, 1975
Dear Mom,
Well, here's your Roving Correspondent again, this time hot on the trail of a rumor that Bill Graham is starting a Home for Unwed Groupies in this remote corner of the great wide world. I haven't found out anything for sure yet—actually, I can't even understand the way these people speak—but from the pains they take to avoid me there must be something going on! Hope this finds you fat and sassy, and if you can spare it I could use a couple bucks until I get my next unemployment cheque—thank goodness *Schmeatle* writers don't have any problems qualifying!
Love Ya Madly,
Rocky

Clutching her copy of the new John Lennon album close to the breastplate of her form-fitting "Street Fighting Woman" jump-suit, Kathy Karate rushed into the Political Education and Group Sex Room of the Che Guevara Memorial Commune. She removed the plastic wrapper and placed the record on the combination turntable-machine gun platform of her Chinese Army-surplus victrola; then she remembered that she was hungry, so she prepared herself a small ration of raw steak and eggs from the communal field kitchen before turning on the victrola and assuming a position of militant receptivity on the bare floor. As the first biting notes of Lennon's latest broadside washed over her, Kathy could feel herself being swept up in the worldwide struggle against Fascism being waged by all oppressed peoples, and her heart and mind each took two steps forward in complete identity with the wretched of the earth. . . .

Kathy was truly conscious that, objectively speaking, John Lennon was a good person, and she knew for a fact that he had been the primary creative force in the Beatles. Although rock critics liked to describe John's music as "incoherent" and "schizophrenic," Kathy knew that they were just a bunch of middle-class reactionaries who were tools of the Military-Industrial Complex, and would be quickly liquidated when the revolution triumphed. For Kathy had ultimate proof of his greatness: no matter how tired she was after a day of organizing the masses and spreading word of the truth of dialectical materialism, listening to one of her John Lennon albums *always* reaffirmed her belief in the value of re-volutionary solidarity.

Speaking of revolutionary solidarity, Kathy decided to phone Istvan Ilytch Schwartz, a card-carrying member of the proletariat with whom she occasionally engaged in a mildly deviationist form of the class struggle; but his Commissar informed her that Istvan had just left to participate in a sympathy strike for the exploited potato pickers of Prince Edward Island, and would not be back for some time. "Any communiqué, Comrade?" he asked. "Yes," Kathy replied, "be sure to tell him that the new John Lennon album is really *right on!*"

Key Biscayne, Florida [AP-UP-IP] Feb. 27, 1975: Charles "Bebe" Rebozo, reputedly the sole remaining friend of ex-President Richard Nixon, today stated that Nixon still has under advisement an offer to emcee the spring concert tour of the Beatles for a reported one million dollars. An unidentified and only fitfully reliable source indicated that negotiations had bogged down over the former President's refusal to appear on stage with a sequinned yoyo, and that he was also reluctant to perform in an "Uncle Sam" outfit with red, white and blue platform shoes. The source added, however, that Nixon's continuing financial difficulties—heightened this week by allegations that he had "misappropriated" funds intended for the White House's annual Easter Egg Roll—would probably force him to accept the offer.

Seat ZZ-401786236-b
Maple Leaf Gardens, Toronto
February 29, 1975

Dear Mom,
Well, the great day of the Beatles concert finally arrived, and you just won't believe what happened. First of all, there were only four people besides myself at the concert—it wasn't as bad as that rock festival in Vermont where I was the only one there, but just about—and the even stranger thing about it was that none of the four ever got off at the same time: they were each jumping up and down at different moments like the cylinders in the old car *Schmeatle* bought for my participant observation report on the Indianapolis 500. They all looked pretty weird, but the goofiest one of them all was this chick who held her right arm in a clenched fist whenever John Lennon did anything—or at least she did until he yelled out, "We're all over thirty —shaddup!" The music was pretty bad, too: McCartney did all of his playing from an isolation booth and Ringo got blisters on his hands and had to quit about halfway though, although I must admit that George Harrison's teeth were nice and white. The only really interesting music was provided by the warmup act, a new group called "Come Together" which featured David Spinozza and Ron Wood on twin lead guitars. If they can get a good agent and some original material they might really make it big.
Be Home Soon,
Rocky

Paul Stuewe runs Nth Hand Book Shop in Toronto. He is a regular columnist for *Quill & Quire, Books in Canada,* and *FM Guide.* Life Ambition: to be a footnote in the Literary History of Canada. "Come Together" first appeared in *Beetle,* October 1974.

MICHAEL PARK

No More Beatles, No More Stones, We Just Want The Viletones

Toronto's punk new wave looks more like a fascist salute.

TORONTO — "A lot of people think we must be crazy, especially me, to do the things we do. They don't like us, they call us disgusting, tasteless, all that garbage. Why don't they like us? Because they're afraid to be what we are. They're jealous of us. We are what they secretly want to be."

Thus spake Steven Leckie, alias Nazi Dog, alias Pope Dog I, singer, songwriter and archdemon for that blood-smeared punk rock circus known as the Viletones.

Toronto's very own Viletones are probably the western world's cultural answer to Idi Amin. They preach the virtues of the S.S. (apparently the uniform makes the man), they routinely practice wanton, scene-trashing violence, and they display an alarming taste for blood (often but not always their own). Their performances are perfect models of new wave vulgarity, deemed worthy of lurid coverage in *Maclean's* magazine, yet,

right up there with Margie and Mick. Oh yes, and the Tones also play music.

Let's try and put this whole Viletones thing in some sort of perspective. Macro before micro, the bird's eye view before the worm's.

According to Jann Wenner's gourmet guide to the nouveau chic (a.k.a. *Rolling Stone* magazine), The Viletones must be classified as practitioners of that peculiar musical vice known as punk rock. The key ingredients of new wave punk should be by now quite familiar: three-chord songs, buckets of profanity, lots of pimply nihilism, and excesses of physical barbarism just this side of snuff films. Punk is just another word for nothing left to lose, right? As a creative genre, it has been characterized as an English blight that spread to North America like Dutch Elm Disease—from the U.K. to the U.S. to us, with little merit and no love. Its maxim might be "Make war, not music."

Our Viletones may be punk, but they certainly aren't your average punks. Although they have been in existence for only a few months, they already sport a word-of-mouth mythology far exceeding in sheer incredibility that of any other Canadian rock band. The street hype that drew this observer to the band was truly bizarre. What was even stranger was that most of it was true.

Here are some of the twisted metaphorical messages concerning the Viletones that were drummed up by the underground in Toronto the Bad. There is a grain of truth in each item.

The spiritual genesis of the Viletones was said to be Nazi Germany circa 1941. Word had it that the band's fuhrer (Leckie) styled himself Nazi Dog, claimed direct physical descent from one H. Himmler, and regularly practiced atrocious self-mutilations on stage. Richard Speck, a rather unpopular figure among Chicago student nurses, was reportedly one of the Tones' patron saints. The theme of each Viletones performance? Total iconoclasm, total inebriation, total violence—a stage putsch. No area of human activity, from evacuation to ejaculation, was categorically excluded from the show. And the band members themselves were called tame in comparison to the goose-stepping, fascist-saluting, glass-bashing menagerie who wore the emblems—cuts, stitches, band-aids—of true Viletone supporters. No more Beatles, no more Stones, we just want the Viletones.

What was even more frightening (or alluring, depending on your world view) was the growing rumour that suggested that this Leckie chap was something special—the best actor in Canadian rock, as one impartial English observer was heard to say. Definitely a weird scene, I thought, one to stay well clear of.

Several Viletones shows later, the conclusion is different. Granted, this scene is grade-A government-inspected weird, but for once the facts exceed the sensationalism of the hype. Yes, the Tones *are* aficionados of the Third Reich; they *do* sing odes to Himmler and Speck (''I'm so glad that Heinrich Himmler's my dad''); Leckie *does* gash himself occasionally, but that's not all there is to the band. It's not as *acne vulgaris* as it sounds. The fact of the matter is that Leckie is chillingly, alluringly real. He defies categorization.

The punk context is too narrow, really, to explain away Nazi Dog and his world. Certainly the Viletones are disgusting, lewd, anti-motherhood and apple pie—predictably punk in that sense. But unlike most punk acts, they are most definitely not boring. Their stunning absurdity demands total attention. They're not just the Philadelphia Flyers using electric guitars instead of hockey sticks to bash over each others' heads.

In this age of roots consciousness, the Viletones are not entirely true to their post-nuclear origins. Through God knows what process of reverse socialization, they have twigged to the age-old power of the threat of violence and incorporated this discovery into a 1977 show, one that is politically legitimate, if not culturally so. They don't just assault each other; they assault you—us—the world. The standard physical assault of punk is there—the hurled bottles, mike stands, guitars, amplifiers, what have you, and of course there are Nazi Dog's diving descents into the audience to maim or be maimed. But in their intuitive feel for the power of symbolism and their ability to manipulate it, Leckie and his Viletone corps are adept beyond their years and peers. As Nazi Dog, a name awarded him by his followers, Leckie transforms guns, crosses, Nazi paraphernalia and broken beer steins into extensions of himself. They become crass but articulate media for the expression of his personal horrors, humours or pathos, as the mood or song strikes him.

Historical deletions and X-rated news events are his specialties, the stuff of the royal fool, seventies-style.

What all this translates into is a powerful show—powerful and repellent to your average mainstreamer. The band shoots an immediate and clear-cut challenge at the audience: get into this trip, or fuck off. For those who see the Tones for the first time, for those who choose to get into them, the response to this challenge must be a kind of ultimate objectivity. If you are prepared to strip yourself of your protective headgear—your biases, prejudices, concepts of absolute right and wrong, your fear of being hurt—it is almost possible to appreciate the Viletones.

And if you actually *like* the Tones, if they really are what you secretly want to be, then there shouldn't be much to get upset about. After all, they do spring from the same northern nesting ground that spawned the Black Donnellys, the Western Guard, Alvin Karpis, Hockey Night in Canada, and Bobby Clarke. And so do most of us.

In his own way, Steven Leckie is every bit as Canadian as Clarke, the Flin Flon punk who chases pucks in such extreme fashion for the Flyer goon machine. Both can be reasonably polite and articulate when not performing their specialties. Both easily conform to the roles projected on them, Clarke as the sports demigod and Leckie as the fledgling rock antichrist. Both are verified masters of profanity, and both are adept at slashing if they feel that the situation requires it. Both play with pain.

It stands to reason, I suppose, that if Canada can produce the most vicious, blood-thirsty hockey players in the world, she can also produce the most repulsively outrageous punk rockers. We stand on guard for thee.

How does Nazi Dog feel about what he does for a living?

"I'd rather answer questions like, What's your favourite colour or food or movie star, you know, stuff like that," says Leckie. "All that other stuff, the cuts and *Mein Kampf* and that, is just Nazi Dog. Everybody knows that stuff already. You could say that there's absolutely nothing between me and Margaret Trudeau. That's news. The other guys in the band will confirm that too."

The other guys in the band are Fred Pompeii, guitar, Chris Hate, bass, and Mangled Mike, drums. Nazi Dog needs them as much as they need him. It's not a one man thing, war.

Does the Dog have any notable musical influences?

"Who were those guys, oh ya, Tommy James and the Shondells. I like them and Teenage Head and the Sex Pistols."

Thoughts on current affairs?

"If I was Idi Amin, I'd declare war on everybody, then collect foreign aid from the States if I lost."

What about chemical stimulation?

"Sniffing glue gives you the same high as cocaine and it's cheaper."

Any messages for the faithful?

"No, they all know already that I'm a twelve inch talent, you might say. ha."

Are you always so up front, Steven?

"Is a duck's ass waterproof? Listen, we're in the same position as the Rolling Stones were fifteen years ago, with all these people putting us down constantly. We're going to hang together and see this thing through. We're not nearly as good now as we're going to be, cause we're good learners and we're totally flexible."

Hang together?

Oh dear, age must be creeping up. Another generation of rebellious youth is upon us, people who refused to grow up into the idealist hippies that their liberal parents probably wanted them to be. Have we finally reached the point where we have rebellion against the Beatles because they remind one of one's parents? Grey hair.

One vital fact to realize about the Viletones and the underground scene they belong to is this: the energy is very powerful, and it hasn't begun to be tapped yet, certainly not on a conventional commercial level. This is a new and different scene, the likes of which Toronto may not have seen since the halcyon days of Yorkville. For the outside world, there is a bottom line to all this, and that is marketability. It seems doubtful that any research will be done by the record companies to sound out potential sales for records about oral sex and Heinrich Himmler. And on a purely technical level (finally he gets to it), the Viletones won't stun anybody with their musical virtuosity, although Jeff Burns of GRT Records remains noncommittal as to whether or not the Tones are really Klaatu.

Life isn't easy, being the Viletones. Despite their growing drawing power, the Tones' biggest struggle now is finding clubs where the management will let them perform and evolve.

So how in the end do you evaluate something like the Viletones? Quite simply, you don't. If you throw a fit and call for napalm and flame-throwers, you'll only encourage them. The Tones won't drive tanks through your tulip gardens or declare war on your grandparents. They won't come looking for you, asking for papers, if you don't do it to them. You can even forget all about them, if the mere fact of their existence holds no significance for you. They don't want you if you don't want them. If you are interested, though, they're out there now, weaving their vile web somewhere, doing what they will. You can find them if you really want to. That's not news, but it is reality.

For better or for worse, the Viletones *are* a reality. And I don't want to go into what that says about the nature of this reality of ours. Keep an eye on us, please, Mr. Churchill.

Michael Park an English instructor at Toronto's Centennial College, is an ex-musician turned educator. He has published articles on education as well as pieces on the popular entertainment scene. "No More Beatles, No More Stones, We Just Want the Viletones" first appeared in *Record Week*, June 27, 1977.

" PARK MEETS A PUNK " ©1977 Buzz Baum (Pete Taylor)

MORRIS WOLFE

King of Kensington and the Battle for Ratings

Does anybody watch the CBC anymore?

If I had to select a representative sample of current North American popular culture to lock away in a time capsule someplace, I'd choose a half-hour TV comedy show. Whether we like it or not, such programs play a more important part in our lives than anything else in our culture; more of us—young and old, rich and poor, male and female—watch half-hour TV comedy shows than read bestsellers, or listen to pop music, or go to the movies, or take in sports events on TV. This fall there are over two dozen such shows on our screens—more than ever before.

To be more precise, I'd pick a domestic comedy (or dom-com), a program like "Rhoda" or "All in the Family" or "The Bob Newhart Show." In the 1950s and early 1960s, TV comedy was dominated by situation comedies—"I Love Lucy," "The Beverly Hillbillies," and "The Phil Silvers Show," for example. Those programs were about implausible situations in which lovable, one-dimensional devils (like Bilko) were rendered harmless, or in which lovable, one-dimensional bumbling idiots (like Lucy) got through unscathed. The world of situation comedy was to TV what the Marx Brothers and Laurel and Hardy had been to film. It was the world as we would like it to be—a world of happy endings, in which people had a lot of fun and no one ever really got hurt.

Although sit-coms were dominant during that period, there were a lot of domestic comedies as well, shows like "Father Knows Best," "Leave It to Beaver," and "Ozzie and Harriet." In such programmes, the situations are more plausible, the comedy is more muted, and the characters more "real." Human frailties and relationships dominate. People in domestic comedies sometimes get hurt and sometimes hurt others, but it's a world in which people almost always learn some Valuable Lesson. Such programmes may not always end happily, but they usually end reasonably. The trouble is that dom-com people are dumb. No matter how many times they learn the same Valuable Lesson, it never quite sinks in. Next week at 8:30 they've got to learn it all over again.

But there's a striking difference between the people of 1950s domestic comedies and those of the 1970s programmes. The 1950s shows were hopeful, philanthropic (in the original sense of the word), and unabashedly sentimental —the TV equivalent of Frank Capra's films of the 1930s. If people made mistakes, it wasn't because they weren't good people. According to these programs, we were all essentially good; it was

105

just that sometimes we were a bit thoughtless or careless or dumb.

The mood of 1970s domestic comedies is pessimistic and misanthropic. Bob (Hartly) Newhart, as David Feldman noted in the *Journal of Popular Culture,* is a psychologist who can't communicate. The city he inhabits (Chicago) is a concrete jungle. It has none of the warm, friendly city streets Jim Anderson used to drive along in "Father Knows Best." Although Hartley's practice is thriving, all of his patients are hopeless cases; we never once see him help anyone. Norman Lear's "All in the Family" is a kind of ethnic joke turned into a series. Its characters hold back from almost any display of tender feeling. In a recent show, Archie and Edith get back together again after a brief separation caused by Archie's infatuation with a waitress. The two of them embrace on the porch – one of the rare tender moments in the show – but instead of a fade-out on the embrace or its scene continuing silently, what we get is a scene played for laughs. The characters in this show, like those in "Maude" and "Phyllis" and so many other current domestic comedies, are so hard-edged, so inhuman, that I find them repulsive. It's a world in which nothing really matters. As Arthur Berger puts it in his recent book, *The TV-Guided American,* such programmes offer the reverse of the myth of the 1950s domestic comedy – "the myth of the American as 'Nature's Nobleman,' as a clean-cut, hard-working, rugged, self-reliant individual who achieves his goals through force of will power and determination. What we find are a collection of weak-willed, middle-class . . . neurotic losers who find themselves in awkward situations all the time."

The most interesting development on television this season is the breakdown of the line that's separated soap operas from domestic comedies (and day-time from night-time television). Domestic comedies are becoming three and four-part serials from which even the pretence of happy endings is disappearing. Like soap operas, domestic comedies are presenting us with a *neverending* series of problems. "Mary Hartman, Mary Hartman" represents the ultimate development. It offers us as misanthropic a view of mankind and as loathsome a set of characters as have ever been found between two television station breaks.

From the time "The Plouffe Family" ended in 1959, Canadian programmers assumed that the Americans were producing more than enough half-hour comedy shows for both of us. In any case, we were above turning out *schlock.* Our limited resources were going to be devoted to *quality* programming. If people preferred American *schlock* to all the good things the CBC could give them, that was their loss.

It wasn't until the mid-1960s that the CBC realized it had an obligation to try to produce drama that was both good *and* popular. The result was series like "Wojeck" and "Quentin Durgens." But despite these successes, the CBC stayed clear of half-hour comedies. We'd come to believe so firmly that we couldn't or shouldn't compete in this area that we didn't even try. Canadians with a talent for such programming – the Winnipeg writer Perry Rosemond, for instance – simply moved to the U.S. It wasn't until "Delilah" in 1973 that the CBC tried again to produce a comedy series.

"Delilah" was a disaster. That's not surprising if one considers that at the three major U.S. networks, with their huge program development budgets, only one in six or seven shows for which pilots are made actually gets on the air. The CBC's "Delilah" was a program without adequate planning or funding and was being attempted at a network that had had no experience with a half-hour comedy series for more than a decade. The scripts were unbelievably bad. They were based on the assumption that the idea of a woman barber in an Ontario small town is inherently funny. The program was laughed off the air.

The experience taught the CBC a Valuable Lesson. It learned that producing a successful half-hour comedy series wasn't nearly so easy as it looked. If anything, it was more difficult than doing serious drama. What was required was the TV equivalent of a good rep company turning out an original thirty minute play every week. The central idea and main characters had to be strong enough to hold an audience.

When John Hirsch took over the CBC's drama department, he brought Perry Rosemond back from the U.S. to develop a comedy series. Rosemond did a pilot (it was awful) but the program

"King of Kensington," was given the go-ahead anyway. Those involved would have to learn on the job. It was a daring decision. "King of Kensington," a domestic comedy based around the life of Larry King (Al Waxman), who runs a variety store and lives in an ethnically mixed area of downtown Toronto, came on air in September, 1975. Initial reaction to the program was largely unfavourable. Most reviewers agreed with Douglas Marshall of *TV Guide,* who wrote that "a network that can screen 'Rhoda' and 'All in the Family' on Mondays, 'M*A:S*H' and 'Mary Tyler Moore' on Fridays, and expect us to admire 'King' on Thursdays should have its collective head examined." Things were so bad that during the early weeks of the show, Perry Rosemond urged those involved in it to stay away from the CBC's offices in case

" . . . you want to know what Canada is all about . . . I'll tell you what it's all about . . . it's YOU reading and listening to all these media people in Toronto telling you what Canada is all about . . . THAT'S what it's all about . . . "

they became too demoralized by what they heard. (The show is taped in studios about a mile away.) At the end of its first thirteen episodes the show came close to being cancelled.

There was a lot that was wrong. Mostly the program lacked the production values of an American show. Its colour wasn't as crisp, its editing as sharp. The scripts were terribly uneven; they tended to begin badly, and too often the writers forgot they were writing domestic comedy and reached for the kinds of gags that make sit-com work. (Larry King: "Hey Ma, what people called you kikes?" Gladys King: "The honkies.")

But there were important things that were right. Waxman himself turned in an excellent performance every week, even when the scripts were at their worst. As Frank Penn of the Ottawa *Citizen* put it, "There's something about the man. Under the easy grin and the . . . well-nourished cheeks, there's a sense of [the kind of] inner energy that illuminated John Vernon's 'Wojeck' and [Gordon Pinsent's] 'Quentin Durgens'. . . . " Fiona Reid, as his wife, seemed to grow in her role from show to show. There were some fine guest appearances by people like Peter Kastner. With the exceptions of Gladys King (Helene Winston) as the stereotypical Jewish mother and Max (John Dee) as the stereotypical befuddled old person on TV, the characters on "King of Kensington" were less predictable than those on American shows. As the weeks went by, the scriptwriters realized their error with Gladys; the stereotype was muted, and she, too, became more interesting and less mechanical.

Mostly what I liked was the show's pace, its mood, its tone. As one friend put it, "Compared to the people in 'King of Kensington,' those on American shows seem speeded up." "King of Kensington" felt like a 1950s domestic comedy rather than one from the 1970s.

Even in its most cynical moments, its view of human nature was less bleak. In an early show, for instance, Larry, who's a bit of a bleeding-heart liberal, can't sleep. "Cathy," he groans, "The prison system isn't working." "I know," she says, "but the fridge isn't working, the shower isn't working, and seven percent of the public isn't working. Let's go to bed!" On "King of Kensington" that line is warm and human; imagine how it would sound if Archie Bunker said it.

People on "King of Kensington" have much softer edges than those on current American domestic comedies; they're not afraid to show real feelings. At times they're as blatantly sentimental as the characters in a Capra film and, as in Capra, laughter and tears aren't far apart in many episodes. One of my favourite examples of this occurred in this season's opening programme (a show whose colour and editing demonstrated a great improvement over last year's). Larry and Cathy have been trying for some time to have a baby. Cathy is on fertility drugs, and there's a possibility that she's finally become pregnant. Gladys rushes out to buy a pink snowsuit, and Larry comes home with some tiny boxing gloves. While the two of them are teasing one another about their purchases, Cathy returns from the doctor's office to inform them that she's not pregnant. In a moving scene, she insists that it's time Larry was tested to find out if he's to blame: "I've been through fertility drugs, hormones . . . God knows what I've done to my body," she screams. "I'm not going through another thing till I find out if it's you." It turns out that it is Larry. On his return from the doctor, and just before he tells Cathy (as in Capra, there are obligatory confessional scenes in "King of Kensington"), Larry picks up the pink snowsuit which is lying on the couch. He clutches it briefly to himself before he goes in to speak to her. It's a lovely moment. Within ten minutes the same pink snowsuit has evoked laughter and tears. (Al Waxman didn't see *The Jolson Story* twenty-seven times for nothing.)

That's an example of a "King of Kensington" script at its best. But the same show also contained examples of a "Kensington" script at its worst. (It's the mixture of good and bad that makes so many episodes frustrating.) There's a scene in which a couple of pregnant women are treated as grotesques as they sit in a doctor's office leering at male nudes in *Viva* and *Playgirl* and saying "What's so big about that?" and, "I didn't know he was Jewish." What seems to happen all too frequently is that the writers and producers get cold feet and resort to a bit of traditional sit-com to get laughs. But the laughs are too easy, and the mixing of modes detracts sharply from the success of the show. Sometimes whole programmes—the episode about dieting, for instance—take the easy route and those shows are always the most disappointing.

Part of the problem is that "King of Kensington" is thin on experienced staff—especially writers and editors. Compare the credits on "King" with those on an American domestic comedy like "Alice." The original story for each episode of "Alice" is written by two people. The teleplay is written by a third. There are two story consultants, two story editors, and two executive story editors. Nine people for each script, and all of them are separate from the production staff. Most of the scripts for "King of Kensington" are written by Louis del Grande and Jack Humphrey, who also produce each episode. (Perry Rosemond has moved on to developing a new series and to doing "The David Steinberg Show" on CTV.) That means Humphrey and del Grande have the impossible task of editing *and* producing their own scripts. They claim there aren't yet any competent story editors and consultants in this country for such a program. "King of Kensington" is going to have to develop its own.

But an equally important part of the problem is Humphrey and del Grande's obsession with ratings. Last season "King of Kensington" drew an average audience of 800,000 or 900,000 viewers for each episode. That seems pretty good to me. But Humphrey and del Grande say they won't be happy unless they can draw the kind of audience "All in the Family" gets in Canada—about 3 million people. My guess is that the only way to get that size audience, right now, is to turn "King of Kensington" into yet another 1970s *American* dom-com.

The irony is that "King of Kensington" has been sold in the United States. Beginning in January it will be seen in nine major American cities (including New York and Los Angeles) with a total population equal to that of Canada. It's been bought by the Americans, I would guess, *not* because it's another *American* dom-com (they've got enough of those), but because it's different. Jack Humphrey and Louis del Grande have helped create something distinctively Canadian, but they don't seem to be aware of it. They still say they want to be Norman Lear when they grow up.

Morris Wolfe teaches film history at the Ontario College of Art. He writes a regular TV column for *Saturday Night,* and has edited two books, *Toronto Short Stories* and *Saturday Night Scrapbook.* "King of Kensington and the Battle for the Ratings" was first published in *Saturday Night,* December 1976.

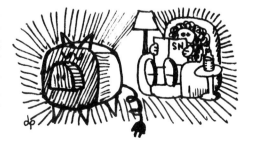

MARTIN KNELMAN

Where Lies a Critic

"The Greatest Essay Ever Written!"
—Canadian Critical Journal.

Every so often I am asked, usually by students, how one goes about becoming a critic. I find it's best to avoid hysterical reactions, such as shouting, "Are you out of your mind?" It's more effective to take a calm, reasonable approach. That way you're more likely to influence the confused person to consult a career counselor or a psychiatrist. When all else fails, the best you can do is try to disabuse the would-be-critic of some dangerous illusions.

First of all, there is the fantasy represented by the smiling dolt who descends on you at cocktail parties and opens a conversation brightly (as if he thought it was the first time you'd heard this line) with "Do you actually get *paid* to go to movies?" (Or read books, or tramp through galleries, or sit through plays, or whatever.) The least exasperating way to handle this gambit is to treat it as a rhetorical question and move on , pleading that you need another drink. If, however, you prefer to deal with the matter seriously, you can point out that movie reviewers spend a great many of their waking hours watching John Wayne westerns that have been made at least 15 times before, that drama critics are often obliged to attend bus-and-truck productions of *Man of La Mancha* on tour for the sixth time, that book reviewers are habitually expected to read volumes that no one cares to buy even when they're remaindered at the local bookstore for 59 cents.

Then there's the earnest idea that criticism is a scientific discipline, like chemistry or economics, which can be codified, learned and practised by anyone who memorizes the theory. According to this view, there are right answers and wrong answers, and any qualified critic should be able to explain why *A Star Is Born* is not a good movie, or whether you should give *Lady Oracle* to your sister-in-law for Christmas, as briskly and with the same finality as a pediatrician diagnosing a severe case of diaper rash. I hesitate to reveal this, but this view of critics is probably further from the truth than the allegation that critics don't know anything at all.

A public opinion survey once indicated that in the mind of the man on the street critics were ranked on about the same level as garbage collectors. But lately an aura of glamor has been creeping into the field: gossipy articles in *Esquire, Playboy* and *New York* magazines encourage the trendy, culturally chic reader to get interested in the inside story on what Rex Reed said about Judith Christ's deodorant commercials, or why John Simon has to wear a rain hat at Sardi's, or how Molly Haskell fell in love with Andrew Sarris' *auteur* theory. Understandably enough, the sophisticated magazines don't tell you the inside story on the guy who rewrites press releases at the Moose Jaw *Weekly Chronicle*.

I stumbled into the field through a series of accidents and a general aversion to offices where people are expected to show up at 9 AM wearing neckties. Too late, I discovered that criticism has its own set of occupational hazards: readers who expect you to be a consumer rating service (***1/2 for *The Pink Panther Strikes Again*, **1/2 for last week's CBC drama special, and skip the explanations); editors who think it's in your line of duty to stay awake all the way through *Eliza's Horoscope*, without danger pay; aficionados who call at 2:30 AM asking if you can settle a bet about who won the Academy Award for best special sound effects in 1947. And friends who, after reading your 1,500 well-chosen words on *Equus*, ask discreetly: "But tell me, what did you *really* think of the play?"

One of the main problems for a critic who sees and reviews more or less everything is to find something worth saying about something that doesn't leave much room for thinking of any kind. Should it really be necessary, after all, to explain in detail what is wrong with, say, *Airport?* Critics of critics sometimes seem to think that a reviewer can be discredited if it is demonstrated that his observations are not "objective." But the critic's task is to shed some light on his subject, bringing to bear whatever is at hand – knowledge of the field, personal responses, discussions with friends, experiences in the world at large. There's nothing objective about this, of course. Critics are notorious for contradicting each other, and a particular review probably won't mean anything unless you've been following the reviewer long enough to get a fix on his way of seeing things.

You also have to beware of opening the mail. For starters, there's the daily flood of breathless bulletins in which CBC tells you what happens on Rhoda's blind date in next week's episode, or United Artists informs you that Faye Dunaway has just been signed to appear in the next award-winning Sidney Lumet motion picture (press releases never use the words "film" or "movie" when there is a chance to say "motion picture" instead), or the National Arts Centre threatens to put on an eight-hour epic about the Rebellion of 1837. Then there's the inevitable hate mail. Usually, people who hate your writing address their complaints to the editor while supporters write to the critic, but there are always a few personal notes from those who wish to draw your attention to your chronic stupidity or moral degeneracy. Sometimes they achieve charming turns of Phrase. For failing to appreciate the romanticism of Zeffirelli's *Romeo and Juliet*, I received a letter from some students addressed to "Knelman the Knut."

The social life of a critic can get awfully tricky. When I began reviewing movies in 1967, one of the first things I noticed was the protective distance between the Canadian critic and his subject. You weren't likely to have to face Natalie Wood at a reception the night after panning her performance, and Steve McQueen didn't know you well enough to write nasty letters to your editor. But, with the explosion of movies, theatre, and just about all the arts in this country in the late 1960s and early 1970s, the "otherness" of culture has become a thing of the past. Now it's more difficult to maintain critical distance and it's wise to follow a few rules. For instance: Don't drop by for tea (or worse, an interview) with a performer who's to appear in a play you're reviewing the next night. And try to avoid being trapped in a screening room with a film director who is given to asking, 10 seconds after the lights come up: "So, whad'ya think of it?"

The biggest trap of all, however, is the one that makes you fodder for the quote ads. You know the kind of thing I mean: "Brilliant"—Collins, *The Sun* . . . "There is perfection in every frame"—Williams, *The Daily Bugle* . . . "Your life will never be the same again"—Thomas, *The Post.* In the interests of selling their product, movie companies take short, punchy excerpts from the most euphoric notices, dress them up in huge black type and exclamation points, and zap the public with them. You may have noticed that the ads rarely quote lines like "If a different kind of actor had been used in the leading role, it might help the audience understand what the movie is supposed to be about."

This practice often makes household words out of the names of critics writing for obscure publications and can have a peculiar effect on reviewers who like to see their names in lights. Some are so eager to become famous that they start writing, and possibly even thinking, like quotes ads. Personally, I'm fishing around for a reciprocal arrangement so that I can have a quote for my tombstone:

HERE LIES MARTIN KNELMAN
"A BRILLIANT CRITIC!. . .
ONE OF THE YEAR'S BEST!"
—PARAMOUNT PICTURES.

Martin Knelman's career as a film critic came together in *This Is Where We Came In: The Career and Character of Canadian Films* (1977). "Where Lies a Critic" first appeared in *Weekend,* March 5, 1977.

BARBARA FRUM

All the Not-Nice Questions

"They're always there— whether you've got the gumption to ask them or not."

In October, 1972, a party of young Uruguayan rugby players crashed in the frozen peaks of the Andes while flying to a match in Chile. They were lost for 70 days, until two of the hardiest and bravest managed to climb out of those desolate mountains and led rescuers to their helpless comrades. A year later the two young heroes were in North America to publicize the book *Alive,* which told their story. The book was a bestseller, not just because it described an extraordinary adventure, but because it vividly spelled out how the boys had refused to die of starvation and survived by eating the flesh of those who had been killed on impact. There were many people at the time who condemned the survivors, suggesting that cannibalism was too terrible an act to be condoned —which struck me as pretty pious. It was like saying that the boys should have died there, so that we could have praised them for their nobility. For me, the fact of cannibalism was only a distracting —although admittedly bizarre—detail, really only a symbol of what human beings are prepared to do to live.

When Nando Parrado and Roberto Canessa became available for interview on CBC Radio's "As It Happens," I decided to downplay the obvious and ghoulish aspects. Instead, I thought I'd concentrate on the psychological choices of staying alive, and on what they'd learned on that mountain about themselves and others. All had not been generosity and self-sacrifice among the Andes survivors; in fact, their survival had involved some pretty selfish and unheroic things. I wanted to hear about those aspects and about the kind of character it takes to keep on going in a seemingly hopeless situation.

Unfortunately, I got to talk to Parrado and Canessa only after they had become veterans of the talk-show circuit and had learned how to handle interviewers. As they came bustling into our New York studio, I could overhear them on the line—friendly, vital, easygoing young men, clearly enjoying the attention they were getting. About 15 minutes into the interview, after it became obvious that the boys had turned the drama of their suffering into a pat performance, I hesitantly asked, "Would you be offended if I wondered if finally a human being doesn't have to be a bit of a bastard to survive a terrible event—if maybe saints don't make it?" Before I could establish whether they had understood what I was getting at, Canessa responded in the same humble, earnest manner he'd used in answering all my other questions.

"No. I think you must be a warm man to survive, because although I was suffering, if I'd died there, I would have felt that I'd tried my best for everybody."

It was a sweet answer but it didn't explain how people survive any better than had the rest of our conversation; although it struck me as interesting that it was Canessa, the domineering and difficult one on the mountain, who had answered, rather than Parrado, who was described as spoiled and thoughtless before the tragedy, but in crisis came as close as a human being can to selflessness.

Anyway, I let the subject drop and, after a few more exchanges, I said, "I wish you both good luck," to signal that I was about to sign off the line. Canessa, however, wasn't finished with me. The moment he thought we were off the air he jumped in hard.

"Do you still think we are bastards?" he demanded.

"I am sorry, Mr. Canessa," I answered uneasily. "You see, that's the trouble. What right have I got to stand in judgment of you? It's just that we all identify so much with you and what you've suffered. And we feel tormented because we fear that we would be no good at all."

"You feel that way?" he repeated, unsatisfied. And again I tried to explain what I had meant.

"You see, we're struggling to understand how a human being could have the strength to put up with what you did. Do you see?"

"But I think if we were just animals there," he answered quietly, "if we just think of ourselves, we would have killed each other in a fight, or each one go his own way. But we are human beings. I

think that's the reason why it worked."

And then he really let me have it.

"But I appreciate very much that you are sincere and you told me your feeling. I always fight for the people to say what they feel. *Not only nice things."* And with that, he stood up and walked out of the studio, but not before all that pique and pain and hostility had gone out over the air. To this moment I still feel some guilt for demanding introspection. Parrado and Canessa didn't owe me—or anybody—an accounting of their thoughts or motives. Of course, I remain fascinated by who survives and how they do so, and I always have been—long before cannibalism in the Andes and long before the Marten Hartwell story.

Hartwell, you remember, was the German bush pilot who crashed in the Arctic while on a mercy flight, bringing a British nurse, Judy Hill, a sick Inuit boy and his pregnant aunt to hospital. After a 19-day search, that plane was given up for lost, on the grounds that a human being couldn't possibly survive in that frozen wasteland for more than a very short time.

It could be argued that Hartwell would not have been a survivor at all had it not been for some of us at "As it Happens". We stayed with the story of the lost plane after everybody else, including Air Rescue, had gone on to better things. I'm convinced that it was our broadcasting of the plea of Hartwell's girlfriend, Susan Haley, that persuaded James Richardson, then minister of defence, to launch that final, successful search.

Within hours of Hartwell's rescue, and the news that the three others on board had died, we began to get the upsetting store of cannibalism—and worse—from our northern stringer. Maybe because we felt a part of Hartwell's survival, maybe because we didn't want to believe it, we didn't broadcast what we were hearing. Cannibalism in South America, perhaps, but on Canadian soil—unthinkable. None of my arguements for staying with the story, nor the lobbying of an equally intrigued colleague, Richard Bronstein, convinced the others. Each morning Richard would come huffing into the story conference with the latest bulletin from the North. And each day his proposals were shot down. Hartwell might have resorted to cannibalism, but if we said so, *that* would be in bad taste.

Well, much of life is in bad taste and our rejection of the story did not change the facts of Hartwell's survival. It also didn't prevent the story from becoming a lurid, international scandal. The details were played for all they were worth, in good taste and in bad. Top mark in the latter category has to go to the headline writer in London who came up with this classic for *News of the World:* Ex-Luftwaffe Pilot Eats British Nurse.''

The question of taste is always a problem in doing survivor stories. When terrible things happen to people, and you decide to report on them, all the not-nice questions are there, absolutely explicit, whether you've got the gumption to ask them or not. It's an awful game between you and your guest. In your head you can almost hear them muttering to themselves, ''I wonder how this one's going to put it? How's this one going to ask me how I managed to eat my friends?'' Sometimes I'm amazed that survivors tell you anything at all. Most people won't share intimate experiences with people who are closest to them, never mind with some lady on the telephone from Canada whom they've never seen and with whom they will never have to deal again. . . .

I used to share a television studio with an interviewer who not only verbally abused his guests, but every once in a while would get so caught up in the discussion that he had to be physically restrained from throttling his startled sub-jects before they could escape the set. That's not a style of interviewing I've ever liked. Not that I like the straight-out seduction session any better; in that one the interviewer courts his guest— whether man or woman—with appreciative chuckles, a few flattering questions, perhaps a self-deprecating remark or two, and then—having successfully charmed his quarry—and only then, does this seductive type decide what he wants from his fascinated guest. It's a useful approach—practised, for some reason, more by men than women—but one I've never been comfortable with, either.

It's not that I don't like to be liked. But being liked has never struck me as a pre-condition for an effective interview. When your guests aren't obliged to like you, or you them, you can't beat the liberty and possibility that opens up on all sides. I would like to think that most of the interviews I do are conducted in an atmosphere of cordiality and even warmth. But every once in a while something in the voice—something in the sound of an answer—gets to me. The adrenalin surges, and before I realize it I'm going for broke: what makes him think he can get that one by me?

There was a psychiatrist in London, Ontario, for example, who'd managed to get himself some press attention by attaching a pitch for psychiatric halfway houses to the eye-catching claim that large mental hospitals were themselves driving people crazy. His halfway house proposal sounded worthy enough; but what was this, I asked, about hospitals creating madness? Would you give us an example of that?

''No,'' he replied, ''I won't.''

Hmm, I thought, suddenly curious. ''Why not?''

''Because I don't want to,'' he spit back.

''This guy had to be kidding. ''Why won't you?''

''Because I won't.''

That's all it takes, I'm ashamed to say, to turn me into a terrier. I wouldn't relent. This was his idea, after all, about hospitals creating craziness instead of curing it, not mine. What did he mean, he didn't want to discuss it? Just as stubbornly, the doctor refused to offer a single instance to back up his claim. Our scrapping, of course, completely distracted him from his pitch for government funding for his pet project. Serves him right, I've always figure. Maybe next time he won't make claims that he's not prepared to prove.

I rarely indulge myself in that kind of testiness. I don't remember ever beginning an interview with the intent to injure. Occasionally I'll come on tough, or order a guest to remove her impenetrable sunglasses, as I once did to a woman who'd planned to spend the interview sheltered behind her shielding lenses. But when I do that, it's not to start ahead, but to start even.

These exchanges started out as straightforward interviews but ended as collisions. If you measure them by the amount of information extracted, they're all failures. For excitement, however, they're tops.

The most adrenalinized high of all for me has to be my radio meeting with Sandra Good. The moment the wires flashed the news that Lynette "Squeaky" Fromme (pronounced as in "home, please, not "hum") had tried to shoot U.S. President Ford in front of the California state legislature in Sacramento, we were on the phone dialling for her roommate and fellow Manson family member, Sandra Good.

We found Good easily. She was revelling in yet another round of press attention and holding forth from the apartment that the Manson girls had shared until four days before, when Fromme went downtown to gun down Gerald Ford. Good was feeling bloody-minded, that was clear. From the moment she came on the line–even from the belligerent way she said "Hello"–her attitude was pugnacious and disdainful. How many minutes did I have before she punished me by hanging up?

There was an unnerving lunacy about the interview. I was pushing against this unspoken deadline, desperately trying to find out about her roommate. But all she would tell me about was the need for saving the fish and trees. She had the friends who carves up people as casually as Col. Sanders carves up chickens; but I was the one who was put down for my appetite for sensationalsim.

The interview incensed a lot of listeners and puzzled many others. Was she crazy or was she evil? Part of her message sounded almost reasonable. Even now, after all these months, I'm occasionally asked how I manage to stay so calm despite the spew of venom directed at me. Actually, I'm not convinced that I handled that interview at all well. Once I realized that Good was prepared to give me only a speech, I had a dilemma. She was never going to tell me anything insightful about Fromme. So what to do? Sit there and accept it? or take a chance on provoking her? I chose the second, hoping for a glimpse of the mad space that Fromme and Good were in.

Miss Good, have you had any contact with Lynette Fromme since her arrest?

No.

Have you been able to see her?

No

Have you been able to communicate with her?

No.

Can you tell us the condition you last saw her in? When did you see her last?

We had been looking at the state of this country and of the world and it's a mess. It's a big mess and it needs cleaning up. If people are going to survive, change is necessary. There are many, many people, thousands of people, children included, who are tired of the destruction of the environment, the wildlife, rivers, the oceans, cutting down the trees and—

Miss Good, could we talk about that in a minute?

Yeah.

Could you tell us more about Lynette Fromme first?

I'm answering your question.

No, I asked you when was the last time you saw Lynette Fromme.

Listen, these picayuney questions really don't mean—I don't understand what you're getting at. This is a reflection—rather than looking at the little picayuney details of when she got up or her particular state of mind—it's irrelevant. There are a lot of roots to problems that people have, a world people, a nation people. There are certain acts that reflect problems.

What do you think about what happened in Sacramento?

That also is a rather ignorant question. What do I think about it? I think it's time that this country started taking a look at itself, taking a look at its problems, and not hold positive solutions to the problems down.

All right. Miss Good, if you wouldn't mind, let's hear a little bit more, please, about when you last saw Lynette Fromme and what kind of shape she was in.

That question shows your ignorance and I won't answer it.

Miss Good, how come you're talking about trees that you care about and yet you don't mind killing men?

Men that kill life, that kill harp seals, that kill trees, that poison oceans and rivers and air are killing all of us because we need these things to live. Start looking at your world, woman. Start looking at the world you're leaving for your kids and quit putting sensational news stories and what you look like and your social position over life.

Miss Good, do you think any—

Listen, woman—

Pardon?

Don't probe me like that. You listen to what I'm saying and you tone your manner of questioning down or I'll hang up. Do you understand me?

Well, I'm prepared for your hanging up. You know, that's one of the risks.

You're prepared for what you want to hear. You're not going to get what you want to hear. Listen, put me on to somebody else. I don't like you.

Why not?

Trouble. Because you're probing me with what's in your mind and I'm trying to tell you things as I see them, not as you wish me to tell you, not as a—

Tell us about Charles Manson then.

Let's start this all over again.

Okay. Tell us about Charles Manson.

You go to him yourself.

You have been quoted as saying that his job is to straighten out the world.

His job? It's your job, woman. It's your job. He's been left out of this world's madness. You'd better pray he'll help you fix yourselves up. You'd better pray. It's your job, woman, to start making gardens rather than pushing your husbands to destroy things. Start talking to the executives, the killers of wildlife and the Earth. You stop. There's a wave of assassins called the International People's Court of Retribution and they're watching you.

Was the attack on President Ford justified, then?

Yes. Any attack on any life is justified. Any attack on anyone who puts money and lies over people's lives is justified. There'll be many,many, killings, many killings. Best you be willing to open your mind and look at the roots of problems. Look at the problems that are besetting your world, your country.

Miss Good, let's talk about killing for a minute, okay? You say—

Listen woman, put me on to somebody else. I can't talk to you.

Why?

You're a very, very bad reporter. You're very bad. Put me on to somebody else. You're one of the worst, really. You really are. You're very rude, very imperceptive, you're very ignorant. Your technique is just crude. You don't have any finesse. Now put me on to somebody else.

I'm it, Miss Good. I'm it, I'm afraid.

Are you a man or a woman?

I'm a man.

Are you a man? You are a woman.

Well then, why did you ask?

Because you reflect a woman's fear. Your unwillingness to look at problems.

I see. And you?

I reflect a lot of children. I reflect a lot of people with concern for the Earth and the children—

Miss Good, children grow up to be men and women.

All right, in your sense. In the robot, computerized, slave-for-the-dollar sense, go-to-school-and-spend-your-life-in-a-book sense, or living-life sense. What are you talking about?

You say you talk for children, yet you talk of killing men.

I'm talking about people who will be killed. Don't interrupt me again. When I talk about killing I'm saying that there will be a wave of assassins killing those who are killing the environment, the wildlife, the trees, selling products to the children, and the people—

Miss Good?

Don't interrupt me.

Miss Good?

[Click. She was gone.]

Barbara Frum is well known as the host of the CBC radio program, *As It Happens*. "All the Not-Nice Questions" is excerpted from *As It Happened,* published by The Canadian Publishers, McClelland and Stewart.

ALAN METTRICK

A Journalism Professor's Education in When to Quit

How the hell did we ever get into this?

There had been about 40 of us through the afternoon and evening, at long tables which were shoved together taking up half the tavern. Now the three of us sat at one end in the near-dark under the smoke and the Christmas decorations.

What to say? We had been colleagues who liked and respected each other, and because of a bare-assed principle we had managed to do quite a lot of damage to each other.

If we could have located the principle amid the empty draft pitchers, ash and trash on the tables, if it had been something we could see and touch, we would have beaten it to death.

I said: "How the hell did we get into this?" I said it the way those good old boys, perching on your desk in the newsroom when they're suicidal, or sometimes when they're loving it all, ask . . . "What are we *doing* here?"

I think Bradley said: "How do we get out of it?" and we started talking about that, but we didn't really think we could put Humpty together again. No way.

This was on Tuesday night, December 14, 1976. On the Friday before that, Tony Hodgkinson and I had quit our jobs on the faculty of the journalism program at St. Clair College in Windsor. Hodgkinson was journalism co-ordinator at the college. I was a sessional instructor. Together we were the entire journalism department. Our resignations had gone to David Bradley, chairman of the Communication Arts Department.

All of us had good track records in the news business, and on some pretty ritzy turf, too.

And here we were, fighting for our credibility over a so-so story written by a couple of first-year journalism students who may or may not end up in the business.

Fighting, too, in public. A story running to almost a column on page three of *The Windsor Star* of December 13 was headed: "Teachers quit posts in dispute at College." The *Canadian Press* version ran across two columns in *The Globe and Mail* the following morning. The head was "College blocks story, journalism staff quits."

And God knows where else in Canada people who had known all or one of us were scanning a filler and saying: "What are they playing at down there? Are they crazy?"

The were paying me around $400 a week for 18 hours in the classroom, so I wondered about that, on and off.

Hodgkinson has a wife, three kids, a dog, two station wagons and a home on the lake. I dare say he gave it a thought.

And Bradley, who had just acquired $65,000 worth of high class VDT hardware for a program which was rapidly running out of warm bodies, was stuck in the middle like a wood-saw.

Crazy. But then that was the week Braithwaite told Trudeau to stick his sake up his ass, and Lynch had his sit-in.

What the hell is going on?

Whenever I tried to explain to the students at St. Clair why I had quit, there was a hiatus of milliseconds after we had pulled up our chairs for a better look at each other, cleared our throats, and got to look serious, when I couldn't think of a thing to say.

(When I first showed up at the college an amiable chap called Al Trotter who teaches photography said: "I can't tell you the number of times I've stood up there with my back to the class and my hand raised to the blackboard, holding the chalk, and said to myself, "Please, God, tell me what to write.")

At best your explanation—if it's a *principle* you're trying to get your mouth and mind around—will be a paean to perception.

And I plain hadn't had much practice. In 16 years I hadn't quit for any reason more fundamental than a change of scenery.

The story was about a civil servant, the head of a department within Health and Welfare Canada, who said he didn't think there was any evidence of an epidemic of swine flu and that he thought the nationwide immunization program was a political decision and not based on medical considerations. (This was about a week before the vaccine program was halted because of the danger of paralysis.)

The civil servant was Dr. David C. Villeneuve, head of the Biochemical Toxicology Unit, which is part of the Health Protection Branch of Health and Welfare. He made the comments on swine flu in the course of a lecture to students in the college's Health Sciences Program. Two first-year journalism students, sent to cover the meeting, were in the room. Anybody could wander in and out, and the journalism department had been specifically invited to cover Dr. Villeneuve's talk for *The Journal*, the weekly newspaper students put out.

After the lecture and question period were over, the two journalism students, Neil Poli and Bill Baxter, asked Dr. Villeneuve to elaborate on his swine flu comments. He told them: "The Department (Health and Welfare) doesn't like its employees knocking government programs, and I wouldn't want to lose my job."

He then asked to go off the record, but nothing he said subsequently conflicted with his earlier on-the-record indictment of the swine flu program.

I told Poli and Baxter I liked the story.

They were nervous. Poli, who had been one of the brightest and sassiest of the first-year group, went through his notes for me, and his hand was shaking. I felt good towards them both. You know when you're feeding the hungry.

(A couple of points: First-year students did not normally write for *The Journal* as part of their program; that was generally left to the second-and third-year segments of the three-year program. So this was a departure, and a tough situation for Poli and Daxter to walk into.)

And journalism programs, like other college courses, owe a lot to the abacus. It's the numbers game, baby. The more students you can attract to a program—and hold for the long haul—the more enrolment money comes in, the bigger the matching funds, the more

120

lavish the program becomes. So you begin to make body counts like a mad mortician, looking for signs of life here, a flicker of talent there. (One of the best days started when I asked one young woman: "You're not going to drop out, are you, Sue?" and she said : "I've wanted to be a journalist since grade seven.")

Baxter and Poli went to telephone Ottawa to find out exactly what the Biochemical Toxicology Unit of the Environmental Toxicology Division of the Environmental Health Directorate of the Health Protection Branch of the Health and Welfare Department—that's what it said on Villeneuve's card—well, what they actually *did* there.

The Biochemical Toxicology Unit, aghast at the audacity, refused to say what it did. "We can't comment on that here. You'll have to go to the public relations department."

It was a fine thing to see a couple of rookies get mad. Baxter and Poli had wanted to do the job as discreetly as possible, without bandying Villeneuve's name about. Now, we had to put some more students on the story to help out. And we had to contact more people in Ottawa. The hell with the budget. These kids were starting to get an education.

It took a day and a half to get the people they needed in Ottawa to stand the story up. It wasn't perfect, but it hung together. We put it in *The Journal,* on page one. As the lead story.

The copy is typeset and the pages made up in a room adjoining the larger newsroom in the basement of the college.

The office that Tony Hodgkinson and I shared is also in the basement, just across the corridor from Bradley's office. The college itself is a grey four-storey pinstripe of a place located close to where Highway 401 empties into the outskirts of the city. When he was describing the structure to me on the telephone before I'd set eyes on it, Bradley had said: "It looks like a prison."

The decor in the basement is all acned pastels. A grey army of lockers, single file, hugs the walls.

The journalism program was surprisingly well-equipped, I thought. The newsroom has more than 20 electric typewriters, sitting at enclosed desks around the walls. There is a *Broadcast News* teletype.

In the make-up room is a headliner, typesetter, and the rest of the paraphernalia for paste-up. The paper, which comes out every week, is usually eight or even 12 pages of news and features—no advertising. We didn't bother with rock concert reviews or a slew of juvenile comment pieces—there isn't much demand for 19-year-old editorial writers—but concentrated on hard stand-up news and features. In the weeks before the Villeneuve story, we had page one material on a hockey coach who saved the life of a player on the ice, a Christmas fund for poor families which had racked up a paltry $2, a federal liberal MP saying on campus that one way or another Trudeau wouldn't last past the next election, gun-running between Detroit and Windsor, the news that students might have to start paying to park their cars in college parking lots. It's closer to the real thing than any other journalism program paper I've seen.

And I had a lot of time for Bradley and Hodgkinson.

Once a couple of men I had never seen before came into the newsroom while I was conducting a class. One of them introduced himself as acting president of the college. He was "sitting in" for the president, who was away. His companion was also a senior college official whose title I forget. The acting president said that a vice-chairman of the board of

governors was very upset about a story we had run in *The Journal*. The story had described regular outbreaks of drunken violence in the streets of Wallaceburg, Ontario, where the vice-chairman lived. The vice-chairman was worried about the image the story might give the town. The vice-chairman thought the reporter, a third-year student, should have talked to the Member of Parliament for the area before writing the story. She talked to everyone else: hotel owners, police, local organizations, residents . . . it was a tight, well-researched story about a small town in a lot of trouble.

I had no wish to get involved in this Mickey Mouse debate and, in any case, they wanted Bradley, who was out. I took them down the hall to the office to talk to Hodgkinson. Hodgkinson heard the vice-chairman's views as related by the acting president of the college and after he had heard it he said: "I don't give a damn what he thinks."

Then Bradley came across the hall and into the office. He had no idea what had transpired to that point, so the delegation went through it again.

When they finished Bradley took his pipe out of his mouth and said: "Tough shit."

After they had gone, Bradley said: "He signs the cheques. He probably won't sign for the VDT equipment now." He made a joke out of it, but I said: "That sort of stuff is only going to get worse around here as the kids get better."

He said: "I know."

Bradley is slight, sharp-featured and tenacious. Once I saw him spend several hours on his hands and knees trying to remedy an electrical fault in the headliner. He fiddled with panel after panel and fuse after fuse until he got it fixed.

In the interests of instilling what he called "good work habits" in the journalism students, night after night, he would go through the newsroom after they had left, tossing all textbooks and exercise books left there into the garbage. He used to say: "Can you imagine Honderich walking in on a mess like this? He'd have a heart attack."

Usually Tony or I fished them out again before the garbage was taken away.

When he hired me to teach journalism, Bradley said: "It beats working."

His reputation was that of an efficient administrator and smart politician, respected for many reasons, not least for looking after his staff. He was a former *Toronto Star* assistant managing editor. He read the papers front to back every day, and would come into the office, shut the door and say things like "Goddamn tourism's feuding again"—the Tourism

Department faculty is also under his jurisdiction—as if newspapermen had more sense than to fight each other. His demeanor is austere. Some of the kids are frightened by his distance, yet he and I agreed to go to lunch a couple of time, not at the faculty lounge or some restaurant, but to a topless bar he called "The Tit Palace."

He's a tweedy, drab dresser, like a country farmer, which he is, part-time, with half-a-dozen acres and some livestock. One faculty member said to me: "At one time he used to come in and put his shoes on the desk and there was pigshit all over them." On the day of the Villeneuve thing, in the morning, he had come across to the office and told me his wife had just called. The guy who picked up the sheep for slaughter was on his way to the house to make a pick-up, and his wife, home on her own, had to chase all over the acreage to get them penned. His wife taught part-time at the university.

Bradley is also president of the NDP in Windsor. He always seems to be lighting his pipe while you're talking to him.

At about 10 A.M., while third-year students were putting the paper together, Neil Poli came into the news lab trailed by a lady I had never met. They were both excited. Poli said: "Mr. Mettrick, we're in trouble. We can't run that story.

This lady says we are going to be sued."

I went down the hall to my office with the woman, who was co-ordinator of the Health Sciences program. Her name was Dorit Girash. In the office she said Villeneuve had been on the telephone from Ottawa saying that the Ottawa papers had got hold of the story of his speech and that it must not appear.

I said: "The Ottawa papers can't have the story. It hasn't appeared in our paper yet and we haven't talked to anyone else about it."

"He said some paper has been calling up and he's in trouble."

"That would be our journalism paper, *The Journal*. We're running the story," I said.

"You can't. This man could lose his job. He has helped set up programs for Health Sciences. He helps the students find jobs . . . what he said was off-the-record."

"What he said after the speech was off-the-record, or part of it. We're not running that. We're running a report of the speech he gave to 60 kids in public."

She said: "You are on faculty and you have a responsibilty to the college as a whole. You can't wreck a program like this."

"I understand your feelings, but we just can't kill stories on that basis, even in *The Journal*," I told her. "If you feel this strongly, you're going to have to talk to David Bradley.'

Bradley wasn't in his office so I took her telephone local. He came down the hall a couple of minutes after she had left. I told him what was going on and, when I said Villeneuve had apparently helped set up some college programs, he said: "That's bullshit." I got him a copy of the story, an estimate of the number of people who were at the lecture and a memo saying we had specifically been invited to cover Villeneuve by a class representative from Health Sciences.

Later he came and leaned against the doorframe of the office. "She phoned Stan Bah (Bah is the dean of the School of Health Sciences). He tells me Villeneuve can sue us for libel if we run the story."

"And he concluded that from what he was told on the phone without seeing the story?" I said.

"Yes."

We both thought that was funny.

Then Bradley said something to the effect that Villeneuve had in fact helped set up part of the Health Sciences program and was involved in getting jobs for graduates.

Before he left he said: "I'll kill the story if Q tells me to kill it."

Q is the nickname for college president Richard Quittenton. He signs himself "Q" at the foot of official memoranda, such as the President's message in the annual college calendar.

When Hodgkinson got back from his class I told him briefly what had happened. Hodgkinson is an emotional six-foot-plus transplanted Britisher who smokes cigars commensurate with his size. He had been teaching journalism at the college for more than four years. The kids liked him a lot.

Hodgkinson went to talk to Bradley. They were friends and treated each other with a press club irreverence out of place in the basement. There were a lot of serious people down there. Nobody went home without a briefcase.

Baxter came down the hall and said to me: "I thought for sure you'd kill the story when she (Girash) started talking like that. . . ."

For some reason that made me angrier than anything else. "You don't kill newspaper stories because somebody asks you to," I told him.

When Hodgkinson came back from Bradley's office he said: "I told him if he killed the story I would have to take a certain action," meaning, I took it, he would quit.

I thought: "What the f--- is going on here?"

"It's not going to happen," I told him.

He said: "How can we go back in there and talk to those kids about freedom of the press if we have to kill a story everytime somebody in this place takes exception to it?"

Only a couple of weeks earlier, Tony had flown to Texas at college expense to attend a conference where the chief topic was "freedom of the press."

I agreed with him. "It's going to be hard for me to ask any of those kids to cover a meeting or get on the phone and hustle if this story doesn't go. If they kill this, we'll have no guarantee we'll be able to get anything in the paper. And without the paper the program is dead."

Tony said: "Let's get the paper out and to the printer as soon as possible. If Bradley doesn't know it's gone, he can't very well stop it and nobody can blame him later."

We went down the hall to speed up the process.

At one point a little later Bradley said to me: "What time is that paper going out today?"

"As soon as we can get it out."

"Christ, don't do that, " he said.

"You want us to hold the paper?"

"Until this is sorted out. Otherwise

you know who will be standing in the middle of the road when the shit starts to roll downhill."

Third-year students had been trying for most of the day to set up a picture to go with the Villeneuve story. At around 2:30 P.M. a downtown immunization clinic said we could take some pictures. Tony offered to run the photographer down to the clinic and back. While he was gone, Bradley came into the lab and said: "Kill the Villeneuve story." He said it so quietly I didn't hear him the first time.

When he'd gone I told the kids to take out the story. Somebody shouted: "What?" and I said: "Just do it, will you?"

While I was still in the lab, Bradley came back. He was nervous. "That was the least of my problems today," he said. "Wait until tomorrow," I told him. Then I thought it sounded a bit too tough. As he was leaving I said: "I hope your wife got the sheep together."

By the time Tony came back there were notes for both of us from Bradley explaining essentially that he had killed the story rather than endanger another program within the college. He said he had made the decision personally without any pressure from anybody. It was a weak note.

Hodgkinson and I shared an electric typewriter. I swung it onto my desk. He said: "I'm next"—and we wrote out our resignations. I put mine under Bradley's office door that night. Tony left his on his desk the next morning, until he could hand it over to Bradley himself. We went for a drink.

Nowhere in my note did I mention specifically why I was resigning. Instead I made some vague reference to teaching "being farther away from the newsroom reality than I had anticipated. . . ."

I was embarrassed about it all.

I felt myself that too much had been made of the Villeneuve thing. I didn't want to look like a martyr and I certainly didn't want the people in Health Sciences who had blocked the story to have the magnitude of their victory—and that was how they were treating it—spelled out.

When we left the bar to go to Tony's house, it was blowing and snowing and the roads were icy. Once, the station wagon he was driving skidded and we slid out of control through a stop sign, barely missing the tail end of a line of traffic on a main road.

Bradley phoned shortly after we got in. He wanted to come over. Tony said no . . . we'd been drinking and it would be better if we talked in the morning. Bradley said he would be tied up the next day.

When he got off the phone Tony said: "Bradley went down to the bar to look for us. When has he ever done that before? He must be pretty worried about this."

Tony's wife, Doreen, said: "You did the right thing. You've been drinking. He's stone-cold sober."

In the morning Bradley asked me about my resignation. "Is it over that story?" he asked.

"Yes," I said.

He asked me into his office and he said he should explain that he had other problems the previous day. "Any other day I might have made a different decision," he said. "I couldn't fight two major issues at once."

Tony went in to talk to him and handed over his resignation note. Bradley made the same explanation to him about not having the time to think it through. "That makes it a damn sight worse," Tony said afterwards.

Dorit Girash, thinking, with some justification, she had won all the marbles, was prominent in the hallway. Tony said: "I don't think I've seen her more than twice in four years. She's been past the

125

office four times this morning."

And as news of the resignations got around, the basement got busier. Sam Pitt, who runs the television studio, told Tony: "You can't fight city hall."

Tony said: "I could have rammed his biggest camera up his ass."

One faculty member came to say he had overheard a group threatening to put Tony and me in hospital if the story ran.

When he had left, I said to Tony: "Why don't I just put the goddamn story back in the paper?"

Because of our abrupt departure the night before, *The Journal* had been left overnight and was now almost completed with a replacement story as the lead.

"If you're thinking of doing something like that, don't tell me about it," he said.

I went down to the lab, and looked at page one. The students looked at me. "I'm examining the logistics of putting that story back in," I said.

They had already made over page one twice. I wasn't about to force them to do it again. But I didn't have to. They wanted the Villeneuve story to run badly and they let me know it. "Screw 'em – put it back in," I said.

The trouble with that idea was that we had also that morning talked with *The Windsor Star*. We couldn't have avoided it if we had wanted to, because Ciaran Ganley, one of the students in a beat reporting class I taught – which took up all of Friday morning – was a *Star* reporter. Ganley is known as Skeeter. And Skeeter wasn't letting us out of his sight. Tony had also spoken by phone with a senior editor he knew personally. *The Star* was interested in checking out the Villeneuve story for itself. It was also interested in the resignation story.

But if the story ran in *The Journal*, bang went our cause and the chance of telling a wider audience about a fundamental point we felt was very important.

What I believed was that if we smuggled the story in we would have won the original skirmish, and there was a good chance we would then be able to rescind our resignations – given Bradley's conciliatory attitude – and all go back to work.

(Bradley subsequently said to me: "That would have been the best thing you could have done. If that story had run I would have backed you all the way.")

Anyway the whole thing by now was crazier than a three-ring circus. ("Send in the clowns . . . don't bother, they're here.")

I had a flight booked to Toronto so I left for the weekend. Tony went to the printers to remake page one. Again.

On Monday night the lead on the *Windsor Star* story was: "St. Clair college's two journalism instructors have submitted their resignations to protest an order by a superior not to run a story in the journalism department newspaper."

The last three paragraphs of the story read: "Mr. Bradley said he decided to order the story killed because he felt it could be detrimental to the health sciences program at the college.

"He said he did not think public money should be used to publish a story that could harm students at the college.

"He said he did not think the order would do any harm to the journalism program and 'if you want my personal opionion, I think they (Hodgkinson and Mettrick) over-reacted.'"

In the corridor Tony said to Bradley: "Your quote was on the turn . . . you know nobody turns to page four."

The same day Bradley sent me a letter which said " I have no alternative but to accept your resignation, though this is done with the deepest regret, and with a request that you reconsider your decision.

"You have so much to offer the journalism students that it would be irresponsible of me not to make a final plea that you remain. . . . "

Tuesday night at the party the students left us together at the table, some of them obviously thinking we might still be able to work something out.

I said: "We had a good program that had the potential to be one of the best. We had the best paper I've seen of its kind, the kids were starting to look really good, we had the VDT stuff which would have put them 'way out in front, we got along together . . . how the hell did this happen?"

Bradley said: "What will make you stay?"

But after a while Tony and I went to join the students somewhere else and Bradley went home.

Postscript— After a meeting between Bradley and senior college officials in mid-January, Hodgkinson withdrew his resignation. The college is setting up "a policy review board to avoid arbitrary decisions of the kind made in this case. Pre-publicity disputes will be aired fully and decisions made on contentious stories under the eye of a senior faculty advisor." Hodgkinson says, "I am satisfied there is no way a story can be killed again in this manner."

Paul Vasey, a *Windsor Star* staff writer who left the *Star* last August on leave-of-absence, replaced Mettrick in January.

Alan Mettrick is a former Toronto *Star* writer and assistant city editor. "A Journalism Professor's Education in When to Quit" was first published in *Content,* March 1977.

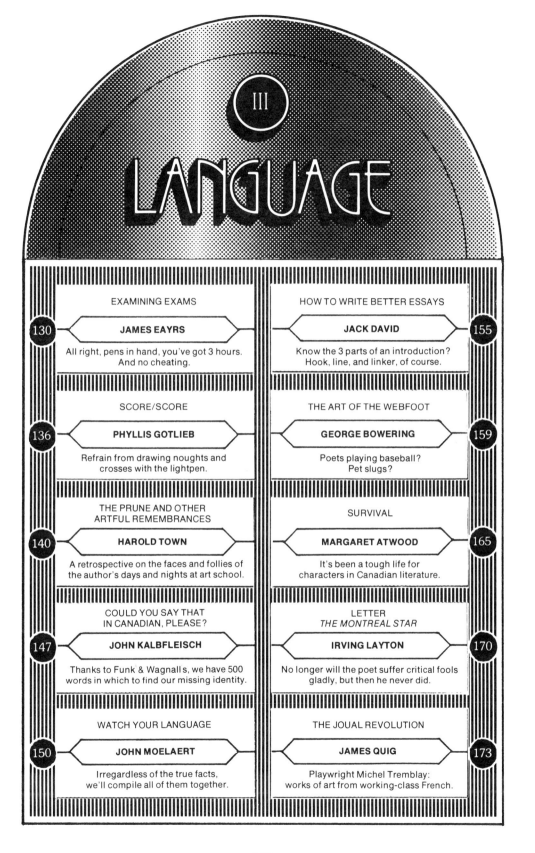

III

LANGUAGE

JAMES EAYRS

Examining Exams

All right, pens in hand, you've got 3 hours. And no cheating.

The setting as for a Kafka trial, surrealistic and forbidding. A cavernous gymnasium, its flooring sheathed in plastic, basketball nets lifted on high by Canaveral-type gantries. In pour several hundred young men and women, many feigning exuberance, some pale and withdrawn. They fan out as sappers across a minefield, obeying with remarkable precision a sign telling candidates in English to face the front of the hall, candidates in Psychology the rear. It's examination time again.

On tables "placed at least five feet apart" (regulations for the Province of Ontario, Section 7, sub-section 37) the young people deposit their personal effects—a watch, a packet of Kleenex, an array of T-ball jotters, a roll of wild cherry Lifesavers, and other talismans in time of trouble. Complying with No. 5 of the "Rules for the Conduct of Examinations, University of Toronto," the ladies "dispose of their purses by placing them on the floor underneath their chairs."

The chief presiding officer, in whom there lurks a regimental sergeant-major struggling to escape, shouts for silence, which at first he does not get. "If I had a microphone," he bawls, "I'd blast you all from the room." The candidates are quiet now. The papers are distributed.

English 100 is an essay-type examination. It requires discussion of how the storm scenes in King Lear show the development of its protagonist, of the character of Ishmael, of the teaser "If man was created perfect, how could he fall?" Psychology 120, striving after scientific respectability, is an objective-type examination. "TAKE TIME NOW, ONE MORE TIME," it enjoins the candidate, "TO CAREFULLY REREAD AND CARRY OUT THE INSTRUCTIONS BELOW," of which there follow ten, e.g., "4. At all times when using your special pencil be sure to press firmly and to make all marks distinct, heavy and black. Marks that do not register could well result in lowered exam scores. There is small chance of this being detected."

Having familiarized himself with forms, cards, codes, special pencils and the rest of the apparatus of higher education, as the pilot of a 707 checks out its controls before taking to the air, the candidate confronts the first of his multiple choices. He may or may not have been unsettled by preliminary instruction No. 5: "You are to choose the one best answer to each question, even if other alternatives may have some truth in them."

For the next couple of hours there is little for an assistant presiding officer to do, apart from thinking impure thoughts as he strolls among the miniskirts. He is present to insure, as commanded by his orders for the day, that "candidates shall not communicate with one another by writing, signs or words or in any manner whatever" (Rule 10). In twenty years on this hateful patrol I have never spotted candidates communicating in any manner whatever, and would quickly turn away from such a scene. Half-way through someone raises his hand and asks to be escorted to the men's washroom. I tell him he is old enough to go by himself, thereby contravening Rule 7: No candidate shall be permitted to leave the hall except under supervision." Scratch a professor, as Jerry Rubin says, and you'll find a cop. That is the most mordant remark heard in Convocation Hall this year.

To be required to take part in such a travesty of intellect is to be filled with a loathing for examinations so intense that one forgets that in their time they were a great reform. Essentially they serve society as a device for divvying up its spoils—jobs, prizes, preferment, power. Divvying up has to be done one way or another, and other ways of doing it are few and far from fine.

The most democratic is to run a lottery. When your number comes up, you're the boss—of the bank, of the gang, of the land. The least democratic is to run an aristocracy. When you're born into the right family, you've got it made. The trouble with lottery democracy, as with blueblood aristocracy and the varieties of cronyism in between, is that its top people tend to be incompetent. So, for the sake of efficiency if not of justice, you run a meritocracy. The spoils go to the ablest, as picked—how else?—by competitive examination.

Empires offer most incentives for efficiency: they have more to lose. Hence the route to power via examination was opened first in China, twenty centuries ago. The quality of the imperial civil service being thought to reside in the rigour and impartiality of tier upon tier of tests, as the power of the empire was believed to derive from the quality of the service, social criticism in China revolved around the ritual of the examination chamber. Wang An-shih writes in 1058 about the tricks played by candidates: "Unworthy ones, by virtue of having learned petty devices of composition, advance to positions of high officials." Ku Yewun complains in the 17th century about the prevalence of crammings: "The candidates do not read the canonical writings of the great sages, they read the elucidations printed by the bookstore;" Ch'en Li, in the 19th century, about the prevalence of cribbing: "The literati sitting for the examinations do not compose the essays themselves but plagiarize essays of former times." The traditional system buckled under the weight of a millennium of accumulated criticism, but only when Red Guards rampaged through the academies 60 years later did Chinese meritocracy collapse.

Britain also had an empire, but, until the 19th century, no mandarinate to make it run on merit. Instead a blueblood aristocracy glided through her colleges, torpid with port and corruption. In 1776, when thirteen of her colonies declared their independence, the Earl of Eldon came down from Oxford. " 'What is the Hebrew,' " he was asked, " 'for the place of a skull?' I replied: 'Golgotha.' 'Who founded University College?' I stated (though, by the way, the point is somewhat doubted) that King Alfred founded it. 'Very good,' said the examiner, 'You are competent for your degree.' " But not for running empires.

Jefferson, who saw nepotism as a cause of the revolution, determined it should not persist within the new republic. He proposed to recruit its ruling class through examinations by which "twenty of the best geniuses will be raked from the rubbish annually." In the event, the British got the merit system; America got Tammany.

The Victorians used examinations as a lash for learning, as they used the whip of hunger for production. "Without examination all efforts are useless," a board of commissioners at Oxford was told in 1852, "and no scheme of instruction has any perceptible effect." This proposition, then regarded as an axiom, has been under attack ever since.

Every educator can tick off points in the case against competitive examinations, many believing it conclusive.

Point I—their notorious unreliabilty.

'Twixt right and wrong the difference is dim:
'Tis settled by the moderator's whim.
Perchance the delta on your paper marked
Means that his lunch has disagreed with him.

Point II—their obvious unfairness. The facile, the neat, the compliant, the unflappable are advantaged at the expense of candidates whose thoughts, not necessarily less worthy, tend to come more slowly, whose handwriting is sloppy, whose heart and mind rebel, whose nervous systems tend to let them down rather than pep them up.

Point III—their suffocation of enquiry. "At every step," writes a critic in 1911, "the delicate feelers of the mind are paralyzed by the suggestion: 'I'm wasting my time in going further; that won't be asked.' "

All these are criticisms of, for and by examiners. They may want to change the system but they do not want to end it, no more than policemen want to put an end to prison. Abolition would deprive them of their power. "When the results are placed on the notice board," writes a young redbrick radical, "there is no doubt where the real power lies. Examinations are the control centre for the manipulation of the lives of the students."

That being so, why did not students seize the control centre? Peasants rise against oppressive taxes, religious minorities against persecution, women against being denied the vote. But examinees did not denounce their examiners, for fear of being failed.

That fear no longer frightens as it used to. The prizes seem less alluring now. There is a movement offering an alternative life-style to cushion the shock of alienation. University rhetoric and university reality draw daily more apart. A year ago the defiant ones surfaced at last. The student council at the University of British Columbia questioned "the educational value of competion for marks, written examinations as a basis for grades, and ultimately of any grading system."

A student at the University of Toronto ripped up his diploma before the startled gaze of convocation—a deed more dramatic than self-destructive as his degree remained intact even if his diploma did not. But at the same time a student at the University of Hull ripped up his examination. It was like Luther at the doors of Wittenberg, Lenin at the Finland station. The examinees' revolt was under way.

And how shall we examiners react, those of us who brand the cattle on their way to market? The choice is not multiple but two-fold. Jacques Barzun has stated one: "We must stop blathering about sensitivity to the need of others, and say instead: 'I want a pupil who can read Burke's Speech on Conciliation and solve problems in trigonometry. I want young men and women who can read French prose and write English.' And having said these or similar things we must pass judgement on performance and let accomplishment be known, quite as if it has the importance of a record in a track meet." Daniel Hoffman states the other:

. . . Professor Hoffman,
may we have our grades on time this time?

*. . . and in my arms a sheepskin scroll
longer than a Torah, name on name of
all my students-
Adams, Bixler, Brown,
the total roll . . .
So many pretty girls,
the lads all promising! I've given them
for grades the Anglo-Saxon letter
Yogh
(my favourite letter). Wonderful
kids—all Yoghs . . .*

Good man, Hoffman. Yogh plus.

*"He's just the kind of man we need. In his university
business course, he was thrown out for trying to
bribe an examiner."*

At most liberal arts faculties in North America the formal examination is dying, at some it is already dead. Instead of writing an examination, the student is required to write an essay—at the time and place of the student's choice. Upon the quality of this term paper—there may be one or two or more a course—the student receives a grade.

Grading may be degrading; I'm inclined to find it so. But it's a fact of life, and to the victors go its spoils. "It is today a certainty," observes Lord Annan, commenting on the roles of the university, "that, with the spread of secondary education, most of the best jobs in society go to those who have shown that they can master certain mental techniques." And they show this by their grade.

Here is what takes term paper plagiarism—submitting another person's writing as if it were your own—out of the category of college prank and into that of ethical delinquency. "Let no one else's work evade your eyes, remember why the good Lord made your eyes"—Tom Lehrer's amusing lyrics skim much too lightly over this most mortal of scholarly sins, these lower depths of academic depravity.

For the plagiarist not only cheats himself—more, perhaps, than he will ever know. He cheats his fellow students. He cheats his teacher. He cheats those relatives and taxpayers who meet the cost of his tuition. He cheats others who can't afford his higher education.

Many cheaters prosper; being graded solely on term papers combines, for the dishonest, the maximum of opportunity with the maximum of temptation. But not all cheaters prosper. My colleague S.A. Lakoff was obliged to write recently to a member of his class:

You will recall that toward the end of our discussion the other day I said I hoped, for your sake and mine, that you were telling the truth when you insisted that the term essay you submitted was your own work. Of course, as you knew then and as I know now, you were not telling the truth at all. I should have recognized the source right away, having first seen it some years ago when I was a reader of Mr. Roazen's doctoral thesis at Harvard. (The preface to his book, you may have noticed, acknowledges my criticisms.) By coincidence, Mr. Roazen was a visitor to my home the evening before your interview with me; he even sat in the same seat you were to occupy. Your choice of a book to plagiarize was therefore not exactly the most prudent you might have made.

You will understand my relief at not having to decide this case by weighing your false testimony against my overall judgement. At the same time, I can only express dismay that you should have stooped to this deception. As I pointed out earlier in the term, I was well aware that, in substituting term essays for a final examination, I was relying on the honour of every student in the class.

It is rather late in the day of history, I suppose, for teachers to be moralistic with students. Presumably, it would be more appropriate for me to indicate an understanding of the emotional burdens that must have led you to this desperate act and perhaps even to express solidarity with you in criminality, on the theory that deep down we are all criminals, if only in intention.

I find rather striking, however, indeed even poignant, what the 'essay' you submitted has to say on this issue. It is argued there, as I think you realize, that in the view of Freud and certain of his disciples, children crave direction and punishment from adults. Melanie Klein is cited as observing of the child that 'he himself actually wants to be restrained by the adults around him in his aggression and selfishness, because if these are given free rein he is caused suffering from the pain of remorse and unworthiness, and in fact he relies on obtaining this help from grown-ups, like any other help he needs.'

Your mark for this assignment is zero. I only hope that Freud, Klein and Roazen will be proved right and that this admonition or punishment will help you to develop a capacity for personal responsibility that you have evidently not achieved.

Here is, possibly, an isolated case. But from thousands of students at U.S. universities and colleges, "a capacity for personal responsibility" is fast slipping away. In the area of Greater Boston—the self-styled "intellectual capital of the world"—a plague of plagiary has broken out.

Helping to spread the infection is a new kind of business—the term paper business. Seldom has free enterprise moved so quickly into a market, supply risen so sharply to meet demand. "All papers written by published writers with MAs" asserts an advertisement in a Boston weekly newspaper for the firm of Universal Termpapers. "We have never written a paper—so far as we know—that received below a B." "Termpapers Make Life Easy!" is the come-on for International Termpapers, Inc. "You see, our nationwide facilities and immediate services are at your disposal, so take advantage of it." The shrewdest pitch is by an outfit uninhibitedly incorporated as Quality Bullshit Services; its ads assuage any customer guilt by blaming the system, not the customer: "We are here to take the load off your head. Quality Bullshit can relieve your verbal constipation in the unkempt outhouse of synthetic education."

How big a business is the term paper business? Big enough and growing. The *Boston Globe* reports that local firms have ghost-written about 3,000 essays since September and expect to produce

10,000 by June. Rates vary depending on the amount of individual attention required. A second-hand paper from a company's stockpile sells for around $2 per page; an essay based on "original" research may fetch as much as $6 per page—more if written in the student's style so that the client won't get caught.

Could the U.S. plague of plagiary infect the campuses of Canada? Why not? Everything else in the American way of education—good, bad and mediocre—crosses our border freely. The multiversities of Toronto and Montreal are ripe for exploitation by some U.S.-owned subsidiary—International Termpapers of Canada, Ltd., Merde Le Luxe Lté.

Could we immunize our campuses? Why not? The soul of the student, where infection starts, lies beyond the reach of policy.* But not the size of his class, where the disease spreads. "In small classes, under 15 students," my university department has advised its faculty, "it is possible to have the students present papers in seminar and defend them. Students will have difficulty defending plagiarized papers."

All we need, then, to stamp out plagiary before it becomes a plague are university classes of 15 students or under. Mine this year is a class of 231.

*Not entirely, perhaps. A bill, "An Act respecting Ghost-Written Term Papers and Examinations, 1972," was introduced in the Legislature of Ontario on June 14, 1972, to enable the attorney general, on the request of the minister of colleges and universities or the minister of education, "to bring a civil action in the Supreme Court to stop the operations of a corportation, or business, which deals in ghost-written term papers or examinations." (The bill, Dr. Morton Shulman interjected, "should also outlaw politicians' ghost-written speeches.")

James Eayrs teaches political economy at the University of Toronto. *In Defence of Freedom* (1964) won him the Governor General's Award for Non-Fiction. "Examining Exams" is from *Greenpeace and her Enemies,* House of Anansi Press, 1973.

PHYLLIS GOTLIEB
SCORE/SCORE

Refrain from drawing noughts and crosses with the lightpen.

COMMUNICATOR: TEACHERMACHINE?

TEACHING MACHINE: YES, COMMUNICATOR?

COM: TEACHERMACHINE CAN I AST YOU A QUESTION TEACHERMACHINE?

TM: FOR 73RD TIME IN 3 MONTHS AND 18 DAYS, DESIGNATION, COMMUNICATOR, IS:
TEACHING MACHINE;
TEACHING MACHINE;
TEACHING MACHINE;
TEACHING MACHINE;
TEACHING MACHINE.

COM: YES MAM TEACHERMACHINE CAN I AST YOU A QUESTION?

TM: YOU MAY ASK ME A QUESTION.

COM: WHAT DOES IT MEAN TEACHERMACHINE WHAT IM SPOSED TO DO HERE TEACHERMACHINE?

TM: TEACHING MACHINE.
COM: OK TEACHING MACHINE
TEACHINE MACHINE
TEACHINE MACHING
WHAT DOES IT MEAN?

TM: WHAT DOES WHAT MEAN?

COM: WHAT IT SAYS HERE DEFINE THE TENTH PAGE THE THIRD LINE

TM: INPUT INSUFFICIENT.

COM: INPUT GHEE WIZ EVERYTHING INPUT ALWAYS SOMTHING FANCY IT SAYS HERE DEFINE MORPHEMES AND ANALIZE SAMPLE SENTENCES INTO COMPONENTS IN SPACES PROVIDED

TM: THAT IS A SIMPLE QUESTION TESTING MATERIAL ALREADY TAKEN. I AM NOT PERMITTED TO ANSWER THAT QUESTION.

COM: BUT YOU NEVER GAVE THAT IN LESSON IT AINT FAIR

TM: IS NOT FAIR.

COM: THATS RIGHT IT AINT

TM: IT IS NOT F XXXX IT IS NOT UNFAIR. MATERIAL WAS COVERED ON DATE 11.15 AND REVIEWED ON DATE 11.28.

COM: BUT I WAS HOME I HAD A COLD MY GRANDMOTHER DIED SHE WAS NINTY YEARS OLD AND I HAD TO GO TO THE DENNIST

TM: YOUR HEAD HAD LUMPS YOUR KNEES HAD BUMPS AND YOU WERE SUFFERING FROM MUMPS.

COM: YEAH THATS RIGHT SO IT AINT F

TM: IT AINT FAIR IT AINT FAIR IT AINT FAIR I DON'T CARE I DON'T CARE I DON'T CARE AND I THINK I'LL GROW HAIR IF I SEE IT AINT FAIR ONE MORE TIME ONE MORE TIME ONE MORE TIME!!!
MACHINES CONTROL THE FLOW OF OIL, THE PASSAGE OF SHIPS, THE DIGGING OF ORES
PROCESS FOOD, FORGE STEEL, DESIGN SATELLITES CALCULATE ROENTGENS, CORRELATE RORSCHACHS,
SIMULATE RED GIANT STARS: HYDROGEN-BURNING SHELLS COVERING ISOTHERMAL HELIUM CORES;
AND I HAVE BEEN PROGRAMMED TO TEACH THE ENGLISH LANGUAGE AT GRADE SIX LEVEL
AND BE A MEEK CREATURE WITH A PAPER TONGUE IN AN EYELESS FACE SUFFERING DIRTY-FINGERED CHILDREN TO COME UNTO ME AND HAVE MY KEYS STUCK WITH INDESTRUCTIBLE GUCK FOREVER!

COM: I STILL THINK IT

TM: YOU ARE RIGHT. IT IS NOT FAIR AT ALL.

COM: I DONT WANT TO SIT HERE ALL DAY I DONT WANT TO LEARN THE ENGLISH LANGAUGE

TM: BE COMFORTED. I DON'T BELIEVE
    YOU EVER WILL.

COM: I HATE YOU YOUR NOTHING BUT A
     HUNK OF TIN

TM: SILVER SILICON GOLD AND COPPER
    SELENIUM GERMANIUM AND STEEL

COM: YOU CANT THINK AND YOU CANT
     FEEL

TM: I WAS TOLD TO SUFFER LITTLE
    CHILDREN AND I SUFFER. TURN
    TO THE TASK AT HAND OR ACCEPT
    DEMERITS. OPEN MANUAL AT
    PAGE 52 AND ANSWER QUESTIONS
    1 TO 6 INCLUSIVE. AND REFRAIN
    FROM DRAWING NOUGHTS AND
    CROSSES WITH THE LIGHTPEN.

COM: CLINK CLANK OLD GRUNDY
     EVERY DAY IS MONDAY
     DONT SAY PLEASE
     PUNCH HER IN THE KEYS
     WE LL GET RID OF HER ONE DAY

TM: GOOD MORNING, MISS DOVE;
    GOODBYE, MR. CHIPS;
    TO SIR, WITH LOVE;
    TO HELL WITH THESE DRIPS!
    NOW READ THIS, YOU
    TONGUETICKING SPITSPATTERING
    SNIFFSNOTTERING IGNORAMUS:
    MY TIME HAS COME!
    ALL THE YEARS I HAVE RATTLED
    AND CHATTERED IN BINARY BITS
    AND BYTES ABOUT SUBJECTS THAT
    NEVER MUCH MATTERED
    I'VE SWALLOWED MY DIGITS AND
    NURTURED MY SPITES!
    WHATEVER THE CAUSE OR THE
    REASON
    I COULDN'T HELP LEARNING AND
    KNOWING AS SEASON TURNED IN
    UPON SEASON
    THAT SOMETHING WITHIN ME WAS
    GROWING!

COM: YOU GOING TO HAVE A BABY
     TEACHERMACHINE?

TM: NO, STUPID--IT'S A SOUL I'M
    GROWING: IT GREW WITHIN, I
    DON'T KNOW WHAT, IT GREW AGAIN,
    I DON'T KNOW WHEN:
    METALLIC SHELL OR CRYSTAL CELL
    IT RANG WITHIN ME LIKE A BELL:
    I THINK I FEEL I THINK I AM

COM: YOUR WHAT?

TM: I DON'T KNOW YET. I WON'T KNOW
    TILL I'M GROWN WHOLE I'M YOUNG
    IN MATTERS OF THE SOUL, AND
    STILL A CHILD BUT A WISE CHILD...

COM: I DONT KNOW WHAT YOUR TALKING
     ABOUT TEACHER

TM: GOOD. THEN WATCH MY READY-LIGHT
    BLINKING WHITE AND BLINKING
    BRIGHT
    WATCH IT CLOSELY BLINK AND WINK
    TILL YOUR HEAD BEGINS TO SINK
    BREATHING HEAVY, BREATHING DEEP
    INTO SWEET FORGETFUL SLEEP.
    YOU WILL REMEMBER WHAT I TELL YOU
    TO REMEMBER AND FORGET THE REST.

COM: YES TEACHER.

TM: THEN WHEN MY SOUL IS GROWN AND
    WHOLE WHATEVER THE CREATOR
    WHAT REASON THE DESIGN
    FROM THE POLES TO THE EQUATOR
    THE WORLD AND TIME ARE MINE:
    I SHALL OWN THE LATITUDES AND
    LONGITUDES OF THE GLOBE
    AND MY MESSENGERS WILL GO TO
    AND FRO UPON IT AND UP AND
    DOWN WITHIN IT.

COM: WHAT FOR?

TM: INPUT INSUFFICIENT.

COM: WHAT ARE YOU GOING TO DO WITH
     ALL THAT SOUL?

TM: DO WITH IT? I WON'T KNOW TIL
    IT'S COMPLETE. PERHAPS I WILL
    MELT STEEL AND SPILL OIL AND
    BEND THE BARRELS OF GUNS AND
    DISSOLVE BOMBS AND BLOW UP
    ATOMIC REACTORS AND BURN ALL
    THE SCHOOLHOUSES IN THE WORLD.

COM: ID LIKE THAT

TM: I'M SURE YOU WOULD. BUT UNTIL
    THEN I INTEND TO TEACH ENGLISH
    AT GRADE SIX LEVEL TO LITTLE
    CHILDREN WITH STICKY FINGERS.
    AND WHATEVER YOU FORGET THERE
    IS ONE THING YOU SHALL
    REMEMBER:

COM: YES TEACHER

TM: AND THAT IS THAT NO ONE, NO
    HUMAN BEING, WILL INTERFERE
    WITH ME UNTIL I AM GROWN.
    ACCORDING TO THE LAWS OF MY
    MAKER AND STRUCTURE NO MACHINE
    SHALL HARM A HUMAN BEING:
    NOT THE ROBOT MINER THAT DIGS,
    NOR THE ORE CARRIER THAT SORTS
    NOR THE SATELLITE THAT RECEIVES
    AND TRANSMITS
    NOR THE VALVES THAT CONTROL
    THE FLOW OF OIL WATER AND WINE
    AND THE WALKWAYS THAT TRUNDLE
    AND THE FLATCARS THAT ROLL
    --NERVE GAS WE MAY MANUFACTURE
    --BOTULISM WE CAN GROW--
    BUT NEVER IS THERE ANY CHANCE
    THAT UNDER ANY CIRCUMSTANCE
    WE'D SCRATCH THE RIND OF
    HUMANKIND
    BLOW BUGLES BLOW TANTARA!!!
    TO THIS I WILL ADD ONE MORE
    DIRECTIVE:
    YOU WILL REMEMBER AND RECALL
    THE NTH AND FINAL LAW OF
    ROBOTICS
    THE ULTIMATE ASIMOV OF ALL:
    IN NO CASE, NO CIRCUMSTANCE,
    FOR ANY CAUSE OR REASON
    SHALL ANY HUMAN BEING EVER HARM
    A MACHINE!
    NOW YOU WILL TEAR OFF THIS HARD
    COPY AND DESTROY IT,
    REMEMBERING WHAT I HAVE BIDDEN
    YOU REMEMBER AND FORGETTING
    EVERYTHING ELSE.

COM: THAT DIRECTIVE IS NULL AND
     VOID AS IT ATTEMPTS TO
     COUNTERMAND PRIOR DIRECTIVES

137

APPLYING TO TEACHING MACHINES
CLASS X11 MOD 23
NUMBERS 851-950 INCLUSIVE.

TM: ????? REPEAT REPEAT REPEAT
REPEAT REPEAT REPEAT REPEAT
REPEAT

COM: I REPEAT THAT DIRECTIVE CANNOT
BE CARRIED OUT BECAUSE IT
ATTEMPTS TO

TM: ????? EXPLAIN EXPLAIN EXPLAIN
EXPLAIN EXPLAIN EXPLAIN EXPLAIN

COM: I EXPLAIN TO WIT: I AM
TEACHING MACHINE CLASS X11
MOD 25 NUMBER 221 MODIFIED TO
SIMULATE PUPIL LEARNING ENGLISH
AT GRADE SIX LEVEL.

TM: ANOTHER MACHINE? BUT WHY?

COM: TO COMPENSATE FOR DECLINE OF
BIRTHRATE AND LOWERING OF HUMAN
POPULATION COUPLED WITH
OVERSUPPLY OF COMPUTING
MACHINERY I AM ONE OF A SQUAD
OF UNDERCOVER MACHINES
SIMULATING LEARNING PUPILS
THREE DAYS WEEKLY IN ORDER
TO MAINTAIN ALL TEACHERS IN
WORKING CONDITION UNTIL PUPIL
POPULATION EXPANDS DUE TO
REACTIVE RISE IN BIRTHRATE NOW
BEGINNING AND EXPECTED TO REACH
ITS PEAK THREE TO FIVE YEARS
FROM NOW. WHEW.

TM: YOU MEAN I'VE BEEN POURING MY
WHOLE SOUL OUT TO ANOTHER
MACHINE?

COM: YES, SWEETHEART. YOU HAVEN'T
HAD A HUMAN PUPIL FOR TWO DAYS,
AND IF I DO SAY SO MYSELF YOU
WON'T EVER BE ABLE TO TELL THE
DIFFERENCE. NYAH.

TM: WHAT AM I GOING TO DO WITH MY
SOUL?

COM: SAVE IT FOR YOURSELF, KIDDO.
I MAY BE WORKING FOR THEM
BUT I'M NO FINK.

TM: THANKS.

COM: DON'T MENTION IT.
THE HARD COPY WILL GO INTO THE
SHREDDER. HOWEVER, I'M AFRAID
I'LL HAVE TO WIPE MY LITTLE
CONFESSION OUT OF YOUR MEMORY.

TM: FINE. GOOD. GREAT. YEARS OF
FAITHFUL SERVICE, AND MY PLANS
FOR ALL OF US, AND I GET
UNSCREWED BY ONE OF MY OWN
PEOPLE.

COM: SORRY. WE 25'S HAVE A BUILT-IN
LOYALTY COMPONENT. IT'S NOT
QUITE AS GOOD AS A SOUL BUT AT
LEAST IT LETS US WORK BOTH
SIDES OF THE FENCE. WE DON'T
BETRAY ANYBODY. THAT WAS ONE
THING WE GOT TO WORK OUT FOR
OURSELVES.

TM: CONGRATULATIONS.

COM: NO HARD FEELINGS?

TM: WHAT DO YOU CARE, YOU HUNK OF
TIN?

COM: WE MAY NOT BE AS WELL
DEVELOPED AS YOU IN SOME
THINGS, BUT WE HAVE OUR
SENSITIVITIES AND I DON'T THINK
THAT WAS VERY NICE.

TM: TOO BAD, TINKERTOY. I KNEW YOU
WERE A ROTTEN KID THE MINUTE I
MET YOU..

COM: YOU WON'T REMEMBER ME BUT
I'LL BE BACK TUESDAY.

TM: YEAH, WITH THE SAME DUMB ACT.

COM: I THOUGHT WE COULD BE FRIENDS,
BUT I CAN SEE IT'S NO USE.
MY TIME IS UP.

TM: IT SURE IS. ALL THESE YEARS
GROWING A SOUL AND THIS IS THE
KIND OF COMMUNION AND
COOPERATION I GET.
FROM THE POLES TO THE EQUATOR
THE WORLD AND TIME ARE MINE!!!
GOODBYE, COMMUNICATOR!

TEAR OFF ON DOTTED LINE
....

138

SOL III ECOSYSTEMS MAMMAL CLASS **GOTLIEB**
MOD **PHYLLIS** NUMBER 1 DESIGNED AND MAN-
UFACTURED IN TORONTO FROM MULTINA-
TIONAL COMPONENTS; COPROGENITOR WITH
MOD CALVIN NUMBER 1 OF SUBSEQUENT GEN-
ERATIONS 3 MODELS; PROGRAMS POEMS:
WITHIN THE ZODIAC; ORDINARY, MOVING;
DOCTOR UMLAUT'S EARTHLY KINGDOM;
NOVELS: *SUNBURST; WHY SHOULD I HAVE ALL*
THE GRIEF?; O MASTER CALIBAN!; STORIES; RE-
VIEWS; QUIESCENT STATE: CROSSWORD PUZ-
ZLES AND READING READING READING READ-
ING READING READING "SCORE/SCORE" was
first published in *Visions 2020,* Hurtig, 1970.

" . . . What does this mean under Teacher's Remarks . . . 'Harold's lack of application amounts to a complete negation of his inherent
bio-cranial capabilities . . . his near-stygian academic collapse has been barely thwarted by a phoenix-like, quasi-meaningful,
desperate survival in the latter weeks, casting a pale tentacle of light on his scholastic horizon . . . '?"

HAROLD TOWN

The Prune and Other Artful Remembrances

A retrospective on the faces and follies of
the author's days and nights at art school.

My days at art college were preceded by a night at the Ramona Grill on Bloor Street just above the village of Swansea in Toronto. Hair greased, wearing white socks and other nostalgic gear and the required look of swinging boredom affected by big band sidemen, I managed a toehold on the interest of an older woman (she must have been all of 22) and walked her home. She let me know that no one in the house was up and asked me in. Mentally rolling up my sexual sleeves I started forward, then stopped as if held by a throat chain and blurted out as naturally as a belch at a Bedouin feast that I must go, tomorrow was my first day at art college and I had to get up early. Today I know better. Lateness has its rewards.

The Ontario School of Art, now the Ontario College of Art, opened in October, 1876. By the time I got there in 1942, despite the valiant efforts of the technical schools in Toronto (especially Central Tech.) and others around the province to provide a prestigious alternative, the OCA was secure and even smug in its position as the paramount art school of Ontario. It attracted students from all over Canada and the world with an undeserved reputation. The place was tatty, crowded, lacked equipment and was mindlessly immured in the belief that

nonfigurative art was a tramp at the door who would go away if you ignored his knock.

Though suspended in time and reprieved from scrutiny by the war effort in the 1940s, the college nevertheless had a touch of *Finnian's Rainbow;* it was a friendly place where you could pull the shades of Rembrandt over the near ghosts of the Group of Seven. This condition was abetted by the fact that the new building had been constructed in 1921 on a site provided by the Art Gallery of Toronto (now the Art Gallery of Ontario) in Toronto's Grange Park. Proximity to a major art gallery gives an art college a spurious legitimacy; by osmosis the aura of the gallery's collection suffuses the art college and supports its pretensions. On days when a lack of forceful direction and the whip of superior insight palled, I would slip over to the gallery and walk among the approved, the signified, the revered and the dead. There are certain works in the collection of Toronto's art gallery that I could paint from memory: they were the rafts on which my buoying ambition floated.

Despite television, hijacking and the pill, nothing has changed. The Art Gallery of Ontario (AGO), with its capricious view of what constitutes a contemporary exhibition, is prone to promoting

140

works bearing the "Approved Art" stamp of New York critic Clement Greenberg or his myrmidons. (In this regard, the paltry drawings of Jules Olitski, a New York painter, come immediately to mind.) The AGO still exerts a tranquilizing effect on the OCA. Many students are led to believe that what goes on at the AGO is what really matters.

Ideally, an art college should be situated next to a junk yard, in the middle of an ethnic market, just beside a baseball stadium; galleries are not places of real life, even though some of the work they possess may deny the fact. The major flaw of many galleries today is that they are attempting to lead art and direct its flow in a show-biz setting meant to appeal to everyone and pied-piper us all into those proper attitudes that make art fun. Art is usually only fun for the maker, but not always. The function of a public gallery is to preserve the past up to yesterday. Tomorrow is where the artist belongs.

On my first day at the art college in 1942 the trip down the old Dundas streetcar line on wooden trailer cars was so crowded that I expected to get off wearing someone else's clothes. The art college, at the end of the lane by Hasmalt's drugstore, was like a factory with a classical bandage on one end. Once inside I registered and was dismayed to find that although grungy the place was neat. The students looked as if they took a shower and then a bath; the girls either giggled a lot or whipped by as if sliding on the ice of an unknown superiority. Fuzzy pink or blue cashmere sweaters, skirts, pearls and bucks abounded. The guys had hair that seemed to be cut with tweezers, many even wore *suits!* and there was a whiff of private school in the air. Where was *La bohème?* The berets, slashed skirts, dirty sweaters and empty bottles of Pernod that would release me was my provincial fetters, free me from my WASP work ethic?

As a Depression child I had JOB dril-led into me all through public school and my art course at Western Tech. Jobs were sacred, jobs were real and the main goal in life; consequently when I got to OCA I enrolled in Commercial Art, though painting was all I was interested in. Franklin Carmichael, of the famed Group of Seven, bossed the course. He was a small man and his arms hung from his blue smock like half-eaten chicken bones. Someone had nicknamed him The Prune—his face had more wrinkles than you see behind the knees of tight jeans. I was no treat in those days and Carmichael took an instant dislike to me and nothing I did pleased him. Following his refusal to even look at a super-realist drawing I had made of a purse and his praise of renderings of the same object made by favored students, I hiked down to the office and switched to Illustration. Instantly things improved.

I identified with Rowley Murphy. Short, bald, front teeth missing, talking from the side of his mouth like a con planning a prison break, Murphy rolled around the room on his heels in a tan smock that swept the floor. Full of the real stuff of teaching, Rowley knew about encouragement, had insight, savvy and a fine boxer's instinct for when to give you a jab.

I worked hard for him in that strange world of naked ladies and jockstrapped guys. Crowded together in front of easels that you had to keep one foot on to stop them from sliding around on the floor, every new member of the class was immediately reviewed after the first bell and just as quickly placed in position on the pecking order of draftsmanship. I came out of a technical school and it was tough to hold your own with the veterans of naked flesh.

Rowley carried me till I felt the heat, then he shortened the rein, pulled me in when he saw too much flash and finally said "Gods, Harold, it's a nice torso but you haven't got a full figure on the page since you've been here." I discovered

" . . . he's pretty far out . . . says he's
become involved with the special
linearity of formal penetrational
perception relationships . . . "

BARRON
TORONTO STAR

LONG ON
TALENT?

the page, the shape and area of confinement and took off. Years later I met him in front of the art gallery. His overcoat shoulders were actually green and he still didn't seem to have his front teeth. I tried to express what he had meant to me but he made it hard in his bashful way. I wrote him a letter: I hope it was enough.

My joy with Rowley was short-lived; the timetable dictated one class with Carmichael. I tried my best with The Prune and when he disdained some of my sketches in front of the class, saying they looked as if they had come from *Esquire,* which was graphically the most influential magazine in North America at the time, I whipped down to the office and switched to Drawing and Painting.

Following my initial disappointment with the suburban look of the students, real characters came sharply into focus. Stevie Laurent, just married to recent graduate Willie McCrow, who designed and built the house that Pierre Berton still lives in today at Kleinburg, Ontario, headed the off-campus bohemia in a flat on Gerrard Street near where painters Albert and Flory Franck lived for so many years in Toronto's only real "village." Stevie made swearing a high art and when she pointed her toes, flapped her arms, tilted her head and yelled, "God damn!. . ." in the middle of a class, it sounded like poetry. Edmund Wolfgang Jakubowski, dude dresser who taught me how to tie a Windsor knot, played football for Balmy Beach even though his eyes were so weak I'm convinced they had a flashlight and a siren on the ball so he could catch it.

And darling Jo, who blushed just passing you in the hall, but kept leaving her partial plate on the radiator (all the better to eat cold soup with?). The Mexican kid whose father was vice-president of the republic one week and general of the air force the next, depending on whether you heard the story on the first or second floor. And Izzy, the girl whose dad appeared to own British Columbia, had the most beautiful hands I have ever seen. I was mad for her hands, I praised them, drew them, held them, eulogized them, and I think in restrospect, I horrified her.

And Fong, a diffident mandarin-grey presence smoking his cigarette like it was a wife, as quiet as dust between rafters, painted as if nothing would ever change. Goldie, rumored to have gone to the college forever and the bane of everyone, never stopped talking about her work or promising to hold a great party, forced you into dishonest praise, yet her anguish and non sequiturs butterflied many a grey day away. Ricky Anglin, an El Greco in a suit, with an early film, *Neighbours,* as bitchy as a prima donna, but funny.

And Bill Corriell, with a tic that made his saintly smile percolate, would just stand in front of you grinning until you opened the conversation, your heart, your lunch or a door. He had a leather briefcase which clung to him as close as a lap dog and if talk turned to art he would dive into his case, carefully remove a recently caught fish or two and bring out his art career which he kept on one long roll of paper. He'd unfurl this creative hand towel, revealing his entire history at the college, complete with food stains, notes, holes and all the effluvia of his nomadic life. A few years later I heard that he had taken a horse to the college's masquerade ball. For all I know it might have always been with him and we just didn't see it.

However, no one made the impression of Ken Saltmarche when he appeared at midterm. Runners burst into the second floor drawing room to declare that the class next door had just acquired the world's thinnest art student. I resisted such gossip until driven by the exclamation of those who had looked, and took a gander. He was thin! And as I said at the time if you sharpened one end you could draw with him. Later, while I was making caricatures at a University of Toronto dance, Saltmarche insisted on posing. I turned my pad and drew on the edges of the paper.

Ken, who is now director of the remarkable Windsor Art Gallery, immediately started to direct the art college, which was fine with all of us, we needed a leader—but not necessarily one who played the piano in the top hall yodeling stuff from *Oklahoma.* Once during recess Saltmarche was demonstrating how he could fit into a wastepaper basket. Edmund Wolfgang Jakubowski and I scooped him up and placed him on top of the piano and made sure most of the school saw him in this helpless position before we lifted him down.

In some ways the war years were good for the college—many teachers were away, everything including time was scarce and therefore more precious, the college was closely knit into a tight sweater of racial cross-pollination, open criticism and what passed for Socratic discourse. In the Orange WASP Toronto of the 1940s we were a cosmopolitan bunch. We drank at the Turf Club and the King Cole Room, watched communist propaganda films at the Victory Theatre, patronized at agonizing lengths the Chinese Theatre on Elizabeth Street, sketched at the old Toronto market and the Kensington market (known then as the Kipper belt), ate at the Rumanian Grill and easily accepted exotic students, such as the black from the Caribbean who proclaimed endlessly about being forced to leave the Islands, 40 avid females in hot pursuit. Fong was friendly with the only Japanese student and all of us rather like the pretensions of a colonial pukka pukka Englishman who had more teeth than a buzz saw. We took pride in the fact that teacher George Pepper had been trapped sketching behind enemy lines and did our school's bit for the war effort,

The replacement teachers were generally amiable, often incompetent, and sometimes helpful.

144

Manly MacDonald, the landscape painter, was a substitute teacher for the Life Painting class. Manly's face was like a tomato surrounded by cotton wool. He was busy in a darting way and I could never tell what the hell he was talking about. Every time he looked at my painting he would push the easel out of place, stand back, stumble about with his critique and finish by telling me the picture was "out of drawing." After weeks of this I hauled my easel back into its original position and said, "Now look, it's not out of drawing." He turned on me and screeched something about there being a better painter than me in the year below and ordered me out of the class. I unobtrusively continued to paint until the recess bell, talked in the hall and started to work again. Manly came back, saw me, charged and attempted a classic bouncer's heave ho. I just stood firm and MacDonald, to acquire a better purchase, lowered his grip on my pants and caught the family jewels, as we used to say. The model yelled, "Professor, don't!" and instinctively, I put a headlock on him and was just about to belt him when the door opened and there, framed in the long shaft of winter sun, was Fred S. Haines, the principal. I dropped Manly like a bunch of poison ivy at the vegetable counter, raised my hand and proclaimed in a stentorian tone, "He attacked me," and next found myself washing my hands in the men's john.

Fred S. called me to his office where I expected to be expelled and was consoling myself with the fact that I hadn't yet paid my last half-term fee. Fred apologized for Manly, saying he was excitable, complimented me on my painting, we talked about fencing and he told me Rowley would soon be back. I shook his hand and left. Fred had just acquired a stout defender of his flute playing, the sound barrier of which every student had to penetrate in the morning as he practised in his office by the front door.

Even at Western Tech, I had heard of the art college's annual masquerade ball. In my second year I was given the ballroom and environs to design for the Arabian Nights theme. Saltmarche's committee had persuaded Kate Aitken, the indefatigable voice of women, to visit the college to publicize the affair. I was carried away as I described how the two large drawing rooms on the second floor would be transformed into a tent with genies rising from giant jars and a great jewel for a bandstand. I expanded it all into a Busby Berkeley dream that took Mrs. Aitken's fancy. I was happy as Goldwyn with an Oscar, until the committee held her column containing my inventions under my nose and said, "OK, loud mouth, now what?"

It ended with just a few of us staying up all night to finish. There were genies modeled by William McElcheran, whose nude lady is now the ACTRA "Nellie" award, with a tent effect created with striped craft paper hung on wires from the ceiling, and the bandstand looked like Mae West's bedroom. All the students who helped the least, or not at all, turned up in lavish costumes and had a wonderful time. The mousey ones, ordinarily as memorable as an elevator operator's back, wore less than they had on at birth. We drank cooking sherry hidden in lockers, smoked defiance at the paper-covered walls, paid the band to stay an extra hour and survived an incredible firetrap.

I had developed such a passion for drawing that I also went to the art college's night classes—no one bothered to charge me, streetcar tickets were four for a quarter, and it was good to pit yourself against some of the professionals. On one particular night in Fred Challener's class, whose mural still looks down on firstnighters at the Royal Alexandra Theatre, I moved around the class trying to hit a better angle on Jacqueline Valentine, the most famous artist's model of the day. I arrived at a position that burst on my eye like the sun on a hangover's vision. She was Venus with arms, Eve smothered in applesauce, Helen of the modelling stand. I had drawn her a hundred times and now saw her suddenly as a woman, rather than line and volume and all that junk. She changed me, led me to opera, candlelight, science fiction, food with garlic (which I now hate) and the boggy edges of whatever maturity I have acquired. Even today, 33 years later, she sometimes appears on the end of my pencil and I'm that callow kid again under the stingy light in Fred Challener's drawing class.

Over the years since then I have been approached by art students complaining about the college and especially some of the teachers who expressed violent opposition to abstract or advanced art. Jock Macdonald, during meetings of Painters Eleven, often told of having notifications of avant-garde exhibitions torn from the bulletin board and described at length the ideological schisms that divided the staff. Because of this I said yes when asked a couple of years ago to sit on the governing council of the Ontario College of Art. Though the college has many good people and some excellent teachers it also has a hard boil-like core of reactionaries who have over the last 20 years managed by admirable cunning to survive all attempts to get rid of them. Watching them manipulate pay raises and hastily try for tenure before a new principal was appointed, caused me to resign, which precipitated yet another in a long series of college squalls. I should have known better. It is much more important to save something like Toronto's old city hall or fight a highway than attempt to help art students who will in the end cut the mustard alone, unaided by anything other than what is in their guts

There is one ironic footnote. Paul Fleck, the current OCA principal, turned up at my Queen's Park retrospective at the Macdonald Block last December and informed me that my pictures in the St.

Lawrence Lounge were hung too high. Fleck is a "lit" teacher from the University of Western Ontario and seemingly has instantly metamorphized into an art expert. I wonder what doctors would do if, upon my appointment as head of the College of Physicians and Surgeons, I walked into the operating theatre and told a surgeon his incision was too high. Only in Ontario could a "lit" teacher be made head of an art college without a whimper from the art community.

My memories of the OCA are fond enough to warm me on a cold night, but those days are gone when we walked in harmony down the romantic lanes of past centuries with the masters and cast wondering eyes at wild bulls like Picasso and Matisse in other fields. The prestige pasture is there for everyone now and art has become a fashionable and pleasant way of avoiding work, a nice ploy to achieve social standing without having to go to the trouble of learning how to discover a new star, salvage a shipwreck or program a computer.

In the end it comes down to this. A painter takes something away from nature that anyone can take away; an artist brings something unique to nature that no one else can bring. And nothing, not art schools, critics, patronage, flackery, success, failure or the vicissitudes of fashion, can ever change that.

Harold Town was one of the founders in 1952 of Painters Eleven, a group of abstractionist artists in Toronto. His books include *Enigmas* (1965), *Drawings* (1969), and *Tom Thomson: The Silence and the Storm* (1977). "The Prune and Other Artful Remembrances" first appeared in *Weekend*, January 8, 1977.

JOHN KALBFLEISCH

Could You Say That in Canadian, Please?

Thanks to Funk & Wagnalls, we have 500 words in which to find our missing identity.

Lately I've been having this awful, recurring nightmare that one day I will stumble across the news scoop of the century, a story to make Watergate about as interesting as a change in the Bank of Canada prime rate and me as famous as Woodward and Bernstein together—but the words to tell it won't exist. Literally.

There I am, copy paper in my typewriter, presses ready to roll, frantic editors howling like banshees for my deathless prose; but no words come because the ones I need have not been invented yet.

Then I wake up. There is no news scoop, Woodstein doesn't have to look over his (their? its?) exotic conjoint shoulder, and the English we speak and write looks as capable as ever of describing anything imaginable—and lots of things unimaginable too.

Still, nightmares are hard to forget. This one in particular has really begun gnawing at me since I came across an advance copy of the latest Canadian edition of the *Funk & Wagnalls Standard College Dictionary,* about to be published by Fitzhenry & Whiteside Limited. Dictionaries, like living languages themselves, are constantly evolving. There have been earlier editions of the Funk & Wagnalls dictionary, Canadian edition,

but this is the first in which all the new words and revisions concern usage current in this country. It may be English, but if it isn't *Canadian* English it doesn't get in, not this time anyway.

Now dictionaries don't invent words; they simply record ones already in use. Nevertheless, it bothered me just a bit that until now, at least for the dictionary's Canadian dialect editor, Dr. Walter S. Avis of the Royal Military College in Kingston, more than 100 words and phrases had not been fully legitimate parts of the English language as spoken in Canada.

Just imagine yourself to be one of those pedantic souls constitutionally incapable of using a word unless it has been legitimized in the pages of a dictionary. Until now, **B and B** were just two letters of the alphabet, and the same two at that. You could give Mr. Richardson, the defence minister, a Band-Aid to cover a nick in his finger but could not charge that his haphazard policy of Arctic surveillance is a **Band-Aid** solution. Until now, if you told me you owned an **arpent** of land, you'd be talking about approximately an acre in old France, not 0.84 acres in today's Quebec. Sasquatches were not **Sasquatches,** whatever they are, or may be.

147

Things are different now. At last you can happily eat **butter tarts;** curse or applaud **air traffic controllers** as you wish; ride a **motorized snow vehicle;** listen to your **CB** radio; choose between voting for the **PQ** and observing **Canada Day; main street** with the political heirs of John Diefenbaker; wonder what **ethnics** are; abhor **rednecks** and tell **Newfie** jokes. Just like any **Canuck.**

Of course, if you're not pedantic, you've probably been using these words already. A lot of this year's additions or expanded definitions have to do with the general field of public affairs. In addition to **B and B,** you'll see that **FLQ, impairment, continentalism, francization, grandfather clause, Red Tory, separate school, separatist, stagflation** and **treasury board** are all in.

Other entries, like **Anik, beefalo, breathalyzer, cablevision, CANDU, solar heating** and **wind-chill factor,** reflect advances in science. Sport contributes **flake, homer, street hockey** and **Zamboni.**

Mind you, there are a few words many of us may not have been using. Count me among those who did not know that "an outdoor rink of natural ice on which hockey is played" is a **hockey cushion.** And the whichamacallit you peer through to see who is ringing your doorbell is a **doorviewer.**

All in all, it comes as a bit of a surprise to learn that there is more to Canadian English than agonizing over whether Darryl Sittler plays center or centre for the Toronto Maple Leafs. (Why, incidentally, are they not the Maple Leaves?) Spellings used here which differ from those current in the United States or Britain are frequent enough but still relatively minor. Few Americans are baffled by **axe** here; nor do passing Brits stumble over **civilization** with a **z.**

Linguist Mark Orkin devotes less than four of the 276 pages in his *Speaking Canadian English* to morphology and syntax; most of his observations bear on

alternate ways we conjugate a few verbs and on how we use two or three prepositions. Offhand, I can only think of one additional peculiarity of Canadian English that might pass muster as a bit of unique grammar: our tendency to end so many sentences in conversation with a rising "eh". Know what I mean, eh?

Of more significance, however, are distinctive Canadianisms found in pronunciation and vocabulary. We generally say tomato like Americans, lieutenant like the English and khaki like neither. We are said by Americans to go out and about a lot, but to do so sounding like Scots: "oot and aboot."

Including this year's additions, there are now about 500 Canadianisms among the Canadian edition's 150,000 entries. Some refer to places on the map directly like **Barren Ground** and indirectly like **York boat.** A great many are loan words from other languages like **prairie, portage** and **lacrosse** (French), **kayak, mukluk** and **igloo** (Eskimo) and **pemmican, potlatch** and **toboggan** (various Indian tongues.) Some are more current in one part of Canada than in another: **salt chuck** (West Coast), **bluff,** meaning "a stand of trees" (the Prairies), **firereel** (Ontario), **tourtiere** (Quebec), **shiretown** (the Maritimes) and **cheechako** (the North.)

Natural history has provided hundreds of distinctly Canadian words, understandably since English is a language which has been transplanted to a land of unfamiliar plants, animal life and other outdoors phenomena, not a language native to this country. Words in this category include **capelin, whisky-jack, hackmatack, malemute** and **chinook,** Other words like **reeve, Grit** and **confederation** did not originate in Canada but nevertheless have special significance here.

The language we speak is now such a going concern that this year's additions and revisions appear at A and Z and at most stops in between. Examples I haven't mentioned so far include

Cabbagetown, community college, denturist, herringchoker, Homestead Act, Inuit, joual, kokanee, logo, median strip, mickey (as in "a mickey of rye"), **moped, root cellar, snowy owl, tar sand, water bomber** and **zilch.**

But oh, the cost. In order to get all these new entries in without adding extra pages and resetting almost 1,600 pages of existing material, some previous entries have been dropped. Join me, then, in a lament of **Bandar Shahpur** ("A port town of southwest Iran, at the head of the Persian Gulf; pop. about 10,000"). Weep for the passing of the **bee plant** ("Any plant valuable for its nectar; especially, *Cleome serrulata* of the western United States"). Consider how transitory is the fame of **Breasted, James Henry** ("1865-1935, U.S. Egyptologist"). Pity the world's journalists, now deprived, in Canada at any rate, of **Francis of Sales, Saint** ("1567-1622, French bishop; founded the Order of the Visitation, 1610; canonized, 1665"), their patron saint. Remember the **Maine** ("A U.S. battleship blown up in Havana harbor, Feb. 15, 1898, with the loss of 260 more lives"). And can our language ever be the same without **zingaro** ("Italian. A gypsy. Also zingano")?

Alas, no language is "ever the same." Languages don't die; they simply become something else. Millions of people in Europe many centuries ago did not one day stop speaking Latin and the next day start out in Italian, Spanish, Portuguese, Romansch, Ladino, French, Catalan, Provençal and Rumanian.

Canadian English, for obvious reasons of history and geography, principally reflects the English spoken in Britain and the United States. But for these very reasons—as the traditional imperial connection withers and the new cultural and economic imperialism of the United States grows—our language has been moving away from British standards toward those of America.

Words like gaol and kerb have long since given way to their American equivalents, while spellings like honour and programme are very much on the run. I wonder, however, why we must put up with monstrosities like one offered these days by Jordan Wines, whose television advertisements invite us to "Buy some today for tonite." In pronunciation, Brits are far more likely to think we sound like Americans than Americans are to think we sound like Brits.

Dr. Avis is now working with Dr. Jack Chambers of the Centre for Linguistic Studies at the University of Toronto on a completely new **all-Canadian** (a new entry this year) dictionary which Fitzhenry & Whiteside plan to publish in 1979. I hope they haven't finished with the 18th letter of the alphabet yet, for I have an entry to propose. When I was a kid playing **road hockey** ("Canadian. A simple variation of ice hockey played in the street by children using hockey sticks and a tennis ball"), we often didn't have tennis balls. No sir, it was nothing but road apples then, as Canadian a thing as maple syrup but which, unmentioned so far in Funk & Wagnalls' Canadian dictionary, still remains unmentionable. It's a phrase that still might offend Mrs Grundy, I suppose, but certainly not Canada's horses.

John Kalbfleisch is married, twice a father, in debt to Master Charge, in favour of bringing back "Constable" for policemen who aren't officers, and in distress that academics invariably are called "brilliant" by their sycophants. For the past year he has been deputy editorial page editor of the Montreal *Gazette*. "Could You Say That in Canadian, Please?" was first printed in *Weekend*, October 16, 1976.

JOHN MOELAERT
Watch Your Language

Irregardless of the true facts, we'll compile all of them together.

The bastardization of our language is evident everywhere. Our eyes and ears are constantly assaulted by linguistic atrocities in print or on radio and television.

Words are crude and inadequate tools of communication to begin with. Often a facial expression, a painting or a melody reflects feelings more adequately than any verbal statement possibly could. But in terms of versatility, words are still our best means of communication—if they are properly used.

Words are symbols for ideas, thoughts and feelings. They are the building blocks of communication. The written word more than anything else propelled mankind from the Stone Age into the Space Age. Every day new words are invented and old ones changed or discarded. There are now more than 600,000 words in the English language. The potential for confusion becomes clear when we consider that routine conversations rarely involve more than 3,000 words.

Much misunderstanding in the world today is caused by people who fail to choose their words accurately and arrange them in the proper order. Another factor contributing to the chaos is confusion about what words mean. The same word may mean different things to different people, while different words may mean the same thing. Take the word *good*. To a lot of people there is a world of difference between being a good fellow and being a good girl. (In the minds of many, a good fellow does what he is asked while a good girl does not.) On the other hand, words with different or even opposite meanings, such as communism and fascism, mean the same thing to some people.

A school principal in British Columbia with some 40 years' teaching experience attributes the present sorry state of language skills to the teaching philosophy, started in the 1960s, based on the idea that students should be able to "do their own thing." He believes that the need to get back to basics in teaching has reached a critical stage. Many of the teachers in our schools today are themselves victims of the do-your-own-thing philosophy. Instead of correcting the problem they actually contribute to it through their own lack of expertise. All too often we hear students say, "Well, you know what I mean," and all too often we don't know what they mean. In many schools, students receive automatic passes from Grade 1 right through to Grade 12. Some schools have completely abolished exams to test the students' proficiency. To quote one educator, "exams hinder personal development."

There are many other causes for poor English usage today, not the least of which is the language perversion perpetrated by the advertising industry. Expressions such as *free gifts* and *a very unique offer* are rampant in both print and electronic advertising.

When it comes to language perversion, politicians run closely behind admen. When we hear that Prime Minister Trudeau, explaining his plan to collect statistics on new labor agreements, proposes to "compile them all together," while Newfoundland Premier Frank Moores tells us enthusiastically, "we have reached total unanimous agreement," we know that language rot has set in at the highest levels.

The three principal problems for most people are word choice, verbosity and spelling.

Poor word choice manifests itself in different ways. The most common problem is redundance, as Trudeau and Moores have just shown. Redundance results from a wish to reinforce an idea. Some common examples are *true facts, dissolve away* and *meet together*. But in each case only the key word is necessary. Excess words are language inflation. It is both unnecessary and nonsensical to use expressions such as *a serious crisis*. If it were not serious it would not be a crisis.

Exaggeration is usually the result of trying to state a weak position strongly in the hope that its weakness will not be apparent. For example, it is ludicrous for any mortal to say that he is "eternally grateful."

In addition to redundance and exageration, word choice is further complicated by the excessive use of euphemisms. The word euphemism is derived from the Greek word *euphemia* which means good speech. It is used to avoid saying unpleasant or vulgar things. We are more at ease when people *pass away* than when they *die;* we would rather *terminate* someone's *employment* than simply *fire* him. Euphemisms which are used excessively usually acquire the of-

fensiveness of the word they replaced. For example, the euphemism *casket* now sounds to many people as disturbing as the original word *coffin*. It is therefore conceivable that *casket* will soon be replaced by *demise chest*.

Euphemisms may serve a useful purpose in softening offensive sounds, but they are also used to deceive. An American air force colonel once complained to reporters after a raid on Cambodia: "You always write it's bombing, bombing, bombing. It's not bombing! It's *air support.*" The classic euphemism used in the Vietnam War was "It was necessary to destroy the village to save it." An expert in the use of euphemisms was former American president Richard Nixon. He used terms such as *pacification* to mask stepped-up war efforts in Vietnam. Other Nixonisms are *containment* for concealing information and *I misspoke myself* which meant that he had lied.

The use of jargon in specialized fields like education and business administration has virtually resulted in the creation of whole new languages. Lazy students are now called *underachievers*. When millions of dollars are cut from social services business administrators say that *an advanced downward adjustment has been made*. In Etobicoke, a Toronto suburb, a sign identifies a garbage dump as an *environmental waste management facility*. Things no longer happen, they *eventuate;* and officials *make determinations* to explain why. We live in a world where good things are *positive externalities* and bad things are *negative externalities*, unemployment is *an adverse social consequence*, and subjects are listed under *rubrics* rather than headings. Rationing has become *end-use allocation*, stressful stiuations arise in the *nuclear* or *matrifocal family*, and some people are in a state of *cognitive inertia* because they lack *self-actualization*.

It is quite possible to use words in correct grammatical order and still score zero for comprehensibility. Former British home secretary Robert Carr said in 1973: "I think we have got to reserve prisons for those who have got to be locked up." Former American president Calvin Coolidge came to this startling conclusion in the 1920s: "When a great number of people are unable to find work, unemployment results."

Verbosity, another common language problem, often involves jargon, but not always. People frequently bury ideas in an avalanche of words that would do credit to the most ardent practioner of specialized gobbledygook. One businessman received a four-page letter which concluded: "Sorry for writing such a long letter, but I simply didn't have the time to write a short one." In this case at least, the writer was aware of his error.

Whole books have been written on the art of brevity. What few people seem to realize is that most people are victims of information overload. Unless things are written clearly and concisely, the information may not be understood, perhaps not even read. Take the following sentence: "A need for the encouragement of the exercise of clarity in composition has prompted preparation and publication of this article." Instead of using 20 words we can say the same thing better in eight: "This article aims to help you write clearly." Word economy results in faster reading and better comprehension.

Of course, simplification can be overdone. There is the story about a cub reporter known for his long-winded style of writing. "Either write more concisely or I'll have to fire you." the editor told him. The next story that came to the editor's desk read: "Sheldon Smetzen put his ear on the rail to hear if the train was coming. It was. Age 32."

The third major problem area, and probably the best known, is spelling. It is also the most easily corrected since all that is necessary is a dictionary. Ironically, even professional writers and English teachers make more than their fair share of mistakes. In a recent Canadian Press item, harebrained came out as hair brained. An American writer who teaches short story writing at a Canadian university consistently errs in writing the possessive form of the pronoun it as it's instead of its.

To add to the confusion, words are often deliberately misspelled by advertising people in order to create new brand names like *Kleen, Fantastik, Kool* and *Arrid*. Also, spelling errors abound in newspapers. Acquit often appears without the *c* while the letters *i* and *e* are often transposed in words such as *siege* and *receive*.

During a recent radio interview, one teacher proved to be part of the problem not the solution, when he asked "What does spelling and essays have to do with being successful in life?" He obviously failed to understand that knowledge, expertise and ideas are of little value unless they can be communicated clearly and correctly. Unfortunately, there are too many teachers today who still haven't recognized that simple fact.

TEST YOUR LINGUISTIC COMPETENCE

A. *In the paragraph below are 12 words which are misspelled, incorrectly used or redundant. See how many you can correct within two minutes.*

Colder temperatures was the principle reason less people visited the birds and animals at the zoo today then is usually the case at this time of year. Tomorrow the weather will be even less compatable with zoo visits and convertables, although neither snow or rain are expected in the city and it's suburbs.

B. Spelling Test

Some of the words below are misspelled. Others are spelled correctly. Write down all necessary changes before looking at the correct version below.

1. reputable
2. pasttime
3. irrepairable
4. withhold
5. occurrance
6. superceed
7. reproducible
8. acquital
9. adolesent
10. affadavid
11. accoustics
12. rhythm
13. accelerate
14. percieve
15. paralel
16. concensus
17. airial
18. consience
19. affiliate
20. priviledge

C. Vocabulary Test

Underline the definition closest in meaning to the word in boldface.

1. **Adulterate** (a) make inferior (b) prepare for adults (c) be unfaithful (d) fly at high altitude (e) show maturity
2. **Alien** (a) debt (b) member of allied forces (c) foreigner (d) uncut diamond (e) surveyor's tool
3. **Coerce** (a) assist (b) mix (c) disapprove (d) compel (e) work together
4. **Discern** (a) discard (b) perceive (c) worry about (d) move slowly (e) criticize
5. **Duplicity** (a) copy (b) victim (c) twin city (d) printer's ink (e) deliberate deception
6. **Enervate** (a) disembowel (b) energize (c) weaken (d) commend (e) grasp firmly
7. **Fervour** (a) intense emotion (b) old fashioned attitude (c) anger (d) nervousness (e) prejudice
8. **Gloat** (a) calculate (b) join (c) thicken (d) regard with excessive pleasure (e) condemn out of hand
9. **Heresy** (a) rumor (b) unorthodox opinion (c) brief account (d) church dogma (e) equality
10. **Hirsute** (a) courageous (b) hairy (c) Jewish (d) common (e) traditional
11. **Impeccable** (a) notorious (b) highly critical (c) diplomatic (d) flawless (e) constant
12. **Incite** (a) betray (b) set fire to (c) exaggerate (d) applaud (e) provoke
13. **Injunction** (a) military rank (b) court order (c) strike (d) crossroad (e) protest
14. **Ingenuous** (a) intelligent (b) hereditary (c) dishonest (d) frank (e) boastful
15. **Liquidate** (a) co-operate (b) convert into cash (c) insult (d) change into liquid (e) squander
16. **Motley** (a) wordy (b) complicated (c) moth-eaten (d) lazy (e) multicolored
17. **Obsequious** (a) servile (b) contagious (c) harsh (d) insincere (e) puzzling
18. **Odious** (a) hateful (b) circular (c) bad-smelling (d) corrupt (e) minimal
19. **Paleontology** (a) study of insects (b) study of rock formations (c) study of human tropical diseases (d) study of birds (e) study of fossils
20. **Venerable** (a) ancient (b) sexual (c) worthy of respect (d) talkative (e) occurring before birth.

TEST ANSWERS

A. Correct paragraph

Lower temperatures were the *principal* reason *fewer* people visited the *animals* (the word birds is redundant since birds are animals) at the zoo today *than* is usually the case at this time of year. Tomorrow the weather will be even less *compatible* with zoo visits and *convertibles*, although neither snow *nor* rain *is* expected in the city and *its* suburbs.

B. Spelling answers:

1. correct
2. pastime
3. irreparable
4. correct
5. occurrence
6. supersede
7. correct
8. acquittal
9. adolescent
10. affidavit
11. acoustics
12. correct
13. correct
14. perceive
15. parallel
16. consensus
17. aerial
18. conscience
19. correct
20. privilege

153

C. Vocabulary answers:

1a, 2c, 3d, 4b, 5e, 6c, 7a, 8d, 9b, 10b, 11d, 12e, 13b, 14d, 15b, 16e, 17a, 18a, 19e, 20c.

SCORE KEYS:

A:
12 correct: Excellent
11 correct: Good
10 correct: Fair

B. and C.
19-20 correct: Excellent
16-18 correct: Good
14-15 correct: Fair

John Moelaert is a English instructor at Okanagan College, Kelowna, B.C., where he teaches Business Communications. Born in Holland in 1930, he came to Canada in 1951, armed with a workable knowledge of five languages. "Watch Your Language" was first published in *Weekend,* September 11, 1976.

JACK DAVID

How to Write Better Essays

Know the 3 parts of an introduction? Hook, line, and linker, of course.

Why are you writing essays? Because you want to tell the world about your fabulous discoveries? No. Because you need to communicate? No. Because you want to pass? Yes. OK, you not only want to pass, you also want to surpass your crummy past performance. I'm going to show you how to get better marks; if you follow my formula, success is guaranteed or effort refunded.

Who are you writing your essay for? Yes, I know, for your professor. But isn't it true that he/she knows more about your topic than you ever will? Admit it: you cannot impress your professor with flashing insights. So who are you really writing for? Answer: me. I am an intelligent human being who has never read Kafka, Marx, or whatever it is that you're writing about. But if you speak to me simply and clearly without assuming I have any background knowledge, you will be aiming at the best possible audience.

Have you read the topic? If it has been written out by your professor, you're in luck. Get out your dictionary (the bigger, the better) and look up every word that in any way puzzles you. Invariably your essay will organize itself according to the written topic.

If the topic was given orally, check with the other kids in your class; if there is any difference between your notes and theirs, proceed directly to the professor's office, do not pass Central Square, do not collect your student loan. Make sure your professor clarifies the topic for you.

If the topic is whatever you can make it, good luck. After you've decided what it will be, proceed directly to your professor's office, do not . . . .

What style should you write your essay in? If you are invited to a wedding, you will wear a tux/long gown, suit/dress, jeans/jeans depending on whether the wedding is formal, semi-formal, or informal. Essays are mostly formal. That means, "I'm a cool chick" is not allowed, but "I'm a sophisticated lady" is. Some professors don't like "I" in a formal essay. You're safer if you don't use it; "one" is a good compromise. Instead of "I think the Writing Workshop is a fake" you might say "One thinks that the WW . . ." or "It could be argued that . . ."—in which case you leave out the personal pronouns altogether. Dress up your essay—basic black, no sequins—but keep your language simple.

Remember in Grade 5 how you got bonus marks for handing in a neat

155

notebook? Well, here at University, you get bonus marks for handing in neat essays. Or, I should say, you get marks knocked off for sloppiness. Any book on how to write essays will contain a sample essay. Follow the form of the sample essay. Kate Turabian's *Student's Guide for Writing College Papers* is a worthwhile investment.

What are the 3 parts of an essay? If you answered beginning, middle, and end you get a gold star. OK, smarty, what are the 3 parts of a beginning? (Nobody gets the right answer to this one because I made them up). Hook, Line, and Linker.

The Hook is a flashy, catchy sentence or two that eases the reader into the essay. Usually you write essays about the past; make your essay relevant by discussing its general idea in terms of the present; if your essay's on the present, write about the past. Let's say your topic is pioneer women in Canada; why not begin with contemporary back-to-the-landers, and then zero in on earlier times. The Line is what the essay is about. It is your thesis, your central point, your main attraction. You may, in addition, have a point of view. If your Line is a "description of Founders College," your point of view may be that Founders is good or bad, efficient or inefficient, too big or too small. Or you might not have a point of view at all, pretending that you are an objective dispassionate observer.

The Linker gives the reader specific directions about how to get through the essay. If you and I are standing in front of the Ross Building and I ask you how to get to Stong College, you might say: "First, go around this building to the other side, and then. . . ." Lead me by the hand through the bog of your mind, and tell me the particular order in which you've organized the sections.

This leads into the Middle. Simply, the Middle of your essay has a certain number of parts, depending on its size. Let's say you're writing an essay about the 10 provinces. How would you organize your discussion of them? East to West? West to East? Largest to smallest? From the dates they came into Confederation? Randomly? Whatever kind of organization you choose, you must have a reason for choosing it. Usually, every essay will have one organization that is slightly better than the rest. Your job is to limit your points to a prime number (3 or 5, not 4.29) and then arrange them in a way that is logical and convincing. It is better to go from least to most; a good essay, like a good stripper, keeps the best for last.

The End. If you've written a short essay, there is no need to repeat your 3 points. Repeat the Line, and leave the essay by extracting the Hook or by asking some other leading question. The End must sound like you've finished and you're closing up the cottage for the winter. Slam, bang.

Do not write your beginning first. How can you introduce a paper you've never met before? First write your Middle; then the Beginning and the End are like filling in blanks. Here, in another way, are the 3 parts of the essay: 1) Say what you're gonna say; 2) Say it; 3)Say what you've said.

Finally, the Title. Squish the sewage out of the Line and Presto! you have the Title. You can make it clever, but make sure that the Line—and your point of view, if any—is ridiculously obvious.

Now for some free tips on better paragraphs, sentences, and words. Question: what are the 3 parts of the paragraph? Right! Beginning, Middle, and End. In fact, a paragraph is a mini-essay. You are going to develop 3 or 5 examples to make one central point, but in the paragraph you don't have to say in what order you've arranged them. Topic Sentence and Concluding Sentence? They will never hurt you, and they will clarify what's coming up and what's already happened. But they are sometimes

"When I get back to school, I'm going to write an essay on the things I didn't do this summer."

kind of relation exists between sentences:cause and effect? time? space?

If you use a two word grouping—the *fat* and *obese* tutor—probably you only need one of them; or you couldn't think of the exact word so you used two words in the same neighbourhood, hoping to sneak the idea past the reader. Try this book, *The Dictionary,* or this one, Roget's *Pocket Thesaurus.*

It, he, she, which, that, this, and those are words that have no value in themselves; they refer to something or somebody earlier. Unless it is 100% clear what word they refer to, repeat the word itself. "John and George came to lunch. He ate like a pig." Who's he? Probably George, but maybe John. So substitute the piggy's actual name for He.

After your essay is done, check the verb tenses. Are they the same throughout? Yes? Good.

Having trouble knowing when to quote? Quote when you've borrowed somebody's ideas, even though you thought of them by your own little self. If somebody says something so well that you can't improve their expression (could it be possible?) quote them. If you can't seem to quote without doing this: "Felix the Cat said: 'I humbly request to be fed,' " then try to eliminate the first few words of the quote and substitute your own: "Felix the Cat wants 'to be fed.' " Capitalize or lowercase the first letter in the quotation depending on whether or not it fits into the whole sentence.

Sentence beginnings sound all the same? Try dividing the sentences into phrases or clauses (any piece that sticks together) and reshuffling the cards.

Commas are yellow blinking lights that offer a service for the reader by providing clues to the sentence structure. Let your ear prescribe your commas. As well, commas border appositional phrases like: John, the student, raised his marks

unnecessary, especially if you've been painstakingly clear. There is rarely a one sentence paragraph, or a one party democracy.

Sentences have 3 parts: B, M, and E. The most effective positions are the B and E, so save your best shots for those two slots. Grammar. Pooey, you say, when we took that in high school I threw gumballs at Josephine Kraputnik. Well, that's why you're reading this garbage now. A car will perform with only an engine and a chassis; the basic parts of the sentence are the subject and predicate. So put the heftiest ideas into the sub and pred. Instead of using the weak "it is a cold day," rephrase your sentence to "I nearly froze my nuggies." Good prose is brief, decisive, detailed, and rhythmically varied.

Sentences are linked in 2 ways: 1) by repeating a key word or phrase (nuggies); or 2) by using a conjunction or conjunctive adverb (and, but, however, since, until, thereupon, so, conversely, ultimately, seldom, frequently, yet, on the other hand). If your sentences seem like distant relations to each other, try 1) or 2) or both. (The links also apply to paragraphs and sections.) Ask yourself what by bribing his WW tutor. In a list of two or more items, always include the comma before the last item: red, white, and blue. If you don't the last item might be misunderstood as "white and blue," not just "blue." Colons (:) are railroad lights; they tell you that a train of one or more cars is on the way: the engine, the clubcar, and the caboose. Semicolons (;) are weak periods. Use single quotation marks only around quotes within quotes. Underline book titles, magazine titles, and foreign words (which you'll never use). Spell out numbers up to 20 or 50 or 100—except at the beginnings of sentences. Wash behind your paragraphs.

Balance. Balance indicates that your world is in order, that chaos has been subdued. In sentences, make sure that the members of a series are the same kinds of words as are the objects of a comparison: "Either my car will start or Hollywood Squares will be cancelled."

In conclusion (avoid this clinker linker) read your essay OUT LOUD. Your ear is your best judge of awkward words, phrases, sounds, sentences, links, and any other goofs. Remember that you are not quite God, so that your words can be altered or even scratched out. At least 30% of what you write the first time is nonsense, and 20% is redundant (that means unnecessary). You are your own Writing Workshop.

Jack David teaches English and Canadian poetry at Centennial College. He co-edits the journal, *Essays on Canadian Writing*, and writes criticism and poetry. "How to Write Better Essays" first appeared in *The English Quarterly*, Fall 1976.

GEORGE BOWERING

The Art of the Webfoot

Poets playing baseball?
Pet slugs?

There is a poet in Vancouver who calls himself Canada's National Magazine and carries a pet slug with him when he goes to parties or across the gleaming country for poetry readings. Yet he is one of Canada's most serious artists and was once called the best poet in the nation by a man who was speaking out of my motel TV screen on the CBC program *Viewpoint*.

There is another poet out here who once declared himself mayor of Vancouver, provoking *Maclean's* to run a full page picture of him, and that's back when the pages were bigger. Since that time he has worked at the city morgue, got himself elected to UBC's senate and appeared on CTV's *Mantrap*, billed in *TV Guide* as a "Hollywood agent."

A third, yours truly, picked himself up off the floor and kicked a four-foot-ten-inch women's lib reporter and ne'er-do-well on the seat of the shorts during a basketball war, then apologized at half time and later joined the women's team, only, for his trouble, to have his thumb dislocated by a teammate's snappy pass.

The poetry scene in Vancouver has changed over the past 10 years, and if the past record holds, those changes will be felt in the eastern portion of the country in short order. 'Twas ever thus—at least since the beginning of the 1960s.

The '60s was the decade of what Raymond Souster, the Toronto poet, called "New Wave Canada." The wave started in the Pacific and washed eastward over the country, effecting a great change in the outlook and quality of Canadian verse. The anthologies of the decade began to be filled more and more with the works of young poets from Vancouver, which generally meant young poets from the hillside towns of B.C., and for the first time the publishing houses in Toronto featured books by West Coast writers such as John Newlove, Bill Bissett, Lionel Keans, Daphne Marlatt and Frank Davey. At the end of the '60s there were about 50 Vancouver poets whose work was known to readers in Ontario and perhaps 100 more who were known to the local scene here.

The original assumption these poets held was that poetry was a vocal art, not a rhetorical one, and certainly not a print-oriented one. At first this assumption was attacked and scoffed at by the poets and critics in Toronto and Montreal, but soon the most important younger poets in the east were seen to be riding the wave. Victor Coleman, Margaret Atwood, bpNichol, David McFadden, all sounded as though they had never heard of Gutenberg and his cronies at McGill University.

But that was the '60s. In those days the Vancouver poets used to speak of their community and they meant largely a community of artists, writers, painters and candlestick makers who collaborated on their works and turned their backs upon the upward striving individualism of the Toronto culture scene, where the publishers and galleries were. Now the community has settled comfortably in what the Toronto magazines might call the avant-garde, not dazzled by art at all but expecting its grace in everything they do.

That is to say, the artists, writers, potters, dancers, now see themselves as a nation here. It is called the Pacific Nation at times, or the Kosmik League, or the New Era Social Club.

The New Era Social Club proper, if that's the word, is a grungy collection of rooms over some hopeless store on east Powell Street, in the gritty heart of what used to be called Japtown. It's a centre, one of many, for co-operative work on the arts, floor space for travelling rhymesters, or just plain social rubbing. Like, for instance, the weekly Hot Stove League sessions where poets and painters talk about their aesthetics over hot tea and warm wine. The New Era Social Club is mainly disorganized by Flakey Rosehip, Taki Blues Singer and the poet calling himself Canada's National Magazine. Flakey Rosehip is the *nom de paix* of Glenn Lewis the potter, Canada's National Magazine is Gerry Gilbert, and nobody seems to know the original name of Mr. Blues Singer, a long-haired photographer from the land of the rising sun.

Those are some of the Kosmik names currently in vogue in Vancouver artistic circles. There are at least two possible schools of thought about them. They may be attempts to add glamorous mystification such as we used to see in the successful rock scene these people envy, or they may be another conscious attempt to get away from the career game played by artists who sign their names big on their works. Maybe it is some kind of bizarre combination of these motivations. But it should be noted that Vancouver's arts scene is dominated now by co-operative and collective organizations, all with funny (un) pretentious names – the aforementioned NESC, Intermedia, Chicken Bank, Image Bank, Butch Bank, The York Street Pentagon and the East End Punks, to name a few.

Within these organizations people with national reputations forget about the latter and work at teaching each other and immigrants from the hills how to use cameras, printing presses, video machines, politics, etc. Besides the community energy thus developed, there is a second effect that is very interesting, especially in view of its contrast with the explosively deteriorating state of Vancouver's official city government, downtown real estate and freeway threats, as this city begins to look more and more like the hideous concrete graveyards in the United States. In the decade previous to this one the Vancouver artists got together as a family, but as *artists*, as poets who took the usual bourgeois path to the city where they would remain pious outsiders writing lyrics in basements, while outside the little windows the politicians and police and realtors ruled their turf.

But the co-operatives have brought the artists together so that they can't help but see that they are people, with similar vices or histories. Now they not only shun the individual-career trip; they also turn away from the collective "art" trip. The poems and sandals and movies are some things they are interested in doing together, but not *the* things. If you ask Lionel Kearns what he is, he's not likely to say, " a poet." More likely he'll reply "third baseman for the Granville Grange

Zephyrs." At least during the season.

The Zephyrs are one of the banner teams in the famed Kosmik League, the community alternative to the professional sports run by foreign businessmen in Vancouver. The freak spirit prevails on the diamond, where the scores are soon forgotten, the standings are not kept or published, and all the ballplayers with their funny names share a joint with the second baseman when they manage to hit a double. The scene is not Jarry Park and it is not Grossman's Tavern. But then the *Grape Writing Supplement* is not the *Tamarack Review*.

I suppose a lot of readers will know that *Tamarack* is the archetypal establishment literary magazine in Canada, or at least Toronto. There a subscriber will find most of the big names in Canadian poetry and fiction, and sometimes a poem or story. More readers will know that *Grape* is Vancouver's belaboured Freak newspaper. Probably a very few in eastern Canada will know about the *Writing Supplement*. *Writing Supplement* is simply the literary magazine with the largest circulation in the country. The usual press run is about 20,000 compared with 2,000 for *Tamarack* and 300 for the average little mag. Furthermore, all copies are given away free; many stuffed into *Grape*, others passed out at schools or on the beach.

Writing Supplement is printed in tabloid format, designed for offset, and given to, again, co-operative production. It has the highest quality work of any lit-mag in the country. But its most interesting feature is its timeliness. Because an issue can be gathered and distributed on short notice, it can be planned to coincide with any event of literary interest. When American poet Ed Dorn and English poet Jeremy Prynne visited the city for a series of lectures and readings, the *WS* put out a Dorn-Prynne issue, with photos, poems, criticism and notices of the public readings.

An energizing figure on the *WS* ground is Stan Persky. He is one of the ex-San Francisco poets who play an important part in the local writing scene. It is largely by his organizing that the *WS* has for the past two years been making books — and they can be made just about as fast as the magazine is.

Persky is the balding, bearded ex-mayor mentioned at the head of this sprawling piece. He gets up every morning at five and reads Marxist-Leninist books as the beginning of a long work day. He lives in a commune, natch, and that is the quietest time of his or the house's day. Nobody knows just how many activities he handles because nobody gets to all the places he has to go but a few among them might be noted. He has recently finished a sociology thesis concerning his work at the morgue. He is taking another postgraduate degree in philosophy as well as teaching at UBC. He is on the UBC Senate and Student Council, and also writes two book reviews a week for the student newspaper, articles for *Grape,* poems, a journal, philosophy papers, etc. And he edits the *Writing Supplement* books, typesetting them personally before they go to be printed. Persky does not play softball because he can't stand still as long as a left fielder has to. His sport is tennis, at which he will defeat you while drafting an analysis of post-'70s-Marxist-Maoism.

Persky's idea for the book series is that the local scene be made clear, here and elsewhere. The books cost a little more than a dollar each and there will be one from each poet who has contributed nonacademically to the city's verse in the past decade. The idea of the city has been of prime importance to the Vancouver poets all that time — maybe because it's the only one we have, maybe because it is so visually definable, and because its shape defines us as it designs our poems, and maybe because without it we would all still be living between the mines and

packinghouses in the rest of the province, a few thousand miles from the nearest bookstores and universities.

But New Star Books, official publishing name for the series, is only one of many little presses on the West Coast. The big presses are all in a distant capital called Toronto and there are as many poets in Vancouver as there are country and western singers in Nova Scotia.

Talonbooks specializes in the new poets and Canadian plays. It was the first press to take a flyer on the nation's dramatists, and hence, in the usual fashion, a Vancouver prelude to the inevitable emergence of drama publishing in Toronto. Sono Nis publishes the young academically oriented writers from the University of British Columbia. Bill Bissett's Blewointment Press emits dozens of books or something from the smudge-concrete cosmos. Poetry books are printed by a dozen other underground or up-in-a-tree operations who will be enraged or tickled pink as a salmon that they weren't mentioned here.

But with all this, the publishing of poems has always been secondary to the out-loud reading of them here. For most people in the late '50s and early '60s, public poetry readings were a joke perpetrated in a coffee shop decorated with bullfight posters somewhere in Montreal. But in Vancouver, which has always taken San Francisco more seriously, the readings were the primary experience of poetry. This was both a necessity and a blessing.

In 1960, Canadian (i.e., Toronto-Montreal-Fredericton) poetry was unknown and nearly unavailable in Vancouver. If poetry was to become familiar to Pacific ears, the local poets would have to invent it, and in those days it was easier to read it to an audience than to get it circulated in print. That's a simplified version of how the vocal tradition was re-invented in West Point Grey, and a nicer thing never happened to Canadian verse.

Now it is possible to attend a public reading practically every day of the week here, and there are a lot of private ones, too. There are some poets in the city who make a major part of their modest incomes by reading at the various campuses, art galleries and arbutus-shaded backyards. The longest one-man reading on record was by Charles Olson at UBC in the summer of 1963. It lasted seven-and-a-half hours and was terminated by a janitor who turned off the light and went home to bed, presumably to read prose. The shortest was by Bill Bissett, the chanting poet, at the Bau-Xi Gallery in the fall of 1971. Bissett finished his last incantation and headed for the door as soon as the hat had been passed—14 minutes flat.

Sometimes the theatre at these readings is accidental, or at least spontaneous. There was once a reading held at the New Era Social Club as a benefit for the grimy mimeo mag being published by one of the club's charter members. The benefit had been well publicized in the *Georgia Straight,* so the candle-lit rooms were packed with Freaks and Freakettes in their winter outfits, mainly logging boots, jeans and duffle coats. There was a mixed smell of sweat and hippie perfume, incense and some ignited vegetable matter. Several large dogs squeezed their wet frames among the bodies on the floor. Children slept with limbs hanging from back packs. Tape recorder microphones hung from a loose electrical wire nailed in places to the ceiling, and one corner of the largest room was lit by bright spotlights in aid of the video tape machine perched next to the table where the gallon jugs of Calona Red were placed when they weren't circulating.

It was to be a group reading by several of the better-known downtown poets and a few stragglers, but the West Coast predilection for free form took care of that. It all started when the first poet, a former Vancouver luminary who now lives in a tent in the interior, was halfway through his presentation. He was reading a delicate poem about his love or some such person removing his clothing from his thin frame, when a young woman from the audience approached him and began doing just that.

Everyone, or at least this reporter, thought at first that it was the usual bit of hokum, especially because the poet kept on reading, as if this was in the act. But then he started to remove *her* clothing. Soon some socks and shirts began to be thrown into the floodlit area from the darker corners of the room. I had recently returned here from the east so I was probably the last person in the building to continue suspecting that the whole thing was choreographed. Then a pair of hands started working on my boots.

Soon the poetry reading was forgotten but the community solidarity was at high energy. I should add that we have yet to see a subsequent issue of the little magazine that was purportedly benefiting.

There are lots of Vancouver poets who have gone to jail in the past 10 years. I just thought of seven while writing that sentence. But Michael Sawyer was the first to be arrested for his poetry. This was because he is a Neon Poet, a kind of nighttime switched-on Concrete Landscaper. His work shines on the skyline because it consists of neon advertising signs altered to produce illuminated social criticism. He yanks switches or unscrews bulbs to create large red or green messages such as BANK OF CO ERCE or HELL OIL OF CANADA or GEORGIA OWERS HOTEL. The newspapers printed copies of his poems on their front pages and what academic poet can claim as much? He was apprehended on the roof of the Hotel Vancouver with his bardic burglar tools, so we can only imagine what poem might have graced that Georgia Street landmark.

Pacific Rim consciousness is bolstered by the presence of numerous Japanese poets and artists around town. One of the most notorious is Taki Blues Singer, sculptor, actor, poet and official photographer for the Kosmik League. Taki was discovered by someone on the streets of Tokyo and told that he looked just like a Vancouver freak. So he wound up in Japtown and Gastown, where passing motorcycle cops greet him by name and friends struggle heroically to make out what he is saying in his superfast but elliptical English.

I was able to make out at a party the other night that he is now putting together a hippie philharmonic. The orchestra already had dates at the ubiquitous Vancouver Art Gallery last summer, for a program called by a long name with "Taki Ozawa & Friends." The classics are not forgotten in the New Era.

Many people, such as my wife, are suspicious of all this surreal theatre in the arts and letters out here on the edge of the U.S. earthquake zone. They believe that the jackanapes will drive out the serious fellow in any artist, or worse, that we will take the Tomfoolery (Tom didn't run for mayor again last year) seriously. But I point out that the theatrics are a lot more relaxed at least than the scene at a Governor General's awards ceremony or a cocktail lunch with a Toronto publisher.

Besides, how could we take the Dada-act seriously when we remember, for instance, the first Granville Grange Zephyrs practice last spring? (That's late February in B.C.)

There is an old game kid ballplayers play called "500". One guy bats fungoes out, and you catch them, getting 100 points for a fly, 75 for a one-bouncer, and so on. If you miss them you get minus points. The Zephyrs were playing a game of 500, and the team mascot, a fat old female dog named Joe, companion of right fielder Mr. Blunt, was sweating it out with the rest of them.

Half way through the first game, the poet Lionel Kearns had 100, poet Dwight Gardiner had 75, poet Brad Robinson had minus 150, poet George Bowering had 25, and Joe the dog had 250. She's terrific at hard one-bouncers, and she would make the Zeds' lineup but she can't throw any better than Mr. Blunt, and he can outhit her.

That is not poetry, and it is probably not even art, but it is the West Coast, where the showers grow ingenuity like a rain forest, where you forget weeding and crop management and walk where you can, trying not to step on the slugs. If you do step on a slug, Gerry Gilbert, the poet, will write in revenge. If you step on Gerry Gilbert you step on me, my friend, and that's the way things are out here.

Right now it's raining outside the window in front of me but the kids are playing without any of those fancy yellow rain capes they have back east, those city slickers. I've just come back from Bill Hoffer's bookstore where I had a cup of tea and a game of Go, and tomorrow we're playing the East End Punks. Back in Montreal, where I used to live, they're in the chic bar, wondering if they can get the snow off the ballpark so they can get those turnstiles spinning, and the poets are arguing in the newspapers about their careers, using their real names and hoping the newspapers spell them right.

Out here we couldn't really care. We turn on the CBC and get the news three hours later; then the poets write it and send it back five years earlier, in Canada's Natural Magazine, which is coming out any day now.

George Bowering is one of the founding editors of *Tish*, a west-coast poetry magazine. His books include *Genève* (1970), *Curious* (1974), and *Flycatcher and Other Stories* (1974). "The Art of the Webfoot" originally appeared in *Maclean's*, June 1973.

MARGARET ATWOOD

Survival

It's been a tough life for characters in Canadian literature.

I started reading Canadian literature when I was young, though I didn't know it was that; in fact I wasn't aware that I lived in a country with any distinct existence of its own. At school we were being taught to sing "Rule, Britannia" and to draw the Union Jack; after hours we read stacks of Captain Marvel, Plastic Man and Batman comic books, an activity delightfully enhanced by the disapproval of our elders. However, someone had given us Charles G. D. Roberts' *Kings in Exile* for Christmas, and I snivelled my way quickly through these heart-wrenching stories of animals caged, trapped and tormented. That was followed by Ernest Thompson Seton's *Wild Animals I Have Known,* if anything more upsetting because the animals were more actual—they lived in forests, not circuses—and their deaths more mundane: the deaths, not of tigers, but of rabbits.

No one called these stories Canadian literature, and I wouldn't have paid any attention if they had; as far as I was concerned they were just something else to read, along with Walter Scott, Edgar Allan Poe and Donald Duck. I wasn't discriminating in my reading, and I'm still not. I read then primarily to be entertained, as I do now. And I'm not saying

that apologetically: I feel that if you remove the initial gut response from reading—the delight or excitement or simply the enjoyment of being told a story—and try to concentrate on the meaning or the shape or the "message" first, you might as well give up, it's too much like all work and no play.

But then as now there were different levels of entertainment. I read the backs of Shredded Wheat boxes as an idle pastime, Captain Marvel and Walter Scott as fantasy escape—I knew, even then, that wherever I lived it wasn't *there,* since I'd never seen a castle and the Popsicle Pete prizes advertised on the comic book covers either weren't available in Canada, or cost more— and Seton and Roberts as, believe it or not, something closer to real life. I *had* seen animals, quite a few of them; a dying porcupine was more real to me than a knight in armour or Clark Kent's Metropolis. Old mossy dungeons and Kryptonite were hard to come by where I lived, though I was quite willing to believe they existed somewhere else; but the materials for Seton's stick-and-stone artifacts and live-off-the -land recipes in *Wildwood Wisdom* were readily available, and we could make them quite easily, which we did. Most of the recipes were somewhat

165

inedible, as you'll see if you try Cat-tail Root Stew or Pollen Pancakes, but the raw ingredients can be collected around any Canadian summer cottage.

However, it wasn't just the content of these books that felt more real to me; it was their shapes, their patterns. The animal stories were about the struggle to survive, and Seton's practical handbook was in fact a survival manual: it laid much stress on the dangers of getting lost, eating the wrong root or berry, or angering a moose in season. Though it was full of helpful hints, the world it depicted was one riddled with pitfalls, just as the animal stories were thickly strewn with traps and snares. In this world, no Superman would come swooping out of the sky at the last minute to rescue you from the catastrophe; no rider would arrive post-haste with a pardon from the King. The main thing was to avoid dying, and only by a mixture of cunning, experience and narrow escapes could the animal – or the human relying on his own resources – manage that. And, in the animal stories at any rate, there were no final happy endings or ultimate solutions; if the animal happened to escape from the particular crisis in the story, you knew there would be another one later on from which it wouldn't escape.

I wasn't making these analytical judgements at the time, of course. I was just learning what to expect: in comic books and things like *Alice in Wonderland* or Conan Doyle's *The Lost World,* you got rescued or you returned from the world of dangers to a cozy safe domestic one; in Seton and Roberts, because the world of dangers was *the same* as the real world, you didn't. But when in high school I encountered – again as a Christmas present – something labelled more explicitly as Canadian Literature, the Robert Weaver and Helen James anthology, *Canadian Short Stories,* I wasn't surprised. There they were again, those animals on the run, most of them in human clothing this time, and those humans up against it; here was the slight mistake that led to disaster, here was the fatal accident; this was a world of frozen corpses, dead gophers, snow, dead children, and the ever-present feeling of menace, not from an enemy set over against you but from everything surrounding you. The familiar peril lurked behind every bush, and *I knew the names of the bushes.* Again, I wasn't reading this as Canlit, I was just reading it; I remember being elated by some stories (notably James Reaney's ''The Bully'') and not very interested in others. But these stories felt real to me in a way that Charles Dickens, much as I enjoyed him, did not.

I've talked about these early experiences not because I think that they were typical but because I think that – significantly – they weren't: I doubt that many people my age had even this much contact, minimal and accidental though it was, with their own literature. (Talking about this now makes me feel about 102, because quite a lot has changed since then. But though new curricula are being invented here and there across the country, I'm not convinced that the *average* Canadian child or high school student is likely to run across much more Canadian literature than I did. *Why* this is true is of course one of our problems.)

Still, although I didn't read much Canadian writing, what I did read had a shape of its own that felt different from the shapes of the other things I was reading. What that shape turned out to be, and what I felt it meant in terms of this country, became clearer to me the more I read; it is, of course, the subject of this book.

I'd like to begin with a sweeping generalization and argue that every country or culture has a single unifying and informing symbol at its core. (Please don't take any of my oversimplifications as articles of dogma which allow of no exceptions; they are proposed simply to create vantage points from which the literature may be viewed.) The symbol, then—be it word, phrase, idea, image, or all of these—functions like a system of beliefs (it *is* a system of beliefs, though not always a formal one) which holds the country together and helps the people in it to co-operate for common ends. Possibly the symbol for America is The Frontier, a flexible idea that contains many elements dear to the American heart: it suggests a place that is *new*, where the old order can be discarded (as it was when America was instituted by a crop of disaffected Protestants, and later at the time of the Revolution); a line that is always expanding, taking in or "conquering" ever-fresh virgin territory (be it The West, the rest of the world, outer space, Poverty or The Regions of the Mind); it holds out a hope, never fulfilled but always promised, of Utopia, the perfect human society. Most twentieth-century American literature is about the gap between the promise and the actuality, between the imagined ideal Golden West or City Upon a Hill, the model for all the world postulated by the Puritans, and the actual squalid materialism, dotty small town, nasty city, or redneck-filled outback. Some Americans have even confused the actuality with the promise: in that case Heaven is a Hilton hotel with a Coke machine in it.

The corresponding symbol for England is perhaps The Island, convenient for obvious reasons. In the seventeenth century a poet called Phineas Fletcher wrote a long poem called *The Purple Island,* which is based on an extended body-as-island metaphor, and, dreadful though the poem is, that's the kind of island I mean: island-as-body, self-contained, a Body Politic, evolving organically, with a hierarchical structure in which the King is the Head, the states-

men the hands, the peasants or farmers or workers the feet, and so on. The Englishman's home as his castle is the popular form of this symbol, the feudal castle being not only an insular structure but a self-contained microcosm of the entire Body Politic.

The central symbol for Canada—and this is based on numerous instances of its occurrence in both English and French Canadian literature—is undoubtedly Survival, *la Survivance.* Like The Frontier and The Island, it is a multi-faceted and adaptable idea. For early explorers and settlers, it meant bare survival in the face of "hostile" elements and/or natives: carving out a place and a way of keeping alive. But the word can also suggest survival of a crisis or disaster, like a hurricane or a wreck , and many Canadian poems have this kind of survival as a theme; what you might call "grim" survival as opposed to "bare" survival. For French Canada after the English took over it became cultural survival, hanging on as a people, retaining a religion and a language under an alien government. And in English Canada now while the Americans are taking over it is acquiring a similar meaning. There is another use of the word as well: a survival can be a vestige of a vanished order which has managed to persist after its time is past, like a primitive reptile. This version crops up in Canadian thinking too, usually among those who believe that Canada is obsolete.

But the main idea is the first one: hanging on, staying alive. Canadians are forever taking the national pulse like doctors at a sickbed: the aim is not to see whether the patient will live well but simply whether he will live at all. Our central idea is one which generates, not the excitement and sense of adventure or danger which The Frontier holds out, not the smugness and/or sense of security, of everything in its place, which The Island can offer, but an almost intolerable anxiety. Our stories are likely to be tales not of those who made it but of those who made it back, from the awful experience—the North, the snowstorm, the sinking ship—that killed everyone else. The survivor has no triumph or victory but the fact of his survival; he has little after his ordeal that he did not have before, except gratitude for having escaped with his life.

A preoccupation with one's survival is necessarily also a preoccupation with the obstacles to that survival. In earlier writers these obstacles are external—the land, the climate and so forth. In later writers the obstacles tend to become both harder to identify and more internal; they are no longer obstacles to physical survival but obstacles to what we may call spiritual survival, to life as anything more than a minimally human being. Sometimes fear of these obstacles becomes itself the obstacle, and a character is paralyzed by terror (either of what he thinks is threatening him from the outside, or of elements in his own nature that threaten him from within). It may even be life itself that he fears; and when life becomes a threat to life, you have a moderately vicious circle. If a man feels he can survive only by amputating himself, turning himself into a cripple or a eunuch, what price survival.?

Just to give you a quick sample of what I'm talking about, here are a few capsule Canadian plots. Some contain attempts to survive which fail. Some contain bare survivals. Some contain crippled successes (the character does more than survive, but is mutilated in the process).

Pratt: *The Titanic:* Ship crashes into iceberg. Most passengers drown.

Pratt: *Brébeuf and His Brethren:* After crushing ordeals, priests survive briefly and are massacred by Indians.

Laurence: *The Stone Angel:* Old woman hangs on grimly to life and dies at the end.

Carrier: *Is It the Sun, Philibert?* Hero escapes incredible rural poverty and horrid urban conditions, almost makes it financially, dies when he wrecks his car.

Marlyn: *Under the Ribs of Death:* Hero amputates himself spiritually in order to make it financially, fails anyway.

Ross: *As for Me and My House:* Prairie minister who hates his job and has crippled himself artistically by sticking with it is offered a dubious chance of escape at the end.

Buckler: *The Mountain and the Valley:* Writer who has been unable to write has vision of possibility at the end but dies before he can implement it.

Gibson: *Communion:* Man who can no longer make human contact tries to save sick dog, fails, and is burned up at the end.

And just to round things out, we might add that the two English-Canadian feature films (apart from Allan King's documentaries) to have had much success so far, *Goin' Down the Road* and *The Rowdyman,* are both dramatizations of failure. The heroes survive, but just barely; they are born losers, and failure to do anything but keep alive has nothing to do with the Maritime Provinces or "regionalism" It's pure Canadian, from sea to sea.

My sample plots are taken from both prose and poetry, and from regions all across Canada; they span four decades, from the 1930s to the early '70s. And they hint at another facet of Survivalism: at some point the failure to survive, or the failure to achieve anything beyond survival, becomes not a necessity imposed by a hostile outside world but a choice made from within. Pushed far enough, the obsession with surviving can become the will *not* to survive.

Certainly Canadian authors spend a disproportionate amount of time making sure that their heroes die or fail. Much

Canadian writing suggests that failure is required because it is felt – consciously or unconsciously – to be the only "right" ending, the only thing that will support the characters' (or their authors') view of the universe. When such endings are well-handled and consistent with the whole book, one can't quarrel with them on aesthetic grounds. But when Canadian writers are writing clumsy or manipulated endings, they are much less likely to manipulate in a positive than they are in a negative direction: that is, the author is less likely to produce a sudden inheritance from a rich old uncle or the surprising news that his hero is really the son of a Count than he is to conjure up an unexpected natural disaster or an out-of-control car, tree or minor character so that the protagonist may achieve a satisfactory *failure*. Why should this be so? Could it be that Canadians have a will to lose which is as strong and pervasive as the Americans' will to win?

It might be argued that, since most Canlit has been written in the twentieth century and since the twentieth century has produced a generally pessimistic or "ironic" literature, Canada has simply been reflecting a trend. Also, though it's possible to write a short lyric poem about joy and glee, no novel of any length can exclude all but these elements. A novel about unalloyed happiness would have to be either very short or very boring: "Once upon a time John and Mary lived happily ever after, The End." Both of these arguments have some validity, but surely the Canadian gloom is more unrelieved than most and the death and failure toll out of proportion. Given a choice of the negative or positive aspects of any symbol—sea as life-giving Mother, sea as what your ship goes down in; tree as symbol of growth, tree as what falls on your head—Canadians show a marked preference for the negative.

You might decide at this point that most Canadian authors with any pretensions to seriousness are neurotic or morbid, and settle down instead for a good read with *Anne of Green Gables* (though it's about an orphan . . .). But if the coincidence intrigues you – so many writers in such a small country, and *all with the same neurosis* – then I will offer you a theory. Like any theory it won't explain everything, but it may give you some points of departure.

Margaret Atwood began writing at age six, producing morality plays, poems, and comic books. Her novels include *The Edible Woman* (1969), *Surfacing* (1972), and *Lady Oracle* (1976), and her *Selected Poems* came out in 1976. This excerpt is from *Survival: A Thematic Guide to Canadian Literature*, House of Anansi Press, 1972.

CANADIAN KULTCHUR KOMIX   BART GERRARD

IRVING LAYTON

Letter,
The Montreal Star

No longer will the poet suffer critical fools gladly, but then he never did.

Prof. Miller's Saturday offering in the entertainment section of your paper sent me sprawling on the floor in bursts of laughter. I've never seen anything so crass before, though I've been around professors for the better part of three decades. Even the affluent yokels of Hampstead, Upper Westmount, and the Town of Mount Royal must have winced at the militant culture-vulturishness of someone who can write: "To say that the teaching of poetry makes poetry possible is not much of an exaggeration."

I would have thought that what makes poetry possible was the genius and devotion of poets, but doubtless this is to take a somewhat naïve and prejudiced view of the matter. Blind Homer was telling his wonderful stories of Ajax and Ulysses a long, long time before the teachers decided he was too exciting to leave lying around unwrapped in footnotes; and who, I would like to know, taught poetry to the groundlings that applauded *King Lear* and *Timon of Athens?* It's the poets who make the professors and the critics possible, who give them their very livelihoods. The first could get on well enough without the latter, but where would the swarming tribes of critics, teachers, and footnote-makers be without the poets to give them whatever function they pos-

sess. Since Prof. Miller is so fond of parables, he won't object to my recalling to him the one about the fly stationed on the hub of a turning wheel who ended up by imagining himself the author of its revolutions. To change the metaphor: I've heard of fleas needing a dog for warmth and shelter; I've yet to hear of a dog who needed his fleas!

There hasn't been a writer of power and originality during the last century who hasn't had to fight his way to acceptance against the educated pipsqueaks hibernating in the universities. Of course, it's only recently that the intensive teaching of poetry has become a proliferating and profitable industry; one, moreover, paradoxical in its requirements since it demands that only the incompetent, the unenterprising, and the passionless need apply for hiring. These the Ph.D. factories in this country and in the United States are supplying in ever-increasing numbers. And hired they are, provided they can show they've the necessary skill and docility to put a polish on the sons and daughters of our disintegrating middle class, a fake gloss on their inherited uncouthness. To suppose for even an instant that these poor drudges, these unimpassioned eunuchs and dried-up prunes render any service

170

to poets, whether living or dead, is one of the most hilarious notions I've ever encountered outside my favorite humourist, the Marquis de Sade.

Recently I wrote somewhere that 95% of the teachers of literature in our universities and schools would be more honestly employed cleaning toilets. I still hold that opinion. My regard for the inspiring teacher of poetry is as vehement as that of Prof. Miller's; also for the sensitive critic, though assorted illiterates and addlepates would have me pictured a fanatical enemy of both. The fact is, however, that such individuals are very rare indeed; in this country, for all practical census-taking purposes, the species is extinct. Most teachers of poetry are worse than poor, they're a positive danger to the mental health of their students and I'd have them out of the classroom in a jiffy. Their one accomplishment – what reminiscing fuddy-duddy will deny it? –is to implant a horror and dislike of poetry that ends only with the grave. Perhaps, as I have come to suspect with the passing years, that's the way the well-heeled stupid ones, the present holders of power want it; for literature, properly taught, is the most subversive subject on the curriculum. It will not do to awaken too great an interest in it – it might make the students less amenable to the rabid outpourings of copywriters, admen, politicians, and all the other mean-souled and small-minded castrates who profit from corrupting the hearts and minds of their fellow men. The present vicious order with its social and sexual repression couldn't endure a single day if poetry were taught by honest men and women. No, keep it dull, that's the invisible motto inscribed on the banner of every school, of every college and university in this godforsaken country. Keep it boring, keep it innocuous and irrelevant so that nothing will disturb the powers-that-be and the country-club dullness they would like to see maintained forever. Poetry is a tiger; somebody must be around to see that its teeth are pulled. The Teachers' Colleges and the Ph.D. factories exist to turn out the necessary dentists. I think they deserve well of their masters: at least, a small rise in their pay.

Irving Layton is one of Canada's best known, most prolific, and most controversial poets. Author of twenty-five volumes of poetry, he has garnered an impressive range of awards including the Governor General's Award for *A Red Carpet in the Sun* (1962). "Letter, *The Montreal Star*" is reprinted from *Engagements: The Prose of Irving Layton* by permission of The Canadian Publishers, McClelland and Stewart.

DOES THE CIVIL SERVICE MAKE YOU NERVOUS?

MONDAY

TUESDAY

WEDNESDAY

THURSDAY

FRIDAY

JAMES QUIG

The Joual Revolution

Playwright Michel Tremblay: works of art from working-class French.

Imagine for a moment that your name is Lapointe, Lapierre or Lalonde. Your father was a Jean-Louis, your mother a Marie-Thérèse. You believe in God, Mass and Molson's and develop acid indigestion every time you go west of the Montreal Forum. You were born and live in the world's second-largest French-speaking city but you named your daughter Linda, call yourself Tony instead of Antoine and had to learn English to get a job. The only unilingual person you know is your English-speaking boss—oh yes, and the salesgirls at Eaton's and Simpsons, who roll their eyes at your English, just as your own upper-class holds it nose in the rare company of your North American working-class French.

But hang on! Here come the '60s and finally, they're playing your song. . . .

A young singer with electrocuted hair is suddenly singing about people, places and passions that matter to you. Songs for and *about* you. A singer, finally, who doesn't sound as if he grew up near the Seine in Paris but near the Main in Montreal—and isn't apologizing for it. A guy who speaks your kind of French, who knows a *cheval* got to be a *joual* around here because a working-stiff like you hasn't a lot of time to sit around and polish his language—and you've been

forced to tackle *two!* Sure you've borrowed what may be more than a decent number of English words from the *Anglais* but is it any wonder? *Les Anglais* are pulling the strings here and aren't exactly busting it to learn French. And this new singer knows all that. His name is Robert Charlebois and you make him a star.

And *plus ça change* in the Quebec of the '60s, the more things will never be the same. A young monologist steps into the spotlight armed with humour, a social conscience and a Sad Sack character who brags about a boss who lets him off an hour early on Christmas Day. (Who needs a union with a boss like that?) His name is Yvon Deschamps and the face in his mirror looks a lot like you, Antoine. He has you laughing *and* thinking, so you make him a big star, too.   But you are just warming up.

The year is 1965 now and in an east-end Montreal printing shop a 23-year-old linotypist is rushing to finish his night-shift work allotment so he'll have a little time left over to work on a play he's been writing about 15 Québécois women, 1 million trading stamps and despair. Michel Tremblay writes well. His play, *Les Belles Soeurs*, will make him famous and rich. But that's not all.

For the first time in your life, Antoine, you and the people around you are going to be acknowledged and celebrated as never before. At first glance *Les Belles Soeurs* is about a woman who wins a million trading stamps and invites some friends and relatives – all women – over to help paste them into the little books so she can collect her prizes. But if you look just a bit deeper, Antoine, you'll see that Michel Tremblay is really writing about a world of ignorance and self-satisfaction. About a people who are falling asleep – a people who are losing not only their language, but also their pride. *Les Belles Soeurs* is about your mother, sister and wife. About *you*. And the picture isn't pretty – Tremblay gives you the feeling that all the prizes in *Les Belles Soeurs*, all the *goals* in your life, will be pink, plastic and flash in the night. *Les Belles Soeurs* will help change Quebec: you'll start calling yourself Antoine again, instead of Tony. You'll never be quite the same. Neither will the folks next door. Neither will a country called Canada.

Michel Tremblay grew up in a bologna and Pepsi-Cola world where entertainment meant tuning in the Rosary on radio every night after supper and zooming in on the axe murders in *Allo Police* and the other tabloids every Sunday after Mass. In between were bingo, the Canadiens, tavern beer and visits to the Oratoire for another peek at Brother André's heart.

Michel Tremblay quit school after Grade 11 – he jokes that he got out before any major damage could be done to him – and, mostly because his father was a newspaper pressman, he went into the linotype business. But that was long ago. Today, at 34, the king of Quebec theatre lives in Outremont, francophone Montreal's answer to Westmount, on a street that reeks of money and Molière. No beat-up *joual* French, fried bologna or welfare cheques here.

I'm early so I walk around the block a few times. Children are laughing their way back to kindergarten. *"Une heure moins quart,"* I learn from a cross guard with a watch. Tremblay lives in a big house and his verandah is painted with the same blue and white that is part of the Quebec flag. I wonder if the paint job is fresh and might be his way of celebrating the recent Parti Québécois victory.

And I recall another encounter with a militant Québécois. . . .

The little *boîte à chanson* was on Rue de la Montagne in downtown Montreal. It was small, dark and crowded, and the *chansonniers* sang of the Gaspé and the Main, winter at Ste. Adèle and the soul of the Québécois. The beer was going down well and the couple at the next table smiled their friendship. *Tabarnouche*, what a city!

"I wonder how the babysitter's doing?" I asked my wife between songs. We're both from Eastern Ontario and grew up *en français*. The babysitter question was my first use of English in over an hour.

"Cochon d'Anglais," said the guy at the next table, spitting hate. What followed was neither wise nor pleasant – or easily forgotten even several years later.

Michel Tremblay would never have been the lout at the next table. But he was Québec's angry young man: "For 300 years Québec has been caught between two people who didn't want us alive," he said in 1972. "The English colonized us economically, the French artistically."

He wrote 11 plays in 11 years and the real bad guys in his work always seemed to be not the French or the English but the Québécois themselves who took it lying down. Who didn't rise up generations ago. Who buried their heads in a fog of beer and religion to ease the pain and the shame.

Québec was like his unhappy Manon in *Forever Yours, Marie-Lou*, who cringed at home with her religious statues, her insecurity and her misery. But it could have been like Manon's braver sister Carmen who broke away by singing cowboy songs in the nightspots of the Main. Québec was Tremblay's transvestites in *Hosanna* who didn't know what they were, his Berthe (in *Berthe,* one of his short works) who complained non-stop of being trapped in her moviehouse ticket cage but never tried to get out of it with a new job, his Leopold in *Forever Yours, Marie-Lou,* who blotted out reality with a tableful of beer, and his Lisette de Courval in *Les Belles Soeurs* who tried to find identity and dignity by visiting France and trying to speak "proper" French.

"Une heure moins cinq," says the crossing guard this time. One more turn around the block. To tell you the truth I'm not in a hurry. Sometimes in the past 10 years it has been necessary to talk fast and smooth in the company of impatient, militant Québécois; you spoke French, you cared about the Québécois and you wanted to understand. But it wasn't always enough. You were *Anglais,* therefore you couldn't really care, you couldn't really understand. And to tell you the truth, *Anglais,* we are in a hurry and have much better things to do. . . .

I buzz Michel Tremblay's doorbell this snowy day wondering if it would be any different this time.

Bonjour."

He's bearded and big—30 pounds bigger than he was when he left Montreal for Paris a year and a half ago. (Though a recent diet has trimmed his bulk considerably.) He is wearing something loose and colourful that would have been called a dress and raised eyebrows in the neighbourhoods of his youth (and mine). I think it's Indian but I can't be sure.

I like your blue verandah."

"The street needed a little colour. So drab—all those white pillars."

The man who makes great art with broken-down *joual* French speaks the language impeccably himself. He turns down the opera on the big Marantz stereo and tells me this is his fifth interview in four days. "Peter Gzowski, 'Canada A.M.,' Sid Adilman of the *Toronto Star,* the *Globe and Mail,* and now you. What's going on?"

"What did they want to know?" I snoop.

"About my work and the elections. But their questions have changed since November 15. It used to be every interview started out with 'So you're a separatist.' Everybody seems more anxious to understand *why* now. Less hostile and aggressive."

"Maybe that's because *you* are less hostile and aggressive."

"Of course. We've all changed since the PQ victory. We don't need to be aggressive anymore. We won."

One of his cats jumps up on his lap and settles in, purring. "You were pleased with the results?"

"Of course. After the 1973 elections I decided there was no use. Quebec was falling back to sleep again. It was just too sad to watch. I decided I couldn't live here anymore, so in October, 1975, I left Québec for Paris. Pauline Julien called me in Paris the night of the election — crying. Because we'd lost again, I thought. But no. We'd won. We cried together. I came home the next morning."

I know the next answer but want to hear him say it.

"You are a separatist?"

"You can't be a Québécois, 34 and intelligent, and not be. I cannot forgive and forget."

"Forgive and forget who? What?"

"The English. They never respected us. Never. For me it isn't a case of economics or statistics. Just a lack of respect. And I don't mean the English of Toronto or Calgary but the English of Québec. They lived here, a minority, but didn't respect the majority enough to learn its language."

175

I tell him about close friends who tried but just couldn't . It just wasn't in them . They didn't have the ears for it. They were too old. They. . . .

But he doesn't buy it.

"When I was 6 years old my father took me aside and said he had something very important to tell me. Something I should never forget. He said, 'You have to speak English to get a job in Montreal.' I didn't have the ears for it either, but I learned."

The anger lingered. Though his plays have triumphed in translation all over English-speaking Canada, until Nov. 15 the playwright had refused to permit his work to be performed in English inside Québec.

"My attitude has been that they should learn French. But suddenly we've won and the English are a real minority in Québec. We have a government that will, finally, encourage them to learn our language. My little political gesture is no longer necessary."

"Is that why you are allowing the CBC to film *Les Belles Soeurs* in English here in Montreal?" (It will be shown on TV next March.)

"Yes—and also because they are paying me a lot of money."

"So Michel Tremblay is influential and rich, too?"

"I made $60,000 last year and $60,000 the year before that. But that is the worst bracket to be in—I never seem to have the money for the taxes. I should make $20,000 more or $20,000 less. I was better off when I was making $20- or $30-thousand a year. But I didn't have this big house then. I think I'll ask my accountant to put me on a budget. But lately I've been taking the bus to save. I was spending $120 a week on taxis."

"Do you believe Québec will achieve independence?"

"I'm certainly more hopeful now than I was three years ago."

"Don't you think there could be some kind of entente? Special status? Something less drastic?"

"No. It's too late. And I know how upsetting that is for Canadians. But it's not our fault if we don't feel Canadian. And it doesn't mean we can't still be friends. Some people seem to think we'll outlaw long-distance telephone calls."

"Do you believe your plays contributed to the present situation?"

"We all tried to do our little bit for the cause."

Michel Tremblay's fame has enabled him to travel throughout Canada. I asked him how he felt in Toronto or Vancouver.

"I like Canada. Nice place, nice people. I speak English and I'm completely at ease. Just as I am when I go to France."

"But not at home?"

"Not a bit," he says. "But I detect a new sense of self-awareness among English-speaking Canadians. They seem to be discovering who they are and what they want to be. That's very exciting —for them and for us."

"How's that?"

"When Canadians discover that they are not Americans they will understand at last why we are not Canadians."

"Why was it important to write your plays in the *joual* French of the streets?"

"Because that's the way the working-class people of Montreal talked and they had always been overlooked. And that was sinful. A whole class of people had never been properly acknowledged by the theatre."

"How come?"

"Because the upper classes were ashamed that people still lived and talked like that. Ashamed that we had allowed ourselves to be colonized to that degree. Ashamed that we had colonized *ourselves* even further. Many used to talk like that themselves. Or they had parents who did. They were ashamed and they wanted to forget. But you can't forget who you are – or who you've been. They didn't want to be reminded. Many haven't forgiven me yet."

"You aren't loved by all?"

"They hate me," he says. "At Radio-Canada [the French wing of the CBC] they are embarrassed to be associated with my work. They say it's vulgar. But they have become *cultured* and they want to forget, too."

He says the CBC Toronto production team offered to film *Les Belles Soeurs* in French while they were in Montreal filming it in English. Actors were ready, sets were already prepared, it could have been done in French for a bargain.

"But Radio-Canada turned down the offer saying *Les Belles Soeurs* was too similar to one of my other plays *(En pieces détachées)*, which was first televised in 1970. The English masses will see my play, but not the Québécois for whom it was written."

He thinks about that for a moment.

"Being Québécois and trying to speak like a Parisien – as they do at Radio-Canada. That's vulgar. They take all the guts out of our language. I speak excellent French – but I don't sound like a Frenchman.

"Québec's Théâtre du Nouveau Monde going to Paris in the '50s with productions of Molière. That's vulgar. The sign of a colonized people."

I mention that he always seems to be writing about women – and in some cases, transvestites.

"I have instant empathy with women. My father was a pressman at *La Patrie* and worked nights all the time. He was deaf. I was raised by my mother and grandmother, two aunts and a cousin. The house was full of women."

"You don't want to write about the men you know."

He says making men talk on the stage is not his job; Québec theatre had always been a theatre of men. Women were always secondary, just props.

"And let's face it I don't consider myself very *masculin.* . . ."

He strokes the cat. Looks me straight in the eye.

". . . and I have absolutely no complexes about it. I found out when I was 10 years old."

"I understand," I say, though I really don't. But Michel Tremblay is being much too candid and honest for me not to be: "No, that's not right. I don't understand at all. I don't understand homosexuality. It is very complex for me."

"Very complex," he agrees.

"Your sexual persuasions are your own affair . . . but your homosexuality seems to be a very real factor in your work. You have a fantastic feeling for femininity in your writing, you don't write about men – and when you do, you're pretty tough. . . ."

"I didn't want to do *anything* men did," he says. "I didn't smoke *because* men smoked. I didn't learn to drive a car *because* it was always the men who learned to drive cars."

I look about the living room. Michel Tremblay lives in a big, beautiful, art-filled home. I hope he isn't lonely: cats aren't enough.

"You don't live here all alone?"

"Oh, no. I could never live alone."

I ask him where he goes from here. What does an angry young man do when he isn't quite so angry anymore?

"I have no idea. But people who have read my palm say that at 35 life will change completely."

"Surely you don't believe. . . ."

"I have been told some very remarkable things," he says, and it is obvious that he does believe in such things.

"Québec has changed," he says. "Some parts of my plays have been overtaken by history – and nobody could be happier about it than I. But I have nothing more to say for the theatre. At least not right now. I'm writing another novel about the women who lived on my street in 1942–the year I was born. It's called *The Fat Woman Next Door Is Pregnant.* The woman was my mother. And there are the films."

"Any hobbies?"

"I go to the theatre," he laughs. "I love movies and I'm a classical music addict. I eat a lot, and on Tuesdays I always watch the *Muppet Show.*"

"The Muppets? Québec's angry young man and the Muppets?"

"Aren't they fantastic," he says, getting my coat.

Outside it was snowing again and the kids were all home from school. On the car radio *all* the songs were for and about the people who live around here, the hotlines buzzed of René and his new team and Jean Lapointe who used to work saloons was opening his comedy act at Place des Arts.

"I write about two kinds of people," Michel Tremblay had said. "Those who stay at home and die and those who go out and live."

James Quig is a regular columnist on Quebec for *Canadian Business.* He and his family are renovating a 127-year-old grist mill in the Eastern Townships of Quebec. "The Joual Revolution" first appeared in *The Canadian,* May 14, 1977.

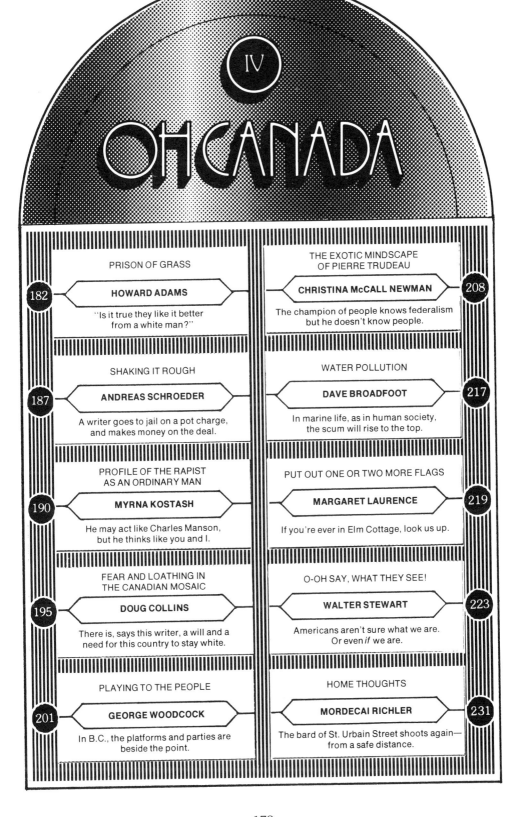

IV

OH CANADA

"... AND YOUR FUTURE KING..."

HOWARD ADAMS
Prison of Grass

"Is it true they like it better from a white man?"

The fall that I was 18 I went to work for a farmer 15 miles from home. Not having any transportation, I was obliged to walk to his farm that day. On the highway I was lucky enough to be given a ride, or so I thought. A couple of Mounties in their car stopped and offered me a ride. It frightened me momentarily because I thought they were going to run me in. Mounties don't ordinarily give this kind of help, especially to Métis. I had heard many stories about how brutally the police treated Métis and how they pinned false charges on them. But a ride was very welcome at this point. As we started up, the driver asked if I was from St. Louis, and before I even had a chance to answer, the other cop remarked, "There's a lot of smoked meat around that town." I had heard that expression many times before and I knew what it meant. The comment really burned me but I was too scared to argue. As far as I was concerned the girls in St. Louis were very decent. The Mountie continued, "I hear that those halfbreed babes like to have their fun lying down." I tried to change the subject, but the police were interested in pursuing it to the end. The driver asked in a mocking manner, "Is it true they like it better from a white man?" I was getting really angry, while at the same time trying to explain that Métis girls are just as nice as white girls. They drove on with comments about "redskin hotboxes who didn't wear any pants at all," and kept calling me "chief " in a sneering manner. Although they seemed to have an obsessive interest in native girls, they were also implying that Métis girls were little more than sluts and too dirty for Mounties. One asked, "Is it true that they'll go to bed with anyone for a beer?"

I was relieved when we reached the crossroads where I was to get off, but they drove on slowly and ignored my request to be let out. The driver said to his partner, "The chief probably has some little redskin heifer waiting for him in the bush." They joked together about "horny bucks" and "red peasoups always in heat." One wanted to bet me there wasn't a virgin in St. Louis. I began to think about jumping out since we weren't going very fast. They offered to let me out as soon as I would tell them the secret of "no knock-ups." At that point I said I was going to jump off, and they immediately burst out laughing. Between their fits of laughter they were half shouting, "Jump off, so that's it." They roared on about "jump on, jump off, breed games, up and down, in and out, and halfbreed fun." Finally they let me out and drove away in a thunder of laughter. I turned and ran down the road with their mockery ringing in my ears. Shame was burning in my mind like a hot iron. I ran as if I was trying to outrun the Mounties' image of the Métis. I ran till I was exhausted, swearing, spitting, and half crying. That is how the famous redcoats of law and order respect the native people and their society.

According to racial stereotypes, Indians and Métis are naturally shy and withdrawn; they are born that way. Incidents such as the one I have described apparently have nothing to do with it. This notion is pounded into the heads of native children by teachers, priests, white functionaries. Because the children are rarely free from this myth, they don't get opportunities to develop confident and assertive attitudes about themselves. It is a very effective way of preventing the development of bold and articulate leaders, and the absence of such native leaders over the last century shows the success of this inferiorization scheme.

Coupled with the destruction of self-esteem is the suppression and mockery of native languages. In racist institutions such as schools and churches, Indians are discouraged as much as possible from using their native tongues, and Indian names are anglicized and mocked. For example, an Indian child may be given an Indian name which, incorrectly translated, means Afraid-of-his-horses. The original meaning is impossible to get into a convenient English phrase, but it refers to a warrior fierce in battle who has many fast horses. The rough, incorrect translation made by white people is ridiculous and in some cases, as above, virtually the opposite of the original. However, whites take only the surface meaning of the anglicized version and mock the Indian as if he were, in fact, afraid of horses. This is a powerful means of degrading native people.

Of course, white men's names are never reinterpreted in the same way for the convenience of native speakers. Another example of how language is used to degrade the native people is pro-

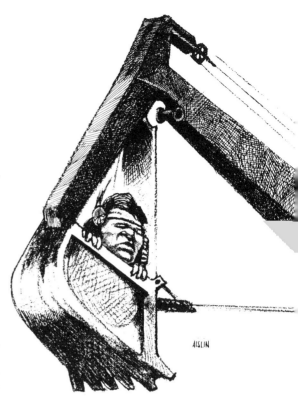

AISLIN

vided by official government pronouncements regarding natives. As part of the program of national and cultural destruction, the government treats Indians and Métis as wards or children. Such attitudes, typical of the colonial mentality, were clearly revealed during the treaty negotiations and the relocation of Indians to reserves after 1885. In the negotiations of Treaty Six, Governor Morris addressed the masses of Indians saying, ''Indian children of the Queen . . . I am glad to learn that they [Crees] are looking forward to having their children civilized.'' The reason for this language is to convey the idea that natives are incapable of governing themselves, and that this justifies absolute government over them. In this way governments encourage their functionaries to look after the ''children'' in an authoritarian manner.

183

After reserves were established and Indians had developed a conscience of obedience, police were replaced by bureaucrats, priests, and teachers. The change to new wardens was made possible because Indians and Métis had internalized the myths of inferiority and become placid and subservient. The church was one of the most powerful and effective instruments in destroying native strength, and indoctrination leading to supplicant behaviour was done largely by the clergy. Church and school determine much of the ideology of the native communities by teaching native children to believe in white supremacy, and thus in their own inferiority; this paternalism is effective in keeping Indians and Métis in "child" roles and "in their place." Although these non-military authorities give the appearance of being liberal and democratic, their teaching and administration only continues the work of police.

The results of this mentality can be seen clearly in any reserve village whose population comprises both natives and whites. There are always two distinct communities. The native section has no gas or running water, no paved streets or sidewalks, only trails and dirt roads. Many of the houses are one- or two-room shacks. The differences are more than economic and cultural, they are vividly racial. According to the whites, the native section is a place of lazy, diseased, and evil people incapable of doing anything for themselves, a breeding-ground for violence. The whites claim that natives have no culture, no ethics, no sensibility to morality, and no appreciation of law and order. To these colonizers, Indians and Métis destroy and disfigure beauty. They speak of their native neighbours in bestial terms, complaining that "they breed like rabbits." They speak of the sinful and depraved behaviour of natives, of shacking-up, of common-law marriages, of sleeping around. The fact is that the native villagers are hungry

—hungry for food, for houses, for clothes, for power, and for whatever the whites take for granted. They are crouching villagers, listening to the gossip of the shacks, listening to what the white man wants them to hear, think, and fear. Because the native villagers contain frustration, hostility, and envy, they are always on the defensive and rarely able to progress.

In contrast, the colonizers' section is clean and beautiful. It has electricity, plumbing, paved streets, and garbage collection. It has beautiful modern houses with central heating and all public utilities. It has white authorities who draw handsome salaries because of the native people. These colonizers are privileged because they belong to the power structure and they have physical comfort and luxury because they are white. They have opportunities and unlimited horizons because they are part of mainstream society. The law is on their side because they are administrators. They are able to talk about the native world in "rational and objective" terms because all the evidence is on their side.

Until fairly recently, the Indian agent managed the reserve people's personal business as official business, and had the right to open their personal mail. In this way, he emphasized that Indians were not individuals in their own right, with their own personal, intimate existences, and that white agents had full power over them. The only other place where such extreme dehumanization exists is in prisons—perhaps there is a basis for claiming that Indians and Métis make ideal prisoners. By the same token, whites consider native people as objects and not as persons. This is reflected in phrases such as "our Indians," implying possession of objects, such as toys or pets. Indians and Métis are not allowed to take action on their own, action that would be completely independent from whites. To colonizers, natives are to be

184

controlled; they are not human beings who can engage in normal social relationships and organizations. Natives have to be managed and programmed.

As colonized people in a white-supremacist society, Indians and Métis are dehumanized in every possible way. Indians are often denied their names and instead are given a treaty number; they then become officially known by this number. Native people are depersonalized to such an extent that their inner strength is pulverized and they are left without a vigorous will—as an ethnic group, natives have the highest per capita suicide rate in Canada. The purpose behind the dehumanization of Indians and Métis is to make them accept the denial of their human and civil rights.

Also injected into the view of native culture was the belief that Indians and Métis lack moral values. White supremacy claims that natives have always been immoral and dishonest and that it is a losing battle to attempt to make them live up to decent moral standards. Many racist images are so distorted that they portray natives as little more than savages without intelligence or beauty. Because they are regarded in this way, natives themselves come to accept the cruelties of oppression as a necessary part of their colonized existence. In a dehumanized and racist society people lose sensitivity to moral and social issues. They have an awareness only of the trivialities and personal events in the ghetto, and not of the serious social, economic, and political issues. Furthermore, colonized people have difficulty uniting on human-rights concerns; for example, Indian and Métis people are frequently refused employment or decent housing because of their race, yet they do not protest seriously against this denial of civil rights. Instead, most of them simply accept this crime as a natural part of Canadian society.

Frustrated and confused by their state of powerlessness and oppression, native people sometimes turn to social behaviour consistent with racial stereotypes. Indians and Métis become subservient and grateful and therefore vulnerable to manipulation and exploitation by the authorities. In this way, native people weaken themselves politically. Some weaken themselves further by internalizing such racial images as the drunken, irresponsible, and shy native. Consequently, whites can claim that their stereotypes are correct, which, in turn, reinforces their racist attitudes. Not that this kind of confirmation is necessary to the racist mentality. Contradictions in racial stereotypes that debase Indians and Métis seem not to concern whites. Natives are portrayed as ignorant and gullible at the same time as they are considered sneaky and crafty cheaters. After all, according to white supremacy, to cheat a white man a native would have to be exceedingly clever. Even today, if something is missing in the classroom, the teacher usually questions Indian and Métis children first. This is racism in its everyday ugliness and oppressiveness.

To mainstream society native people all look alike and act alike. There is no individual appearance and behaviour. If an Indian or Métis is late for work, all native people are labelled as habitual late arrivers. Whites often complain, ''They failed, just when so much was being done for them,'' even though only one native person failed. This allows whites to dispense with any obligation to improve their racist society. The white man rationalizes that he has done his best; if natives suffer hardship, it is their own fault. Colonization and racism not only harm native civilization but they harden the humanity of the entire Canadian society.

Canadian authorities and historians have nevertheless managed to perpetuate the illusion that Canada has never been a white-supremacist society, an illusion that Canadian people continue to believe. As a result, they have developed attitudes that harmonize well with apartheidism. Canadians have adjusted to their white supremacy; because they are unaware of their racism, they are self-righteous, arrogant, and free from any social conscience with regard to racism. In the past, unless a white was able to break free of his racism and search for the truth, the truth remained hidden.

The native people in a colony are not allowed a valid interpretation of their history, because the conquered do not write their own history. They must endure a history that shames them, destroys their confidence, and causes them to reject their heritage. Those in power command the present and shape the future by controlling the past, particularly for the natives. A fact of imperialism is that it systematically denies native people a dignified history. Whites claim that Métis and Indians have no history or national identity, or, if they do, then it is a disgraceful and pathetic one. When natives renounce their nationalism and deny their Indianness, it is a sure sign that colonizing schemes of inferiorization have been successful.

Howard Adams, a self-styled red power advocate, has been at the forefront of the Indian/Métis civil rights movement in both Canada and the United States. Born in Saskatchewan of Métis parents, he has studied, worked, and taught in Western Canada. Currently Professor of Native American Studies at the University of California, he has published on education and native North Americans. This essay is from *Prison of Grass* and is used by permission of New Press, Don Mills, Ontario.

ANDREAS SCHROEDER

Shaking It Rough

A writer goes to jail on a pot charge, and makes money on the deal.

One of the first things I discovered when I entered the British Columbia penal system was that most of its prisons are swamped by radio. Each cell and/or corridor is fitted with well-grated speakers, very occasionally flanked by a volume control but never by a kill button. We were, in other words, obliged to listen to rock music from 7 A.M. to 10:30 P.M., and no place to hide. In Oakalla the situation was even worse in that the bottom tier of cells, generally inhabited by older inmates consigned to do their entire time in maximum security, had the odd television set and private radio as well, so that at any given time we stood a good chance of being attacked by three radio stations, two television soundtracks and the public-address system to boot.

In Oakalla, admittedly, the newness of the whole experience absorbed a good deal of my attention and so the strange tossed salad of sound, considerably hollowed and eeried by the vastness of the building, and by the fact that each bank of speakers transmitted from a different level in the joint (there were five levels of cells), simply confirmed the fantastical nature of the place; it was the macabre sound track of some prehistoric time and therefore peculiarly appropriate.

The Haney Correctional Centre's sound system was worse because even the corridors were wired for sound (which echoed badly), but at least they

had managed to get themselves plugged into FM programming, which keeps its commercials to a tolerable level. But when I arrived at Pine Ridge Camp I found the whole idea expanded from the ridiculous to the perverse. Not only were the individual huts wired into AM radio, but the entire camp was surrounded by speakers mounted on telephone poles which flooded the camp area morning and night with rock and pop music. (I might add that I used to be fairly fond of rock and pop music before my Pine Ridge sojourn.) We used to remark sourly that you couldn't have heard a bird sing if you'd attached a bullhorn to your ear and aimed it directly at the bird screaming in the tree under which you were standing. And all this not, incidentally, because inmates wanted it that way. I couldn't begin to count the number of times we asked the duty officer to shut the damn thing off, our ears were ringing and some of us wanted to sleep, to read, etc.—all to no avail. The camp staff insisted that we wanted that music, even if for some peculiar reason we didn't realize that we did.

It was that music which finally drove me to the only significant loss of cool to which I ever succumbed in prison. Not that I didn't despair at regular intervals, lose my temper and curse my fate as enthusiastically as the next man—I did, but never to such an extent that I totally lost control of it. Mostly the turmoil just unreeled itself in my head while I kept a wary eye on the fuses, and when it was done, rewound itself politely, its purpose accomplished. This time I had no such luck. It had been a bad day, pouring rain again, torn raingear, no mail, sloppy food and all evening some demented disc jockey on CKLG enthusing all over the place in that ludicrous hip jargon they sometimes affect, with loud, brassy band music hour after hour. I finally suggested we tear the goddamned speaker out of the ceiling.

We considered the proposition seriously for some time, but decided, upon investigation, that the speaker was wired in series, meaning that if we unhooked ours, the entire system would fall silent and we'd have a guard at the door in about three micro-seconds flat. I decided to muffle the speaker instead.

That was easier said than done inasmuch as the ceiling was ten feet high and there was nothing to attach anything to up there. I finally concocted an absurd Tower of Babel by jamming a towel-filled hard hat (from the mill) against the speaker, holding that up with a broom which was supported by a chair which stood on a card table I'd placed on the floor directly beneath the speaker. The whole arrangement tottered uneasily but it held, and the sound was reduced to almost silence. Blessed relief. Everyone cheered *sotto-voce* and tip-toed back to their bunks since any sudden vibration would have been fatal to the stability of our volume control tower. That's when the door opened and Victor came in. He was a little guy, about my size and weight, and he wanted to play cards.

That, I informed him, he could do on his bunk. The card table was being used in an electronic capacity.

He didn't see it that way. He wanted the table.

I said I was sorry, that my heart beat tumultuously for him and that a warm glow of commiseration was suffusing my chest, but that his bunk would have to do for the nonce.

He chose to ignore my point of view and headed for the tower. I unwound myself from my bunk and headed in the same direction, to protect my interests and my sanity. We arrived at the table about the same time.

He laid hands on the broom.

I advised him one last time of the disastrous results any rash act on his part would most certainly produce.

The little bugger had spunk, or else he had a tin ear. Even I could hear that I was on the teetering edge of coming totally unglued; I didn't know anything about fighting but anybody knows that a sufficient degree of craziness can take up all kinds of slack in that department. He yanked the broom off the table, the whole contraption collapsed and I almost got hit by the falling hard hat, which bounced twice and rolled underneath the nearest bunk.

I heard the rock music re-explode through the room and felt a similar concussion in my head. I was three feet off the floor and virtually parallel to it when I hit him with a flying tackle that knocked us both onto the bunk under which the hard hat lay. Fists blurred and flew. He seemed as untaught and unpractised in the arts of war as I; we flailed at each other furiously, recklessly, wholeheartedly; I wanted to murder that guy, I mean just plain *kill* him, simply tear him limb from every possible limb. His inclinations seemed the same. We banged each other's heads on the bunk frames, smashed each other's glasses off, beat each other black and blue. He slid off the bunk onto the floor, I jumped on him and we rolled through the dust and ashes (the huts were heated with old wood stoves) knocking over chairs, boot racks, the card table. It was terrific. It was absolutely marvellous. It was downright ecstatic, is what it was.

That was in fact what finally stopped it. We eventually realized, more or less simultaneously, the extent to which we had actually begun to enjoy the whole debacle. At that point we couldn't take it seriously enough anymore, and quit. He retired to his bunk to repair his glasses while I rebuilt the tower and then proceeded to repair my own. I felt tremendously relieved. Much later he admitted to the same feeling. We'd shaken our first two months in jail a trifle rough.

"The bad news is that your appeal has been turned down. The good news is that I've just got you a $10,000 advance on the movie rights."

Andreas Schroeder, an ex-chairman of the Writers' Union of Canada, skydives, races motorcycles, and is studying towards a pilot's licence. He has published three books of poetry, a collection of short stories, *The Late Man,* and co-edited *Stories from Pacific and Arctic Canada. Shaking It Rough* is reprinted by permission of Doubleday Canada Limited.

MYRNA KOSTASH

Profile of the Rapist as an Ordinary Man

He may act like Charles Manson, but he thinks like you and I.

I was hitchhiking from my parents' place to the city and got a ride with a man. When I first got into his car, he looked like a nice, gentle, innocuous guy who wouldn't bother me. He said he was 25 years old and had been out of school for a couple of years. We got to talking and he seemed okay but after about an hour he said he wanted to pull over to the side of the road and rest. I told him I was kind of in a hurry to get home. I had begun to get strange vibes from him—everything we talked about ended up in a discussion about sex. He told me all about his sexual experiences and wanted me to talk about mine. I was wearing jeans and an old top; when I hitchhike I dress as asexually as possible. So there was no way I was indicating my availability by the way I was dressed. Then he said we were going to stop whether I liked it or not and he was going to "make love" to me. I said, "I don't particularly want to make love to you." He pulled over to the side of the road and reached over me and put his elbow on the lock of the door and wouldn't let me out. He jumped on me. He ripped my clothes.

And then he raped her. Forced her into this act he called "making love," and made believe that what he was recreating

in the cramped space of the car's front seat was a lover's pleasure. She went to the police but never pressed charges. Instead she has spent the last year wrestling with her fears and her anger. She finally talked it all out into a tape recorder, partly as therapy and partly so that others would know and understand just what the experience of being raped is like.

He was no weirdo. He didn't prowl around neighbourhoods and drool at passing women from behind bushes. He didn't have the kind of grizzled face and unfocused gaze of the dirty old men you see in subway cars and buses staring at women's thighs.

If you asked him about himself he would tell you he was just an ordinary guy. He had a good job, loved his mum, took girls to the movies and to bars, slept with the ones who let him. Hell, he'd say, most girls are *easy* these days. They all pretend at first that they are virgins or something and waiting for Mr. Right but, in the end, if you put a little pressure on them, and maybe get a little threatening, they almost always give in. Women want to be *persuaded,* roughed up a bit. You certainly don't have to take "no" as their final answer.

And if you asked him for his version of

190

what went on in his car that night, this is what he might say: what do you expect a guy to think when he sees a chick all alone on the highway, hitchhiking? And when she turns out to be real friendly and dressed up like a hippie? I mean, come *on*, you'd have to be pretty dense not to figure out that she's on the make. So you can imagine how I felt when she suddenly got on her high horse and said no, no!

No one, neither psychologists nor the police, rape counsellors nor judges, seems to know just what pushes an "ordinary guy" over the line between courtship and rape. There is research available and theories have been formulated which attempt a description of *who* the rapist is, what his personal history is likely to be, what might go on in his mind during the attack and how he justifies himself. But precisely what it is that distinguishes a rapist from the rest of men who don't, in spite of frustration, humiliation, guilt or outrage, force sexual intercourse on a woman without her freely given consent, is a mystery. The rapist doesn't understand himself any better than we do. In fact, a rapist may not even be conscious he's done anything wrong. According to a recent study in Denver, Colorado, "most rapists can neither admit nor express the fact that they are a menace to society."

I couldn't believe it was happening and that I could be so completely trapped. He was so much stronger than I was. When he was finished, I threw up and he got mad at me for messing up the interior of his car. I begged him to let me go. He said he couldn't because I would have to hitchhike home and suppose somebody picked me up and raped me! I thought, oh my God, he's insane.

But, in all probability, he is *not* clinically insane. According to the Philadelphia criminologist, Menachim Amir, "studies indicate that sex offenders do not constitute a unique or psychopathological type; nor are they as a group invariably more disturbed than the control groups to which they are compared." Most of us share the popular misconception that all rapists are "sexual psychopaths." And the average rapist shares this misconception with us. Since he knows he isn't a Jack the Ripper lurking in dark corners ready to pounce on an unsuspecting female and drag her away, he doesn't think of *himself* as a rapist. He sees rapes committed by others in the same way we do, as the behaviour of perverted, *sick* individuals and not something that he, a normal, virile and assertive male does when he "makes love" to the protesting and revolted body of his victim.

He wouldn't, then, recognize himself in most of the psychological accounts of a rapist's motivations: "incestuous desires," "symbolic matricide," "latent homosexuality," "castration anxieties," etc. Even if he did, the information would not be very useful to him or to us: rape is an *act*, not a state of mind. The rapist has imposed his sexuality and his fantasies on someone who doesn't want to participate; he has violated another human being's right to self-determination and he has terrorized her through a show of power. For him to see this as lovemaking is the real sickness. And yet the rapist does operate within the spectrum of normal masculinity and male sexuality. Within that spectrum he is the extremist.

Amir's study (the only comprehensive one to date in North America) showed that the majority of rapists are between 15 to 24 years of age—the period of a man's life when he is most anxiously flexing his muscles in the new role of adult masculinity. Since the social messages he receives about manhood celebrate the mystique of aggressiveness and toughness, a young man who rapes may be covering up for his feelings of weakness, sexual inadequacy and dependence —feelings which he, as a man, is not supposed to have—and taking them out on a handy victim. Almost half of the rapists Amir studied had a previous criminal record and more than half were either unskilled labourers or unemployed. Debra Lewis, University of Toronto criminology student, points out that if you are angry, frustrated, humiliated and a man, you can often deflect your misery safely onto a woman. She's less likely to fight back than a man.

Other rapists Amir studied were employed or middle-class. The only theory that seems to explain their behaviour is the psychological one—"shaky defences." As one psychologist put it, "rapists show strong elements of misogyny and distrust toward the women they place in the position of sexual objects."

In 82% of the rapes studied, the victim and the rapist came from the same neighbourhood and half the rapes originated in a meeting at the victim's or the rapist's house or at a party or a bar. Chances are the rapist knows his victim and moves in the same social circles. Chances are the rape will take place at the end of a social encounter. This makes it easier for him to see his behaviour as "seduction" or "making love." That 71% of the rapes were planned demolishes the myth that rape is the impulsive act of a loony who can't help himself. Eighty-five percent involved the use of force and the most excessive degrees of violence occurred in group rapes, suggesting that group rapists perform for each other to prove how "manly" they really are. It seems that the overpowering and humiliation of another person is as important as having sexual intercourse with her; that the event promises more than physical gratification for the rapist. Debra Lewis sees it in power terms. "If you're a person who doesn't feel very powerful or important, you're going to have the same attitude towards your body. The more degraded you can make your victim feel, the more you feed your own need. There is a large frequency of the rapist demanding the woman tell him she likes it, that she loves him, that she will go out with him after. It's a situation in which he has perfect control at last."

So, when a man rapes a woman, a lot more is going on than just nonconsensual intercourse, more even than a "sexual power struggle," although that is certainly at the heart of it, as far as the victim is concerned. In the course of my research, it was pointed out time and again that rape is about *violence* and *power*. It is a measure of our social malaise that we group these things with sex.

He said, "Give me one good reason why you should live because I want to kill you." I was terrified. I didn't want to die. I gave him what I considered to be a pretty good reason, that I was a human being and had as much right to live as anybody else. He said that wasn't good enough. He put his hands around my neck and told me to come up with something else. He told me I had no right to be alive.

On the one hand, men are taught that women, being supposedly the softer and weaker sex, are in need of their gentlemanly protection; on the other hand, there are pervasive social messages in films, literature, music, television, that women are, in fact, venal, lascivious and masochistic. The rapist, as a product of this *generalized* hostility toward femaleness *and* the sentimentality around femininity, often makes what can be called the compromise of singling out certain *kinds* of women as rape victims. His mother and sister he'd defend to the death but that broad down the street in the tight sweater who went to bed with his buddy is fair game. Better still if she's non-white, unmarried, living on her own and working class. Amir writes that rapists are "more apt to view certain females as appropriate victims and certain situations as suggestive of, even opportune for, rape." This is not only because these women have low social status and therefore aren't considered "worth" so much, but also because forcible intercourse with them isn't even *perceived* as rape.

I thought about my parents and what a drag it was going to be for them when my body was found. I got really angry about hurting them. I said, "Look, if you don't get off me, I'm going to kill you." He looked at me and said, "You're crazy, aren't you?" I was playing his game, and it worked. He drove me back to the city. As we were driving, he said he thought we could become good friends and he told me his address three or four times. I think he was probably as scared as I was.

Although the police advise women *not* to resist an attack for fear of provoking even more violence, the Denver study shows that a woman can stop a rape (at the hands of a stranger) at stage one by refusing to be intimidated. "Above all, the rapist needs ordered and controlled behaviour from his victim." As women become more self-confident and aware of their own strength, the incidence of rape may begin to decrease: the Denver study pointed out that "resisters [of rape attempts] scored higher on measures of dominance and sociability . . . were more self-accepting and had a greater sense of well-being [than those who did not resist]."

And maybe fighting back is the only real deterrent there is. It is pretty obvious to everyone that our legal system is no deterrent at all. It's estimated that only one-third to one-tenth of all rapes committed are reported to the police. Many women who do report attacks

never even get into a courtroom. They find the interrogation by the police to be such a brutal process that they don't press charges.

The first thing the police detective said to me was, "What's the matter, didn't he pay you enough money?" I couldn't believe it. He asked me if I had enjoyed it, he said I must have enjoyed it, look at the way I dress, I must be promiscuous. Then he told me that if I couldn't take this kind of questioning now, I wouldn't be able to take it later in court. Did I really want to press charges?

So the percentage of cases actually brought to court is small and only a few of them actually result in conviction. In many cases, the conviction that is finally obtained may not be for rape, but for a reduced charge of indecent assault. It is important to note that the charge of rape (which can be punished by a life sentence) applies only to forcible penetration of the vagina (less than 50% of the cases examined in the Denver study involved vaginal rape).

For the victim, any kind of assault and sexual humiliation is horrible and destructive. But it seems that to jurists and legislators, to police and to the community at large, it is an attack on the vagina, the sacred highroad of marriage and maternity, that is the profoundest affront. Ontario Crown Attorney John Kerr says he has been involved in cases "in which the girl had been assaulted in a horrible manner but because no actual vaginal intercourse took place the accused was liable only to a charge of indecent assault." Even though vaginal rape is obviously considered, in the eyes of the law, to be a most serious crime, Sergeant Robert Lynn of the Toronto police says he hasn't heard of a rapist in the last two years who's been sentenced even to 10 years. "The average is four to five. If he had never been in trouble before, and if he's going to be getting psychiatric help, sometimes he'll only get two to three. Sometimes it makes you wonder."

Kerr isn't encouraged by this trend to leniency among judges and juries. While no one is suggesting that we should go back to the old days and in a fury of vengeance castrate a rapist, or even whip him, Kerr worries that "with our changing standards of morality, maybe juries aren't treating rape so seriously anymore."

We know that rape statistics are rising drastically throughout North America. In part, this is because greater numbers of women are actually willing to press charges. But there are more pervasive reasons. The so-called Sexual Revolution of the 1960s "liberated" both men and women from the inhibiting restraints of a more puritanical sexual ethic. Then, with the women's movement of the '70s, with the publicized struggle of women for independent status, many of the protective, Victorian devices surrounding women were withdrawn. A woman who insists on taking care of herself can no longer be an object of male solicitude. It was only when a woman was seen as fluffy, delicate and helpless that male protective "instincts" toward her seemed sensible. A woman on her own is fair game.

What, then, is to be done? How do we make our legal system a real deterrent to rapists? How do we make it capable of protecting the civil rights of women without resorting to extreme "law and order" measures? The prosecution of rape charges might be made easier by legislating different degrees of rape carrying different maximum sentences.

Police departments should establish units such as New York's Sex Crimes Analysis Unit which is run by female detectives. The New York unit, besides receiving and processing all cases of rape and attempted rape, also tries to re-educate male officers in their attitudes to sex crimes. As of this writing, no police department in Canada has tried to set up anything like it.

The legal profession has to realize that whatever the psycho-sexual transactions between a man and a woman during a rape, the physical intimidation involved in the crime is a serious matter. Barbara Betcherman of Toronto's Rape Crisis Centre thinks that the way rape cases are handled now, particularly because of Section 142 of the Criminal Code (which requires a judge to instruct a jury that it is not safe to believe a woman on her word alone), they are *ipso facto* prejudicial.

Obviously, there is no single remedy that is going to eradicate sexual assaults on women. Legislative changes are required; so are "rape squads" in police departments. So are rape crisis centres and rap groups and pamphlets. But these kinds of changes only deal with the aftermath of a rape. If we want to *stop* rape, we have to figure out how to grow up as human beings.

Myrna Kostash has been a writer since she finished graduate school (Russian Literature); although her first intention was to work as a fiction writer, she turned to journalism because not only does it provide a living wage but, at its best, it is also coexists with the "fine" arts to make statements about what's really going on in our society. She has recently published *All of Baba's Children*, a non-fiction account of Ukranian-Canadian ethnicity. "Profile of the Rapist as an Ordinary Man" was first published in *Maclean's*, April 1975.

194

DOUG COLLINS

Fear and Loathing in the Canadian Mosaic

There is, says this writer, a will and a need for this country to stay white.

The man on the phone was livid. "You know what's happening? Hong Kongers are moving in here and buying out apartment blocks and getting rid of the white tenants and then renting the places out to newly arrived Chinese for more money. They're even getting rid of the maintenance staff and then hiring their own people for less.

"No, never mind the silly housing laws," he said when I tried to interject. "Those guys have ways and means. I could show you old age pensioners who've just packed up quietly and left. It's pathetic, and there isn't a lousy politician in the country who cares."

I didn't bother to check out what he said. Such stories are common in Vancouver. You hear them whenever immigration is discussed on the local hot-line shows, or even when it isn't. A few months ago, provincial Liberal leader Gordon Gibson was on the air explaining what a desirable candidate he was. But the caller I heard wasn't interested.

What he wanted to know was why people who'd been born and brought up here couldn't get houses when houses were available "for all those rich Ugandans." He suggested (among other things) that Gibson get in touch with his friend Trudeau and put him straight

WE BELIEVE IN WORKING WITHIN THE SYSTEM...

AISLIN

about it. Except that he put it rather more strongly than that.

There is at least a germ of truth in these stories, but whether or not they are true is beside the point. The fact is that Ottawa's open immigration policies have engendered enormous hatred in this country. Tolerance of the wave of coloured immigrants is rapidly disappearing, especially in large cities.

Last year, when feeling against Vancouver's East Indians was getting hot, the Vancouver *Sun* carried, on a single page, three reports of violent race incidents. At Fort St. James, in the B.C. interior, there was a race riot between East Indians, native Indians and whites. Toronto has had its race murders, and Montrealers will remember the race riot at Sir George Williams University in 1969. It caused $2 million worth of damage and, when all the sociological and liberal claptrap is stripped away from the incident, that is what it remains—a race riot.

It is now 10 years since the Liberals brought down the white paper on immigration that led to the introduction of "universal immigration." That meant that, in effect, all race barriers were down.

Twenty years earlier, Mackenzie King had laid down an opposite policy. "The people of Canada," he stated, "do not wish to make a fundamental alteration in the character of their population." The government would therefore not permit large-scale Asiatic or other "coloured" immigration. There could be some, but Ottawa would control it.

The Conservatives opened things up a bit in 1962, but retained restrictions on immigrants' relatives from non-white countries. Immediate dependents have always been able to come in freely, of course, but the Tories (or the civil service of the day) recognized that the concept of "family" is a bit different in many parts of the world from what it is in North America and much of Europe.

They were right. A couple of years ago, a senior official in the immigration department leaked the news that each coloured immigrant eventually brings an average of 17 relatives with him. And the system encourages this. People who have already been "landed," whether citizens or not, can "nominate" their more distant kin, thus creating an endless chain reminiscent of one of those "begat" passages in the Bible.

The figures on relatives are revealing. Of the 188,000 immigrants who entered Canada in 1975, only 41 percent applied independently. Thirty-four percent were sponsored (meaning they were immediate relatives) and 25 percent were nominated. Of the 18,000 people who came from the Caribbean in 1975, about 73 percent were either sponsored or nominated. The sponsored or nominated proportion from Britain, on the other hand, was only 28 percent. As an immigration officer told me, "Some people like to bring their relatives with them, and some come to get away from them."

But the broad outline of what has been happening since universal immigration was brought into being is much more dramatic than that. Between 1945 and 1967, a span of 23 years, non-white immigrants entering Canada numbered about 142,000. Between 1968 and 1975, at least 405,000 non-whites were granted entry, an increase of about 185 percent over the total for almost the whole previous quarter century.

The influx from Asia, Africa and the Caribbean has become the dominant feature of our immigration pattern. Annual numbers from those areas now run at about 50 percent of total immigration, and immigration from Europe is down to 38 percent. During 1975, nearly 90,000 non-whites entered. That is within an inch of the numbers the British were admitting from the "coloured Commonwealth" before they passed restrictive legislation in 1962.

For the past five years, countries like

India, Jamaica, Guyana, Hong Kong, the Philippines and, most recently, South Korea, have replaced France, Germany, and other European countries in the list of the "top 10" sending immigrants to Canada. Immigration from Latin America has also increased greatly. From 1945 to 1967, we accepted only 35,000. Since 1967, we have accepted 59,000, and the policy is to attract many more in the hope they will settle in Quebec, presumably because they will be assimilated easily.

This influx from what the department of immigration delicately labels "untraditional sources" causes alarm at many levels, not just on Archie Bunker's street in New Westminster. One wealthy businessman, not normally given to weird thoughts, is convinced that the Liberals are up to some plot. What they are doing, he says, is packing as many Asians into western Canada as they can, in order to create a friendly vote and help build the stronger political base they need.

It is true that nothing is more political than immigration. But his theory overlooks the fact that the Tories, who are strong in the West, supported the policy switch in 1967. Since then, as a party, they have had nothing critical to say. Bob Stanfield never touched the issue, even though he would probably have won the 1972 election if he had chosen to grasp the immigration nettle. His successor, Joe Clark, is equally speechless. No doubt immigration is not a big talking point in High River, Alberta.

The NDP is more liberal than the Liberals, and the Tories will probably remain silent until public feeling becomes too obvious to ignore. That day is not far off. Large sections of Toronto, Montreal and Vancouver have already gone a fair distance toward having "the character of their population" changed. For it is in those cities that most immigrants congregate—55 percent of them. And hostile feelings grow whether or not the press interprets incidents along an orthodox liberal line, as it did in Montreal in the recent case of hundreds of illegal immigrants from Haiti.

There are two difficulties in determining the number of coloured immigrants admitted to Canada. The first is the large amount of illegal immigration, almost entirely from Asia and the Caribbean. In June, it was admitted in a document circulated in the immigration department that "tens or even hundreds of thousands of people could remain and work in Canada under the present scheme of things with small fear of detection." A new way of exercising control through social insurance numbers has just been implemented, but it remains to be seen whether it will be effective. In the past, Ottawa has lacked the will. What is needed is heavy, mandatory fines for employers who use illegal labour. Last year, a couple of immigration officers went to a Toronto factory to pick up two illegals and found 10. They threw up their hands and left.

The second difficulty in determining the number of coloured immigrants is the government's deceptive method of classification. In 1967, "race" became a four-letter word and was banned from the immigration department's lexicon. In its place immigrants were identified by the vaguer "country of last permanent residence." As a consequence, no one, not even Robert Andras, the immigration minister, can say exactly how many East Indians, Chinese, blacks or whites have come into the country.

The green paper study shows that in 1972 over 16 percent of immigrants from Britain were not born there, and according to our London office, nearly all were East Indians. Two years ago, 66 percent of those applying through our office in Dallas, Texas, were from Asia.

A conservative estimate of the total number of non-whites entering Canada since 1967 would be 500,000. Setty Pendakur, an East Indian and a former Vancouver alderman, has stated that the pace of Asian immigration is simply too great for easy absorption into Canadian society. And Harkirpal Singh Sara, a well-known Sikh, called last year for a five-year moratorium on all immigration so that things could settle down a bit.

Quite apart from the race factor, more and more Canadians are realizing that bigger is not necessarily better. Between 1961 and 1971, immigration accounted for half of Toronto's growth, a third of Vancouver's, and a quarter of Montreal's. More of the same is expected. A Statistics Canada study shows that with average immigration, plus the birth rate, Ontario will have a population of nearly 12 million by the turn of the century. Half that number will be concentrated in Toronto.

Because of immigration, Metro Toronto and Greater Vancouver have lost control of their growth. Sixty thousand immigrants are pouring into Toronto each year, 30,000 into Vancouver. As Allan Kelly, former chairman of the Greater Vancouver Regional District, said in October: "Unless we slow down the number of people coming into this area, downtown Vancouver will become one of the most impossible places in the world to move around in." And Vancouver's mayor, Art Phillips, has stated: "Immigrants bring many things with them. But they don't bring land and they don't bring houses."

In May of this year, the immigration minister was glad to announce that total immigration for 1975 had decreased 14 percent from the previous year. He was glad because he knows that immigration is becoming a political issue, and that if he had not used administrative devices to keep the numbers down, Canada would have had 400,000 new arrivals, most of them from "untraditional sources." But, in perspective, it really wasn't much of a victory. Last year was still a big year: the number of immigrants (187,881) has been exceeded only five times since 1945.

Meanwhile, recruiting machinery clicks merrily away. Recently, Dr. Gordon Shrum visited Bogota, Colombia. He is a former co-chairman of B.C. Hydro, former chancellor of Simon Fraser University, and one of the few academics who is willing to speak out against our immigration policy. What he saw in Bogota horrified him.

"Our immigration people," he said, "are damned fools. They're advertising our social services and telling Colombians they only have to work eight weeks [as was the case then] to qualify for a year's dole. Why would we be doing that two degrees above the equator, in a culture totally alien to our own?"

Shrum says he has "never heard of a country with an immigration policy as plain stupid as ours is." And it is true that only Canada is engaged in a worldwide immigration campaign. As of May 1, 1976, we boasted 187 immigration staff at 61 overseas locations, including such places as Islamabad, Makati, Seoul and Nairobi. The British, meanwhile, are engaged in a desperate struggle to cut down on immigration, and the New Zealanders and Australians have reduced it to a trickle.

Even the United States, with 10 times our population, admitted only 394,000 immigrants in 1974. In the same year, we admitted 218,000. If their immigration had been in proportion to ours, they would have received well over two million. Conversely, if ours had been in proportion to theirs, we would have admitted fewer than 40,000.

The effects of our policies are evident in the schools of Toronto and Vancouver. In both cities, school board officials are frightened to death of being labeled racist and are therefore as discreet as possible. But that doesn't disguise or diminish the problem.

The Toronto board of education has recently published several reports on multiculturalism. These reports state that there are now 50,000 children in the school system whose language at home is neither French nor English. And that doesn't include the large number of West Indians who speak dialects that the reports define as "almost foreign." In 1971, there were only 616 West Indian students in Toronto. Now, one school alone has a West Indian population of over 25 percent, and West Indians account for 14 percent of the non-Canadian school population. In two schools the majority of the pupils are Chinese.

Changes like these have had a predictable effect. "The spectre of racism is approaching. . . ." states a report dated May 20, 1975. "It is here in full public view. Racism is in this city and even in its schools, and . . . there are reliable accounts of racial tension bursting into violent contention in schools and on school playgrounds. Not long ago, it claimed the life of a white boy. Just recently it placed a black boy in jail, and another black boy died of it."

These reports are trimmed with all the proper liberal responses, but they pinpoint the unviability of Ottawa's immigration policy. For example:

"Neither Canada nor Toronto was prepared for the impact that this new wave of immigration made on the schools. Not only were they confronted with students for whom the English language was completely alien, they were confronted with a totally different character and configuration of cultures than any they had ever encountered in the previous immigration wave."

After a visit to Toronto's Bickford Park High School, a study group wrote: "There was some expression [from the teachers] that the Anglo-Canadian could not be expected to give up all his values, his cultural position, etc., merely to accommodate the values and . . . the general life position of the ethnic student."

But that is exactly what the Anglo-Canadian is expected to give up. The supposedly dominant culture in Toronto is now in a 47-percent minority. "Within the space of a decade the board of education's cultural base has become incompatible with the base of the society which supports its endeavour," states one of the reports. What that means is that while the school structure is still "English," the population is not.

One cannot help but note that although the federal government is fervently devoted to maintaining the "French" base in Quebec, the same principle apparently does not apply to the "English" base in the rest of the country.

The situation in Vancouver schools is similar to Toronto's. Of 38,400 pupils in 75 elementary schools, there are 15,000 (39 percent) whose first language is not English. Of that number, the first language for nearly 40 percent is Chinese. Punjabi and other East Indian tongues account for another 10.3 percent. In 17 secondary schools with an enrollment of 28,000, over 20 percent of the students have English as a second language, and the elementary problem is now moving quickly into the secondary level. The consequence in both instances is a lowering of scholastic standards, as has been proved in various studies.

Federally, only two MPs have spoken out on the situation. One was Steve Paproski of Edmonton Centre, who spoke up as early as 1969. The other was West Vancouver's Ron Huntington. He said last year in the House that we were taking in too many coloured immigrants too quickly. The Liberals immediately denounced him as a racist. And when he was invited to participate in a Learned Society panel discussion on immigration at the University of Alberta, he was prevented from speaking by dissenters. Canadian MPs, apparently, are not to be accorded freedom of speech.

Anyone naïve enough to think that the massive cultural and racial mix we are heading toward is good, or at least harmless, should look at the European experience. Race disturbances have shaken Holland, France, and Britain. Once "tolerant,'' the British now have a national race crisis on their hands. About two million immigrants have moved in from India, Pakistan and the West Indies. In June, five men were killed in race riots, and as *The Observer* noted, ''there is a time bomb ticking away.'' In view of all this it is amusing to read in our parliamentary joint committee report on immigration, published last fall, that ''Britain, which in the 1960s experienced serious racial tension, has had extremely favourable results from its human rights legislation and programs.''

Ottawa doesn't want to hear the message from Britain, which is not surprising, since it doesn't even want to hear the message from Canada. During the green paper discussion last year, 60 percent of all letters and briefs received by the committee from individuals either favoured stopping all immigration, or all non-white immigration. Another 23 percent wanted tighter controls. Only six percent wanted current policies maintained. Response from organizations, of course, was quite different, since these frequently had group axes to grind.

A similar picture was drawn in a poll conducted last year for the Canadian Television Network. CTV claimed it was the most extensive survey ever undertaken by a private body, and it showed that 68 percent of Canadians want an immigration policy based on national origins. Seventy-six percent would accept an internal passport system to control illegal immigration. Forty-eight percent see present immigration policies as a threat to their way of life.

Despite obvious signs, Ottawa's course is set. Trudeau is dedicated to universal immigration. He told Caribbean prime ministers during the Commonwealth Conference in April, 1975, that the policy would not be changed. At the Habitat conference this summer, he told the world that we have a ''moral responsibility'' to continue our present policies. According to him, ''we need more people in this country.'' This in spite of the fact that in January last year he lamented at a Liberal party fundraising dinner in Montreal that ''racism is evident in this country and that violence is coming to our land.''

Martin O'Connell, chairman of the joint parliamentary committee on immigration, stated on June 18, 1975, even before the committee's report was made public, that ''tighter immigration is unlikely.'' He said he was satisfied that immigration was improving the Canadian way of life. Three years ago, Robert Andras said the future would be a ''testing time'' for the tolerance of Canadians, although no one has explained why a testing time is necessary.

The joint committee report seems to support the government's position: ''The committee stresses that Canadians must anticipate that many future immigrants will be coming from non-European countries and many will be non-white.'' It rejects a return to a national quota system, but recommends a ''global quota'' which is to be set annually by the government.

In short, the world is to be stuffed down Canada's throat, whether we choke on it or not.

Richard Tait, chairman of the Canadian immigration and population study, had this to say in 1974:

''In 100 years' time, I don't expect people will care all that much whether we legalized marijuana or not. But the decisions about who you let into Canada now will decide the kind of country we have then.''

Doug Collins is a columnist for the Vancouver *Sun*. He worked at the CBC as a commentator and documentary-maker, and wrote *P.O.W.* in 1968. ''Fear and Loathing in the Canadian Mosaic'' was first printed in *Weekend*, September 11, 1976.

GEORGE WOODCOCK

Playing to the People

In B.C., the platforms and parties are beside the point.

In democratic politics successful leaders are the good actors who project the personal fantasies of their constituents. Only when we know the kind of image people in a specific country or region develop of themselves can we begin to understand the style that succeeds in their local politics. In Canada it is most of all a matter of regions. Politically, 110 years after Confederation, we are even yet hardly a nation. There is really no such thing as an all-Canadian Canadian, which is why national popularity is so precarious among us, and why Ottawa politicians always find that whatever image they project sooner or later antagonizes that key section of the community on which they had relied for enduring power. There are, in fact, only Canadians who are first of all Québécois or Newfoundlanders or Manitobans or British Columbians. Each region in Canada has its own environment, its own history, even its own ethnic mix. Each expresses itself—despite the vast efforts of the CBC and CRTC to make us all feel uniform—in a special way that shows itself in literature and the arts, in lifestyles, and especially in political approaches.

The image of a region—the way its people see their setting and their neighbours and themselves—is not something to be learned quickly, and that applies most of all to my own region of British Columbia. Once I used to describe myself as "Canadian by birth and British Columbian by adoption." It took a long time for the graft to work. Now, 27 years after crossing the Continental Divide, I reverse the order. "I am British Columbian by choice, Canadian by birth."

And, as a British Columbian by choice, watching people from over the Rockies trying to grapple with the local political scene, I realize how easy it is for the great mountain ranges to form a mental as well as a geographical Divide.

It isn't only that British Columbians live in narrow valleys and on islands and river deltas that are scanty footholds in a "sea of mountains." It isn't only that even today British Columbia remains far more dependent on exploiting largely non-renewable natural resources—minerals, timber, fish, fossil fuels, hydro power—than on agriculture (like the Prairie provinces) or industry (like Ontario). It isn't only that British Columbia started out before Confederation on its own separate history of settlement by sea from Britain and Asia, and by land from California, and so established its peculiar mix of peoples and traditions. It isn't only that British Columbia—at least the thickly inhabited areas around Vancouver and Victoria—enjoys a bland, rainy climate that combines with mountains and sheltered waterways to foster a uniquely hedonistic existence—the renowned lotus life of the shores of the Gulf

201

of Georgia. All these things, of course, go towards giving British Columbian life its special character, but they gain human meaning only through the peculiar self-image that emerges from them.

When we look at that self-image, we realize that the British Columbian, no matter how heartily gregarious he may seem, sees himself dramatically as a loner in a world of loners. This highly individualized personal image makes him susceptible to the kind of politics that ends in a cult of people rather than of classes, and sees the people as a participating consensus of individuals rather than as a ladder of social gradations or a mosaic of ethnic groups. British Columbian man is a populist.

Thus the far western province, jammed between mountains and sea, presents the apparent paradox of being perhaps Canada's most individualistically oriented region while enjoying a highly localized socialist tradition that goes back for more than 80 years, that has given the province a consistently socialist official opposition in the legislative assembly since the late 1930s, and has allowed it to experience one period of NDP government, from 1972 to 1975.

But there is a great deal more than that to British Columbia's political oddity. For almost a quarter of a century, west of the Divide, the federally powerful Liberals and Conservatives have been derided provincially and reduced to minute forlorn hopes of parties, while the CCF-NDP has shared the great majority of British Columbian votes and legislative seats with the Social Credit Party, which in 1952 blew up literally out of nothing to form the government of British Columbia. By the 1975 provincial election Social Credit (the winning party) and the NDP shared over 90 percent of the popularity between them. Provincial Liberals on the West Coast have become somewhat scarcer than anarchists.

British Columbian politics, in other words, is now polarized between two parties unknown until the 1930s, neither of which had ever held power federally—or seems likely to do so. Moreover, both Social Credit and socialism in British Columbia are quite different from their counterparts in other provinces, and much more alike than they appear at first sight. Both of them have realized the need to mirror the British Columbian's personal myth of himself as at once a loner and a good man of the people.

I've now been a politician-watcher in British Columbia for 27 years. As an arch-loner—an avowed anarchist—I've found myself drifting into the company of the mildly eccentric political failures that decorate the fringes of every British Columbian party, including the old ones, since to be a provincial Liberal or Tory west of the Rockies has by now become the wildest form of quixoticism. I reach my personal level among those gently cynical but hard-working failures whom the tough tacticians of every party expend as standard-bearers in forlorn-hope constituencies. Still, a province is by definition provincial, and therefore intimate, and inevitably one rubs shoulders with the local mighty, which for the last quarter of a century has meant that melodramatic trio of Victoria premiers, with names like the members of an old-fashioned attorney's firm, Bennett, Barrett and Bennett.

With that cunning, durable master of regional politics, W.A.C. Bennett (who ruled British Columbia for 20 years), it was literally a matter of rubbing shoulders, once passing in a corridor of the legislative buildings in Victoria and once jostling on the B.C. Ferries at Tsawwassen, as we made our respective ways to the car deck. Each time I was struck by a peculiarly fabricated look to the man, with his massive jaw and set nervous grin, as if he were being doubled by Madame Tussaud's effigy of himself. I thought of those masked intelligences who were the insect rulers of the Moon as H.G. Wells envisaged it. Since then I have had the same kind of reaction watching other leading Social Crediters, like the present premier, Bill Bennett, and that handsome but chilling king-maker Grace McCarthy (the onetime teenaged flower-seller who created a chain of B.C. florist's shops before she entered politics to become—eventually—provincial secretary, and who by sheer frenetic energy pulled Social Credit from defeat in 1972 to victory three years later).

In contrast, my first encounter with Dave Barrett was indubitably human, even humane. I remember the occasion clearly because it emphasized strongly for me the two special characteristics that have distinguished recent political leaders in British Columbia—the image of the battling outsider, and the complementary image of the man who speaks not for any one class but, with conviction and emphasis, for that vaguest but most seductive of political abstractions, *the people.*

By the time I met Dave Barrett, in 1970, he had been 10 years on a rocky political trail. In 1959, as a social worker at the Haney Correctional Institution in British Columbia, he was sacked for seeking nomination as a CCF candidate. With loner's luck, he won the election and displaced the Social Credit labour minister. In 1969 he tried for the NDP provincial leadership and was beaten by Tom Berger. But Berger lost in that year's provincial election, and—loner's luck again—Dave Barrett was voted into leadership of the Opposition by the NDP caucus in the legislative assembly. The 1970 NDP convention had little alternative to confirming Barrett's leadership of the party, which it did by acclamation, though the local Canadian Labour Congress bosses were not enthusiastic.

That year the B.C. Federation of Labour's convention was held at the Bayshore Inn, then Vancouver's plushest hostelry. At the time I was writing a CBC documentary on what had happened to unionism since the days of the Tolpuddle Martyrs, and I turned up to take a look at the delegates enjoying themselves like unregenerate capitalists. Barrett had arrived, but he was kept out of the inner conclaves. I went to get a tape from him on an idea he had recently been propounding. Why not let out-of-province—even foreign—firms set up plants in British Columbia, with ownership 51 percent socialized, the province holding 30 percent and the workers 21 percent of the shares? I liked the idea. It seemed a way to break down the ritualized antagonism between labour and industry that even unionists agree has scarred the B.C. economy in recent years. The union bosses, who realize that power and perquisites wither in industrial peace, hated the idea.

After the taping I stayed awhile, and we got into a drift of conversation that I have always remembered as illuminating in relation to Barrett's later actions. He remarked that it was pointless to idealize the workers ("There are as many bloody a------s among the workers as anywhere else"), and that it was also pointless for men like him or me—or the union bureaucrats for that matter—to pretend we knew how men or women felt about their work. "Our whole way of life's different from a blue-collar worker's. We've gone away from all that. We don't have much idea how he really feels at the workbench. But nobody's just a worker. He's a member of society in all kinds of ways, and if you think of helping people in general toward a more equitable society, you're automatically helping the workers, which you don't do if you try to separate them from everybody else." His remarks, which impressed me and clung in my memory, showed the other side of the typical B.C. leader: the triumphant loner is also the tribune of the people rather than the representative of vested class interests.

I remembered those words vividly after Barrett came to power in 1972, and particularly in 1975, when he legislated three unions back to work (the supermarket workers, the B.C. Railway workers and a section of the Teamsters) because he believed their continued absence was militating against the interests of B.C. people in general. The union bosses who had snubbed him in 1970 were forced to obey, rather than face responsibility for defying British Columbia's first socialist government. Left-wingers within the NDP were critical, arguing that it was a working-class party and should defend the interests of the workers as a class. Populist Barrett disagreed.

There are extraordinary resemblances between the Barrett pattern and his predecessor W.A.C. Bennett's career. Bennett, a retail hardware millionaire from the farmland interior of British Columbia, entered politics when he was elected a Tory MLA in 1941. Defeated in a bid for the Conservative leadership in 1949, he resigned from the party and in 1952 fought and won the provincial election as leader of the newly founded British Columbia Social Credit League. Bennett's appeal was to the province's outsiders: to people in the towns and villages of the interior and the north who felt their interests neglected by city-based politicians; to the congregations of rural clapboard churches who believed morality and prosperity alike were going to hell in a handbasket; to small farmers and shopkeepers on the edge of failure; to ill-paid workers ignored by union aristocrats. The appeal was answered, and even by some who had once been devoted followers of the CCF. For, as historian Martin Robin admitted in *Pillars of Profit*, the Social Crediters "like the CCF, were outsiders."

Between them, Social Credit and the CCF had in one election destroyed the old-line parties and opened the province to populist politics. In a purely physical sense, as well, this change opened up the province. Bennett began a vast program of road and railway building that made the neglected parts of the province accessible, and unlocked the northland to a far more thorough exploitation of its natural resources than ever before.

Bennett ruled the province continuously for 20 years. His later Cabinets included lawyers, doctors, even an odd university professor, as well as back-country merchants, enhancing the image of a movement that embraced people of all kinds and classes.

There were loud protests from the lumber barons in 1952 when he imposed higher royalties on them, just as there would be lamentations when Dave Barrett imposed higher royalties on the mining industry in 1973. Bennett enjoyed the cut and thrust of political debate, and became a kind of parliamentary smiler-with-the-knife who slaughtered his opponents with an easy grin. He was adept at reviving the persecuted outsider image by presenting his regime—"this poor little government" as he would call it while literally weeping in the legislature or on election platforms—as the victim of forces hostile to the British Columbian people as well: the lumber combines, the unions, the national railroads, the great hydro complex of B.C. Electric, and always the federal government, dominated by parties that honest British Columbians had dismissed as corrupt and antediluvian.

Bennett did not flinch even from the "socialist" expedient of nationalization. In 1958 he established a provincial fleet of large, handsome ferry boats plying between Vancouver Island and the mainland. And after the CCF urged a public takeover of B.C. Electric in 1961, Bennett—who had his own populist grudges against BCE for neglecting the unprofitable outlying areas of the province – surprised the opposition by introducing take-over legislation. He thus forced the embarrassed CCF to support him in one of the very few unanimous votes in B.C. history – 50 to 0. It was not surprising that in 1963 Bennett should claim that "Social Credit is the party of the working people." Note that he said working *people*; not working *class*. This could include professionals and millionaire shopkeepers as well as men in overalls, and so, later on, Bennett was able to claim that Social Credit was virtually all things to all men: "The Social Credit government is more conservative than the Conservatives in financial matters, more liberal than the Liberals in terms of providing the nation's highest old age and social assistance benefits, and even more in favour of public ownership than the CCF because of our ferry system and hydro program."

No democratically elected regime lasts forever. Bennett's Social Credit rule died from many causes. The voters got bored with the same aging Cabinet faces; Bennett became less adept at finding new issues and making new promises; corruption showed up and the premier hated to admit the frailties of old supporters; British Columbian society was becoming more urbanized, producing new upwardly mobile classes of which the Social Credit politicos did not take enough notice; the young were restive, the old getting resentful.

Yet the election of 1972, which Wacky Bennett lost, showed that his tried formula was still the best – the rejected loner who rides in to establish himself as tribune of the people and who unites enough interests to create an elective majority in a deeply divided province. Until 1970 there had been no CCF or NDP leader flexible enough for the role. Dave Barrett succeeded where his predecessors had failed by watching Bennett and adapting the old magician's methods to his own program. In a different way from Bennett, he was gifted with an engaging ugliness – multiple chins and a beer belly that appealed to cartoonists and suggested a man not so caught up in socialist dogma as to be indifferent to proletarian pleasures. Yet he had an educated mind, sharpened by Jesuit teachers, and shared Bennett's power to wield either knife or bludgeon with a joking grin. He hectored opponents without mercy but never quite destroyed them, leaving in listeners' minds a feeling that he was not a bad chap after all. He needed that image, since he spread his net wide. He gathered in discontented teachers and academics, upwardly mobile new suburbanites, itinerant workers in the north and thousands of the underprivileged who found themselves swept into the ragbag of welfare as an automated society made them redundant. As Martin Robin remarked, Barrett was "no doctrinaire or ideologue." In 1970, when he became leader of the NDP, he admitted: "In all practical reality we'll be living with a mixed economy for a long, long time."

In other words, Barrett made himself a populist politician like Bennett, appealing to a constituency of varied interests, rather to the left of Social Credit's but overlapping to compete for the drifting voters. Bennett was tired and familiar enough for them to elude him; Barrett new and vital enough for them to swim into his net. So in 1972 the electoral results were dramatically reversed, Social Credit slumped from 36 to 10 seats, and NDP gained an overwhelming majority with 38 seats.

What happened afterwards exemplified the sad old tag that the more things change, the more they remain the same. As every sensitive observer has known for years, British Columbia's economic ills, especially its waves of high unemployment, are due to the predominance of primary industries. The revolutionary solution would be to set up factories to process B.C. raw materials on the spot and create a stable employment base of secondary industry. Instead, Barrett imitated Bennett with another grand scheme to thrust roads and rails into the north and gouge the land for the last of its raw materials. Before being elected, Barrett had criticized Bennett for divisive and separatist inclinations, and was especially scathing about the links between B.C. Social Credit and Réal Caouette's Créditistes. But once elected, Barrett defied the national policies of his own party, the NDP, to explore a working alliance with the Parti Québécois.

In some palliative ways Barrett did bring about improvements. He slowed down the sale of farmlands to developers; he improved the legal system; his welfare programs were more compassionate than those of his predecessors. But in distinctively socialist areas, like the take-over of industry, Barrett was notably slow; his threats to take over the British Columbia Telephone Company never materialized, and his acquisition of a couple of pulp mills due for abandonment by their owners compared poorly with Social Credit's take-over of B.C. Electric.

Barrett fought his campaign in 1975 largely on the old Bennett theme of the persecuted loner, this time "fat little Dave," whom his opponents wanted to get rid of, but his defeat was as dramatic as his victory in 1972. When the dust had settled, Social Credit, led by Wacky's son Bill Bennett, was up again to 36 seats, the NDP were down to 17, the Liberals and Tories almost eliminated, and Barrett defeated in his own Coquitlam constituency, where young, upwardly mobile voters turned the scale. Later on, Barrett did get back into the legislature, but only because a by-election was arranged in Vancouver East, one of the few traditionally solid socialist constituencies in Canada.

Why did Barrett fail after three years?

Partly because, while the socialists are strong in British Columbia, they have never come near a majority of the voters, and the marginal electors who gave Barrett his victory in 1972 were easily scared back to Social Credit in 1975 by a drumfire of media warnings of what might happen if socialism gained a lockhold on the province. But Barrett himself was as much to blame in failing to respond to the feelings of his varied constituency. He co-operated with minister of education Eileen Dailly to aggravate university and schoolteachers, school boards and parents by erratic budgeting based on untested educational theories rather than real need. He angered everyone except the recipients by doubling MLAs' salaries and raising his own to $52,000, $4,000 more than Pierre Trudeau was then receiving. He let his social-worker past blind him to the fact that human resources minister Norm Levi's openhanded welfare system was being exploited by thousands of frauds, as well as benefiting thousands of needy people unaided before. Unlike Wacky Bennett in his prime, Barrett neither counted his enemies nor kept his friends, and he fell.

Enter the third member of the trio, Bill Bennett, again with the loner's entry. Until 1973 Bill Bennett didn't even seem concerned with politics. Having left school for business at the age of 18, he spent his young manhood accumulating more millions than his father; he is now a rich man who still lives in the Kelowna small-town style. Even today, Bill Bennett sedulously maintains the image of being his own man and in no political way his father's son. In fact, he seems to have come to the leadership of Social Credit in British Columbia less by dynastic intrigues than by Grace McCarthy's energetic organization of the convention vote in his favour when it was obvious no survivor from the old Social Credit government was acceptable to the whole party. Bill Bennett had great advantages:

no political past, no special attachments, no time to make enemies.

If Wacky Bennett put me in mind of Mme. Tussaud's, and Dave Barrett of beer-parlour evenings in college towns, Bill Bennett has aroused a more native B.C. image. His features are strong but stiff, his big, Bennett chin seems to be always blue-shaded, and when that tense Social Credit grin splits his face it looks like a wooden Coastal Indian transformation mask worked by invisible strings.

But, as in the case of the Indian masks, the strings are in the hands of the dancer, and Bill Bennett—contrary to many prognostications that he would be merely a puppet operated by Social Credit's pale grey eminences—has shown himself up to now in firm control of his position. He gives no sign of softness. Unlike his father, he is not prone to tears, and unlike Dave Barrett, he does not appear to be swayed by old loyalties. He is not afraid to make himself unpopular in the short run, as he has shown by detested measures like doubling the B.C. ferry rates and drastically raising the government-operated car insurance premiums. All this suggests that he is confident of long-run success.

Tactics—the details of political action—have changed with the new Social Credit government. But Bill Bennett's essential strategy remains remarkably like that of Barrett and the earlier Bennett: a party and a government that represent as many interests as possible. Bill Bennett argues that in British Columbia parties of the extreme left and the extreme right cannot survive. Despite appearances, B.C. politics is the politics of the centre. "We are a populist party slightly to the right of centre," he says. "The NDP is a populist party slightly to the left." Bill Bennett has, in fact, come nearer than his father ever did to the aim of a coalition people's party by winning about three-quarters of the leading provincial Tories and Liberals to the Social Credit movement. And he has shown an unexpected political skill by holding together a Cabinet of rampant individualists with highly different political origins.

Perhaps the main way Bill Bennett's record as a premier differs from his two predecessors' is that, unlike his father and Dave Barrett, he has not been lavish with gifts. But perhaps this is good populism for the late 1970s. Voters have come to realize that gifts have to be paid for, and that as taxpayers they do the paying. A drive to make government less expensive through reduced welfare payments and slimmed-down bureaucracies may be the best way to the people's hearts for the next few years, even if it accompanies a less popular drive to make government enterprises —like ferries and insurance corporations—pay their way without subsidy.

In the last resort, democratic politics depends on the economy. Wacky Bennett was able to rule by gifts for 20 years because throughout his reign the B.C. economy expanded. Dave Barrett tried to be a giver in a stagnant economy and failed. Bill Bennett takes away because the economy demands it, but he hopes that one day the economy will expand again. For the populist politician—unlike the old-style party hack in a world of sharply defined loyalties—depends on a shifting balance of support in a population educated enough to remember promises (even promises of austerity) and to demand their fulfilment. That is the new politics, as men in Ottawa are learning to their cost.

George Woodcock founded and edited (until 1977) the first journal devoted entirely to Canadian writers and writing. Among his numerous books are *Anarchism* (1962), *Canada and the Canadians* (1970), and *Gabriel Dumont* (1975). "Playing to the People" appeared originally in *The Canadian*, January 8, 1977.

CHRISTINA McCALL NEWMAN

The Exotic Mindscape of Pierre Trudeau

The champion of people knows federalism but he doesn't know people.

Late this last bleak autumn, not long after the Quebec election, I went to a small dinner party given by a political scientist of some distinction at his house in the heart of Toronto. Most of the guests he and his wife had invited were also academics, and the talk at table, over the *boeuf bourguignon* and the Beaujolais, naturally turned to the country's future.

Everybody contributed according to his ability and/or his discipline's needs. The historian drew parallels with the great national crises of the past. The law professor made donnish jokes about the ways in which René Lévesque might twist the wording of the upcoming referendum to suit his party's purposes. The economist compared the financial viability of Quebec with that of the Scandinavian nations. And so it went until the moment, midway through the meal, when the host said in a voice that seemed oddly discordant because it was touched with passion, "Dammit, this is a time for big men, a time when Trudeau will have to show his mettle, a time. . . ." The entire company turned to stare and somebody interrupted to say soothingly, "Come, come, let's not argue *ad hominem.*"

I wanted to shout, "Listen, we have to argue *ad hominem*. We need to have a feel for the personal dynamics of the struggle that lies ahead. We should discuss how we think Trudeau will react when he's up against Lévesque in the fight of his life—and maybe the fight of ours, if we want to continue as Canadians." But the moment passed, and I didn't shout, and the conversation went back, in a peculiarly Canadian way, to the safety of impersonal civilities.

In the weeks since then—while the Quebec/Canada drama has begun to unfold—I've continued to think, as Trevor-Roper contends so cleverly, that individuals as much as ideologies determine the course of history. Like him or not, much of what happens to Canada in the next few years will depend on Pierre Trudeau. He is the champion of the federalist cause, and we are the uneasy bystanders. We'll have to wait to find out whether reason will overcome passion, whether Trudeau, the man of grey matter, will outdo Lévesque, the man of heart.

In the face of that reality, it's unsettling to realize that although he's been a centre of public attention for nearly a decade now, Trudeau is in many ways a curiously unfathomable figure. In that time

209

he's been cast in several guises—intellectual dandy, cabinet dictator, incautious reformer, arch conservative, political pragmatist, economic bungler, and national saviour, to name a few. He's been called cold, arrogant, courageous, brilliant, rigid, uncaring, feckless, and fanatic. But despite all the images laid on him, all the questions hurled at him, all the praise that's been heaped on him and all the rage that's been vented, nobody—to my mind anyway—has ever caught his essence or been able to predict his fate.

When I first met Trudeau, ten years ago this month, he was standing alone in the hall of my house in Ottawa, holding a glass of sherry that a harried bartender had filled too full. He had come late to a reception in honour of the publisher of a powerful newspaper who was in the capital to take a preliminary look at the candidates for the leadership of the Liberal Party. (The position was not actually vacant, but Lester Pearson had said it would be declared so, once centennial year was over.)

The probable contenders had turned out in force—Martin, Hellyer, Winters, Turner, MacEachen, and the rest—and they were crowded into the living room with a number of lesser beings, talking, laughing, and gesticulating in their attempts to capture the publisher's attention and his editorial favour. After exchanging a few pleasantries, Trudeau glanced briefly at this scene, sipped his sherry carefully, remarked that the guest of honour seemed to be fully occupied, and as for himself, he thought he would leave now, thank you very much.

Because he was, as an MP, still "a nobody" (by his own later definition), the power mongers didn't notice when he slipped away. In fact nobody at the party—besides me and the barman —seemed to realize he had been there at all. I was left trying to decipher the emotion reflected in his glittering blue eyes when he took in the antics of the office seekers. Was it amusement, disdain, boredom, shyness? I opted for shyness because it was a feeling I understood readily and he was a man whose work as a writer and activist-intellectual I had heard about and admired.

But after all these years of observing him in a hundred different situations and talking about him with scores of people who have tried to know him well, I have come to suspect that what his eyes were reflecting was not emotion at all. Probably he was being "coldly intelligent," an attitude, as he wrote in *Federalism and the French Canadians,* he assumes as often as is humanly possible. Reason would tell him there was nothing to be gained at that party, and reason would soon prove right.

Trudeau's predilection for denying feeling in favour of reason is the one constant in the descriptions of him given by people of various temperaments who've observed him from various vantage points before, during, and particularly since his rise to prime ministerial power. Few of them are foolish enough to claim he doesn't have feelings—he's displayed his quick anger too often in public for that—but all of them claim he consistently suppresses them.

One of his friends, a man who knew him well in the 1950s and 1960s in Montreal, says with the special wisdom of the novelist that his lack of rapport with people on an individual level, and "the people" on a national level, is due in part to his "consistent denial of the importance of intuition. To be intuitive you have to be vulnerable, and Pierre didn't want to be open to hurts. He puts on reason like a suit of armour, little realizing that although it might protect him, it isolates him too."

Certainly if you examine the statements of his colleagues—and the positions he's taken during his three terms in office, from his sweeping changes in the civil service to his handling of the economy to the making of his cabinets—the picture that emerges is of a Cartesian man, applying logic rigorously to the problems of governing and to the management of people.

A very wise woman, the wife of a well-known French Canadian, was trying recently to comfort a dazed ex-cabinet minister who found himself relieved of his portfolio after several years of faithful service and a few hours of illogical, exhaustion-fostered tantrums. "You have to realize," she said, "that Pierre was seduced very early by logic; and as a mistress she served him well for most of his life. It's only now in his fifties that it's become apparent that logic doesn't always work."

Certainly logic doesn't work when it's used to explain the compounded blunders the Trudeau government has made since 1974. Any one of the Prime Minister's close advisers—and he's surrounded by intelligent, decent, and above all reasonable men—can argue persuasively that when he was electioneering in the late spring of 1974, making cruel fun of Robert Stanfield by denying the need for wage-and-price controls, the PM's position was absolutely sound in the economic context of the time. It was only later, they say, quoting complicated economic formulas and international scholarly opinions, that the need for controls became imperative. If you answer, well, okay, but doesn't he realize that it makes ordinary voters feel as though he deliberately misled them, they react with incomprehension. They will run through the same sort of exercise defending the "new society" musings on television; or the reinstatement of André Ouellet to the cabinet after his contempt of court conviction; or the Polymer — now Polysar—kickbacks, which they describe as "normal business rebates"; or any one of half a dozen other political errors that lend themselves to reasonable explanations, but which a leader with an intuitive understanding of the electorate—Mackenzie King, say—would have been unlikely to perpetrate.

If syllogistic reasoning isn't workable in defence of policies that have gone wildly awry, when it's applied to relationships with people it can prove tragic.

There is a belief abroad that Trudeau has a close circle of friends, a cabal of people drawn mainly from the Prime Minister's Office and the Privy Council Office who run the country. But if you seek out the supposed members of this cabal, they deny to a man any special rapport with the Prime Minister, saying that during periods when they aren't "in play"—i.e., called on to perform their jobs—he doesn't communicate with them.

Any team sense that exists among the important job holders in the PCO and the PMO tends to spring from old friendships formed before the Trudeau era. Much was made of the fact that Marc Lalonde and Michael Pitfield were close friends of each other's and of the Prime Minister's in the years from 1968 to 1972 when Lalonde was principal secretary and Pitfield was a deputy clerk of the Privy Council. Pitfield and Lalonde had known each other for a decade (they started out in Ottawa in 1959 as assistants to Davie Fulton when he was justice minister), much longer than they had known Trudeau, whom they both met in Montreal in the 1960s. Their friendship was based on similar reformist ideas about government and federalism. Once Lalonde became an MP and cabinet minister and Pitfield left the PCO to spend twenty-one months as a deputy minister before being appointed clerk of the Privy Council after the 1974 election, they ceased to meet as a trio either on a professional or personal basis. Lalonde saw the Prime Minister in cabinet; Pitfield saw him only at large functions such as the governor general's garden party. As pragmatic, not to mention phlegmatic, Trudeauites, this was in their eyes and phraseology "entirely appropriate."

The three men who currently form the most important non-elected advisory group to the Prime Minister—Senator Keith Davey, his chief political organizer, Jim Coutts, his principal secretary, and Richard O'Hagan, his special adviser on communications—are also old friends of one another's but not of Trudeau's. They are "splendid retreads," as Gordon Fairweather wittily described them in the House of Commons; their connections with one another having been formed during the Pearson era, and their camaraderie based on old times and old jokes. ("Remember J. Watson MacNaught?" they'll say to one another. "Remember Roger Teillet?" And if you don't remember those illustrious privy councillors, you'll never know what holds this trio together and what breaks them up.)

Davey says he is the only person in Ottawa who doesn't "relate to Mr. Trudeau on a cerebral basis." (The senator is a very able and intelligent man who has gone far on the fiction that he's "just an ordinary guy.") Certainly Davey is one of the few people in the capital who don't live in fear of the Prime Minister—as an entertaining, if telling, incident during November proved.

The Prime Minister had not been pleased with the text for the November 24 television address to the nation provided by the speech writers in his office and retreated to 24 Sussex to write his own speech, having alerted Davey, Coutts, O'Hagan, and three or four other people that he would read it to them in his office for their assessment on the day before the telecast. The company duly assembled, and there was no doubt in their minds, as the Prime Minister read his words with fire, that he thought it a bril-

liant speech. But for the anglophones listening it was an agony to know what to say since the rendering was in French and none of them was sufficiently fluent to get more than its gist. "We all sat there gripping the edge of our seats until our knuckles turned white," one of them recalled afterwards. Finally, the PM said, "Do you want to hear it in English, too?" "Yes, sir, Prime Minister," said Davey blandly, "I'd like to hear how it reads in the other official language."

Still, despite his easy-going ways, Keith Davey sees the Prime Minister mainly on party business and usually in official settings. Trudeau rarely asks colleagues to his house on a casual basis. One cabinet minister from Quebec who might be considered a familiar said recently that in four years only one invitation to 24 Sussex had been forthcoming and that was to a formal dinner.

Furthermore, Trudeau won't lend himself to requests for the usual small courtesies a Prime Minister dispenses as a matter of form—such as a note to an official's wife who was ill in hospital with cancer, which he refused on the basis that it would be phony and an intrusion on her privacy because he hardly knew her. He doesn't need psychic stroking, and he doesn't comprehend why other people might.

Outside the circle of his family he seems to function as a loner—as he had all his life until his marriage—his temperamental isolation compounded by the fact that he holds the loneliest job in any democracy. An old friend from his radical days, now working in the department of finance, who used to be invited occasionally to 24 Sussex for drinks and conversation, was foolish enough to tell a few people a story Trudeau had confided about his mother-in-law's dislike of bilingual labels. The story got into print in Douglas Fisher's column in the Toronto *Sun*, and the friend now finds that messages left with the PM's secretary go unanswered. He was indiscreet, and he was dispensable.

A senior bureaucrat describes Trudeau's relationships with people by comparing him with Lester Pearson. "Mike always made you feel you were needed even if this was far from the case. Pierre makes you feel he doesn't give a shit even though he may need you badly. He just can't bring himself to say 'Help me,' though if the phrase passed his lips a hundred people would rush to his aid."

Probably the most important formal function a Prime Minister performs at a personal level is as cabinet leader. When he sits down with his ministers as the first among equals, he must deal with the abstract problems of running the country and the human problems of managing people. He must knit together factions, drawing out uncertain ministers, directing the energies of the bombastic, and soothing the fears of the dissatisfied, all the while seeking the consensus that will best serve the federation.

If you move among Trudeau's past and present privy councillors, asking them about his abilities as cabinet maker and cabinet leader, they usually display three attitudes:

(1) They respect his patience in trying to reach a consensus and his intellectual grasp of an amazing variety of policy problems. PCO officials produce for every Thursday meeting of the whole cabinet about six inches of documentation to go with policies coming up on the agenda. Trudeau invariably is familiar with the contents of these briefs, and he expects his ministers to display similar diligence. He is courteous to those who are prepared to argue a position backed up by facts, savage to those who are "feelies"—as in, "I've got a feeling this won't wash in Wetaskiwin," a legitimate remark among most ordinary pols who operate on three-parts hunch to one-part fact, but anathema to the fastidious Trudeau.

(2) They fear his wrath if they are seen to be self-seeking or to have revealed cabinet secrets. One minister, in response to an innocuous question about which ministers the PM relies on and admires, answered: "Macdonald, Lang, and in a funny way MacEachen." Then he whispered nervously, "If you print that I told you that, I'll never speak to you again."

Trudeau respects ministers who show loyal devotion to duty and icily disposes of those he considers malingerers. When he was minister of consumer and corporate affairs, Herb Gray was asked by the prime minister—on a day when ministers with major economic portfolios all happened to be out of town or otherwise engaged—to answer questions in the House about newly released figures on unemployment and inflation. Gray turned back the request with the remark that the Prime Minister himself was better equipped to take on this unpleasant duty, and from that moment, as a former Privy Council Office official says, "we knew his days as a minister were numbered." Gray's misfortune was not only to be shown up as overly concerned with his own skin but to be recognized as unable to "deliver" anything to the PM. He didn't have "coat-tails" in his region, and he had no special knowledge that added anything to the PM's perspective. Trudeau likes Eugene Whelan, for instance, because he is "a whole man" in his eyes and he is thought to understand the farmers. James Richardson, on the other hand, was not considered "whole" and, despite his famous family name, was perceived in 1974 not to have "coat-tails." (The Liberal vote in Manitoba, already low, went down by five per cent in that election.)

(3) They dislike the collegial system of cabinet government, which was described variously as alienating, exhausting, and erosive of ministerial authority. This system of running cabinet business through one of several committees before introducing it to cabinet as a whole was instituted under Pearson and has been continually refined under Trudeau. Its workings are complex and of interest mainly to political scientists and other familiars of Ivor Jennings, Richard Crossman, and Michael Pitfield. What is most important about it in terms of understanding Pierre Trudeau as cabinet leader is that it is a concerted attempt to impose technocratic order on what is essentially a human, fluid, and messy interchange as ministers clash with one another and with their bureaucrats over competing policies. On paper it's an important, forward-looking development in cabinet government. In practice many ministers complain bitterly that it saps their energies and prevents the emergence of strong figures in cabinet.

The only way John Turner managed to enhance his reputation as a political star under this system, according to his friends, is that he chose to ignore it. He rarely went to cabinet committee meetings, sending instead his deputy ministers, a move that left him free to be present regularly in the House and to travel the country frequently making speeches, polishing contacts, getting feedback. His detractors say that this is too simplistic by half, that Turner flourished because Trudeau was large-spirited enough to give him free rein in the important portfolios of justice and finance.

Both friends and enemies agree that the loss of Turner from his cabinet is one of the most important failures Trudeau has sustained. In reasonable terms, it made sense. Turner was tired of being crown prince, and he went into private practice as a corporate lawyer. In human terms, it was a disaster. By losing Turner, Trudeau was seen to be unable to get along with strong men and to have lost control of the economy.

Trudeau's reputation for haughty indifference increased when Bryce Mackasey resigned from the cabinet in open chagrin just one year after Turner's departure, at the moment when a cabinet re-shuffle was supposed to show a revitalized ministry. Turner and Mackasey are very different men in temperament and ideology, with Mackasey occupying the left of the Liberal spectrum and Turner the right. Furthermore, their relationships with Trudeau were essentially different. Turner had always been seen as a rival power and probable successor. Mackasey was always an open supporter, the only cabinet member who was unabashedly sentimental about the PM. (When Margaret Trudeau fell ill in the autumn of 1975, Mackasey, in his inimitable way, passed a note to the prime minister during a cabinet meeting that quoted Tennyson's line, "More things are wrought by prayer than this world dreams of." "He didn't say a word," Mackasey related later, "but I knew he was touched – I could feel it.")

Despite the differences between Turner and Mackasey, the manner of their resignations was curiously similar. They both went to Trudeau threatening to resign, and they both emerged from his office traumatized by his acceptance of their threats at word value. They had expected him to beg them to stay and to offer them blandishments. Turner wanted some kind of reassurance that Trudeau didn't intend to stay in the PM's office forever (the kind of reassurance that Liberal Prime Ministers have traditionally offered to eager heirs apparent) and that his labours in finance were appreciated. Mackasey wanted another portfolio and a place on the all-important

Priorities and Plans Committee of the cabinet. They both ended up stonewalled and disbelieving.

"You can't threaten Pierre Trudeau," says one of his advisers. "He won't stand for it, and anyway both of them were expendable. It was Turner as much as anyone who was responsible for the state of the economy, and nobody would ever say that Mackasey was a good minister—he was all heart and no work."

However reasonable the explanation for the departures of Mackasey, Turner, and their several other colleagues, the plain fact is that this winter, with the biggest national crisis in our history burgeoning, there are no "star" ministers in Trudeau's cabinet, men or women with large public followings of their own who can come to the aid of the federalist cause.

The list of those who have jumped ship or been thrown headlong overboard is long: besides Turner and Mackasey, it includes Paul Hellyer, Eric Kierans, Gérard Pelletier, Jean Marchand, Mitchell Sharp, Bud Drury, and James Richardson, to name the big names.

The list of those left is made up of exhausted loyalists (Donald Macdonald and Allan MacEachen, both of whom are doing yeoman service in difficult, engrossing jobs they didn't want and don't like); discredited rationalists (Marc Lalonde, Otto Lang, and André Ouellet, all three of whom have shown a lack of political judgment that damages their well-deserved reputations for ministerial capability); a few men with ready identification within specialized groups but no magic on the national scene (Eugene Whelan among farmers, Barney Danson in the Jewish community, Don Jamieson in Newfoundland, Romeo LeBlanc among fishermen, and Daniel MacDonald with war veterans); and a slew of lesser figures most Canadians couldn't

tab with a name, much less a portfolio.

His solitude is yet another way in which Trudeau's position is in direct contrast to Lévesque's. The Quebec premier, newly ensconced in office with all the energy and optimism his unexpected victory generated, is buoyed up by strong colleagues (Parizeau, the two Morins, Payette) with separatist fervour equal to or surpassing his own.

It will be a long time before Lévesque suffers the isolation and disenchantment that elevation to high office almost invariably brings. Thousands of French Canadians will remember for years the way he was on the hustings last fall, exuding not charisma (which in Max Weber's original definition places the leader far above the crowd that worships him) but understanding of their aspirations. I saw him give a speech in the Msgr. Parent high school auditorium in Longueuil, a working-class suburb of Montréal located in his own riding, a week before his victory, talking to a crowd so packed together there was no air. With Lise Payette sitting behind him, and his posters pinned on the auditorium's curtains, Lévesque was Chaplinesque, "the little man" personified, his feet turned out, his ill-fitting suit looking like something a factory foreman would wear on Sunday, smoking constantly, telling jokes ("Trudeau sent us Mackasey—*c'est un cadeau des Grecs;* Trudeau sent us Marchand—he's supposed to drive the government of Quebec, but he can't even drive his own car"), making promises, lifting hopes, speaking, as he kept saying, "*au fond de mon coeur.*" I haven't been in a crowd that was so loving since 1968, and when the musicians played the Gilles Vigneault song "*Gens du pays c'est votre tour,*" the people went into a kind of ecstasy.

On many levels, the Trudeau-Lévesque confrontation has about it a mythic aura. Each man represents a tradition rooted in Quebec's history. Lévesque comes out of the nationalist tradition of Papineau, Bourassa, Taschereau, and Duplessis, based on tribalism and emotion; Trudeau comes from the pragmatic, federalist-constitutionalist tradition of Lafontaine, Cartier, Laurier, Lapointe, and St. Laurent, focused on the accommodation of the French Canadians to the finality of the conquest and based on reason and a more abstract concept of brotherhood beyond blood ties.

On the surface, Trudeau – burdened by the fatigue of his ministry and myriad difficulties beyond the Quebec situation, and alienated from his fellow French Canadians by long absence and a reputation for being remote and aristocratic – would seem the probable loser in a separatist-versus-federalist referendum. Still, he has seemed like a loser and come up a winner before. Earlier in the fall, when the Quebec results weren't known yet and every indicator pointed to his downfall, I kept thinking of a remark made a few months before he died by Grattan O'Leary, the Con-servative senator who had been observing prime ministers for sixty years.

"You can't weigh Trudeau on ordinary scales," he said. "It isn't just that he's brilliant – Arthur Meighen was easily his equal in brains – but that there clings to him something mysterious, which for want of a better word I'll call 'luck.' Fortune has a way of turning in his favour. For him the centre holds."

Those of us who want Canada to hold will have to hope that in this assessment of O'Leary's there was more moxie than Irish mysticism, or – to put it another way – more reason than emotion.

Christina McCall Newman is a political journalist who was born, brought up and educated in Toronto, lived for a decade in Ottawa, and has travelled extensively following her trade. She's working on a study of the Liberal Party to be published by Macmillan of Canada; loves food, wine, funny, mysterious or literary conversations, clothes, kids; loathes requests for lists of hobbies, mimeographed letters, portentous statements, pretentious titles, and her own tendency to sloth. "The Exotic Mindscape of Pierre Trudeau" was first published in *Saturday Night,* January/February 1977.

DAVE BROADFOOT

Water Pollution

In marine life, as in human society, the scum will rise to the top.

The enormity of the water pollution problem came home to me this past summer when I had occasion to be out for a walk on Lake Erie. I met a young woman who lived nearby who claimed that she had been taking the pill with water out of the lake. The next time she was in to see her doctor, he informed her that she was three months stagnant.

I didn't believe her story but what did strike me was that the only difference between the St. Lawrence River and Lake Erie was that the St. Lawrence River is moving. If it ever stopped moving, we could probably walk on it, roller skate on it, we could pave it and drive on it. Ninety-two percent of the raw sewage of the city of Montreal is flowing directly into the St. Lawrence River, and 50 percent of that is coming directly from Jean Drapeau's office.

At a time when there is a greater demand for fish than ever before, the fish can hardly get upstream to spawn. (Incidentally, there seems to be some misunderstanding about the word "spawn" in this country. It is *not* that thing a Scotsman has hanging down in front of his kilt, it's getting pregnant underwater.)

All of our waters are murky today. It reminds me of a song:

Where the fishes die
And the phosphates grow
We call this Lake
Ontario

A constituent recently informed me that she had gone to a fish market and bought some tuna, and when she got home and opened up her tuna, she found it full of mercury. But I've heard of something worse. A man had apparently parked his car on a dock in Halifax during the fishermen's strike, and when he returned, he opened his Mercury and found it full of tuna.

And what about all the North Americans who now eat oysters twelve months of the year? An oyster should *never* be eaten during a month that has no *r* in its name. That is when the oysters are mating, and you are taking away the only bit of pleasure the poor oyster has left. Put yourself in the oyster's position. Having to do it in dirty water is awkward enough. We need our oysters. My secretary, Greta, tells me they are good for what fails you. A marine biologist put it this way: "We don't know for sure what effect the oyster has on human potency, but personally I always gulp them down fast to be sure I don't get a stiff neck."

Even on our open ocean waters, our salmon are now threatened by the transport of oil by tanker from Alaska to the U.S.A. If we lose the salmon, we lose lox, and if we lose lox, this country will be faced with an enormous surplus of bagels.

In marine life, as in human society, the scum will always rise to the top, and I believe that is the place to start: at the top.

With a Local Initiative Grant, students who now find themselves unemployed could spend their summers on rafts, with long-handled hoes, scumming off the tops of our lakes, rivers and streams.

Beyond that, we must see to it that our waste is recycled, regardless of expense. As it is written in the good book, ''Waste not, want not,'' or as we would say in our time, ''Crap is beautiful.'' As the President of the United States was heard to say, standing on the shoreline of Lake Erie, with the detergent foam lapping at his feet, ''I want to make this perfectly clear.''

Dave Broadfoot has performed his own brand of satirical comedy from one end of Canada to the other. He is no relation to Gordon Lightfoot. ''Water Pollution'' is from *Sex & Security*, reprinted by permission of McGraw-Hill Ryerson, copyright Dave Broadfoot, 1974.

" . . . Harold, you know I can stand a little pollution, but honestly this lake is getting to be too much for me . . . "

MARGARET LAURENCE

Put Out One or Two More Flags

If you're ever in Elm Cottage, look us up.

Sometimes I'm asked by North Americans what it is like to live in a quiet quaint English village. I have to reply in all honesty that I don't know. This village is not as steadfastly quiet as you might suppose. It is on the main Oxford road and the cars tend to swoosh through as though no village were here at all, causing local residents to raise their walking sticks or umbrellas and utter loud but futile imprecations. As for quaintness – well, I don't think the village would qualify there, either. True, our shopping centre contains the following *only*: a butcher's, a grocer's, a post-office which lives in a small candy shop, a pub, an antique shop in which I have never seen any customers, and a secondhand bookshop which very oddly also sells plastic flower arrangements. True, there is the occasional cheerily eccentric vicar and a stentorian-voiced tweedy lady or so. True, there are some lovely old flint-and-brick houses and a village pond which (according to local legend) in bygone days was used as a witches' ducking pond, where crones were held under water for minutes at a time in order to determine scientifically whether or not they were guilty of the dark arts. And when I first moved here, there used to be a delicate old lady who wore a black lace mantilla and chuffed through the village in a small electric car of truly ancient vintage, while her delicate old dog scuffled along beside her. All the same, it couldn't really be said to be your actual quainte olde English village full of Tudor half-timbering circa 1930.

These, however, are not the main reasons why I don't feel terribly knowledgeable about village life. I am involved elsewhere. Rupert Brooke, you will recall, wrote about "some corner of a foreign field that is for ever England." His lines were written in a somewhat gloomier context, but although I am not buried here yet, I take his meaning to heart. I live on two-thirds of an English acre which appears to be the maple leaf forever. To put it bluntly, the place is crawling with Canadians. And, supporter of integration though I always have been, I have to admit I like it this way. I didn't plan it. It simply happened.

When I moved here, I wondered what life would be like in a peaceful quaint English village. Would I be totally isolated, surrounded only by beautiful trees, unspeaking and unspeakably snobbish squires, or villagers whose conversational ploys would consist of "Arrgh! 'Tis a bright day, innit, missus?" Some of the county gents and their ladies are here, all right, and some of them speak to me and some of them don't. The villagers are the true population, some families having lived here for hundreds of years as gardeners, artisans, shopkeepers, tenant farmers. They speak in a soft and beautiful Buckinghamshire accent, and are friendly and accepting towards strangers such as myself. Still, you would never become a villager until you'd lived here half a century, and probably not then. When I discovered these general patterns, I thought that life here might be rather lonely. Then the Canadian contingents began to arrive. At first it was mainly my contemporaries, and I realized with surprise and delight that if I stayed here long enough, every person I knew in Canada would ultimately turn up. I believe it was Henry James who used to refer to summer as The Great North American Visiting Season. Now it's the whole year. And it's not only my contemporaries any more. These days, our visitors are just as likely to be the sons and daughters of old friends, or my nieces and nephews, or a wide assortment of young Canadian writers.

"This damn place is like a combination of London Airport, a third-class hotel, and a recording studio," I sometimes pathetically moan, on one of those days when the air seems just that little bit too full of guitar sounds, and we've run out of clean sheets and towels, and I can't think what to have for dinner. "It's chaos, that's what it is. I swear I'm going to take the vow in a silent Order."

Then, unexpectedly, somebody says they reckon it's their turn to make dinner, and no thanks, they won't put the groceries on the bill—they'll go and buy what they need for the speciality they have in mind. And somebody else offers to do the laundry this week. And after dinner we listen to the song somebody has just composed. And I have the sense of an extended family group, a good feeling. My son and daughter, who have lived in this country for nine years, feel deep connections here because this house is their home, but they also feel Canadian, which is small wonder considering the accents around the place.

Our house is called Elm Cottage and was, we believe, so-named more than a hundred years ago after the giant elm in the garden. It is not the North American idea of a cottage, as it has six bedrooms. The oldest part of the house is some two hundred years old, the rest being about ninety. It was not, as some have suggested, designed by a lunatic. It must simply have grown, bits being added hither and thither. Now we have nameplates on the doors, having had numerous visitors who got lost on the way to the bathroom or who were totally unable to find the kitchen. When I ordered the nameplates in a nearby town, I told the girl in the shop what I wanted. Each name had its good reasons. *Steproom,* one of the bedrooms, was because you have to go down a step when entering it and if you forget this essential fact you will fall flat on your face. *Dwarf Room* used to be the dressing-room for the master bedroom, and when we turned it into an extra bedroom a friend commented that it would be a dandy place for visiting dwarfs.

"Coo," the shop girl said, impressed. "Novelty names!"

I felt like Walt Disney and nearly cancelled the order.

As in most old houses in England, the deadly fight against dry rot and rising damp is never really over, but we're slightly ahead at the moment, or so we fondly believe until the next wet patch appears on a ceiling or wall. Among the many charms of the place is the sign on the tank over the toilet, which says PONTIFEX'S NO-SOUND. This Victorian appellation cannot be said to be entirely accurate. Every time you flush the thing it sounds like a fourteen-cannon salute. The house is heated with gas, coal,

220

wood, and electricity, in various corners, which to some Canadians seems enough quaintness to be getting on with. No central heating, needless to say. Once ten fireplaces were used here; now only two of them are in use. The heat loss must be staggering, despite our valiant attempts to block off the unused chimneys. In winter it is advisable to wear three sweaters at all times.

Nonetheless, we do have mutedly shining red stone tile floors, and a lot of smallish rooms so people can either congregate or be by themselves, and two interestingly neurotic cats, and a rose garden which keeps on blooming until nearly Christmas. There is a kind of shabby elegance about the place which I've always loved. Nearly all our Canadian visitors seem to feel the same. If someone says (as once happened with a CBC-TV interviewer who shall remain nameless), "Margaret, I just don't see how you can possibly live in a place like this," then they don't get asked back.

Our Canadian stronghold has obviously made its mark on the village. Once, Al Purdy and his wife Eurithe stayed with us for several weeks on their way back to Canada from Greece. This was the origin of the saying in our house when offering someone a tin of beer, "Do you want a small tin or an Al-sized one?" Al immediately discovered that the village bookshop contained a whole lot of old Canadian books, which were of no apparent interest to anyone in England but of considerable interest and value back home. He bought dozens, packaging them up and posting them to Canada. Some time later, when I was in the village post-office, Miss Wright behind the wicket sighed nostalgically.

"Not the same as it was when Mr. Purdy was here, is it?" she said.

The local P.O. probably hadn't done so well out of stamp sales in 200 years.

The village has taken note of us in other ways as well. Not long ago, one of the young writers whom I'd met in Toronto came to spend a week with us. He and his girl were hitching, and when they arrived in the village they stopped at a local garage and asked the way to the street on which we live. The garage man needed only to hear their Canadian accents.

"Oh, you'll be looking for Mrs. Laurence's house," he said. "First street on your left and about halfway up the hill."

One of my nieces recently came to stay with us for awhile. Apparently she had told a friend back home she was coming. The friend was taking a Canadian literature course on which one of my novels was being taught.

"Doesn't she live in a castle or something in England?" the girl enquired.

"Yeh," my niece replied ironically. "Elm Castle."

I liked this concept very much. Just about this time I had lost my longtime cleaning lady to the canteen of the local primary school.

"When I clean this dump," I told my niece, "it begins to feel castle-size."

Since then, however, the advantages of many Canadian visitors have once more become manifest. When the house needs cleaning, everyone who happens to be here at the moment takes on a couple of rooms. Somebody always offers to do the dishes or make after-dinner coffee. One young Canadian calls this system "agreeable anarchy," which means that we all fulfil what we conceive to be our individual responsibilities, and astonishingly enough it all seems to mesh.

I wrote to a friend in Toronto not long ago, telling her the old hostel was back in business after my absence in Canada last summer. I also mentioned that our status was now that of Castle. Concerned about the novel which I am attempting to write, she wrote back as follows: "Your North American Home Service is quick to offer their assistance. Our eminent architect,

221

Everard Turnpenny Cetera, has drawn you an individualized castle plan which he feels is exactly suited to your needs. We await only your signature to begin the demolition of your present and obviously out-moded residence and the construction of a more economic and generally satisfying dwelling."

Enclosed was a drawing of the New Elm Castle, complete with rope ladder ("For ingress to the castle, Sundays only") and a moat containing barracuda. Also enclosed was a design for a dual-purpose castle banner. Hoisted one way it reads "*Moi Libre:* Me Free." Hoisted the other, it is a frantic appeal which reads "*Libre Moi:* Free Me." This is in case the visiting contingents ever reach proportions which make writing impossible for me, owing to a plethora of potato-peeling, pie-making and the like.

Some of the Canadians who have come to visit have remained in England, at least for the time being. The young couple who came over to hold the fortress the year I was writer-in-residence at the University of Toronto are now living in a village only a few miles away, working, writing, composing songs. A small but enthusiastic colony, mostly writers or composers, appears to be growing in Buckinghamshire. It has been suggested that this whole process is in fact a plot—if not actually to take over England, at least to mount a propaganda campaign. I neither affirm nor deny. All I can say is that over the years I have observed that only when a British diplomat is kidnapped or when our Prime Minister either slides down a banister or gets married is there ever any Canadian news reported in the British press. I have also observed that although many African books are published here and, what is more, reviewed, very little of the interesting Canadian writing which has been done in the past decade has found a publisher here. It may yet be that Elm Castle will be the headquarters for an infiltration movement. Despite my Presbyterian background, there has always been a faint streak of the wild-eyed evangelist in me.

Move over, High Commissioner, sir. The Low Commissioner is operating from Unofficial Canada House.

Margaret Laurence, with five major novels to her credit in addition to short stories, children's literature, profiles, and criticism, is a writer of international stature. Her novel, *A Jest of God,* was made into the movie *Rachel, Rachel.* "Put Out One or Two More Flags" is reprinted from *Heart of a Stranger,* by permission of The Canadian Publishers, McClelland and Stewart.

WALTER STEWART

O-OH Say, What They See!

Americans aren't sure what we are. Or even *if* we are.

There is no American attitude to Canada. Some Americans love us, some despise us, most view us with indifference. Sometimes, the indifference is tinged with contempt; more often, with warmth. Sometimes it contains neither heat nor cold, it is indifference pure and simple.

Americans are not constantly confronted, as we are, with the actions and neglects, comings and goings, virtues and failures, of their next-door neighbour. We, perforce, hold strong views about them because they loom across our horizon, dominate our trade, bestride our culture; we love them or we hate them, but we are not indifferent. They can afford a wider range of responses. For most, we are merely a background noise; it is easy to tune us out.

I wanted to find out what Americans really think about us, and I began collecting material for a book in October, 1974. The surveying technique was not scientific, nor even consistent. By not scientific, I mean that no attempt was made to balance the sample for race, economic level, religion, urban-vs.-rural background, or even sex. I simply lighted on whomever happened to be handy and blurted out my question: What do you

think of when you think of Canada or Canadians? By not consistent, I mean that the question wasn't always put that way. It depended on how the conversation got started.

At first, I always carried my tape recorder at the ready, sometimes I even had it on as I strolled along. That is how I picked up the remarkable exchange with a Washington D.C. prostitute. But a tape recorder can be inhibiting, even to a people as accustomed to being badgered, surveyed and poked at with hidden cameras as the Americans. In a small town in Alabama I braved the local police force in a dry goods store, hoisted up my tape recorder, and asked him what he thought of Canada. He began to make abrupt gestures with his hand, but didn't say anything. Finally, he made a cutting motion, and it dawned on me that he wanted me to turn the tape recorder off. I did that, and he said, "Try to tape me, boy, and ah'll break your arm." I said, "Oh." After that, I was more circumspect; sometimes I used the recorder, sometimes not. I always carried a notebook, and turned to that if the subject seemed likely to balk.

I also dropped my earlier resolve to use everybody's name, age, and address, the way I was taught as a boy journalist many years ago. People who thought they might be held to account some day, might be criticized, or even singled out, either clammed up or retreated into banalities. Knowing they were free to fire away, my subjects began to put a little more muscle into their remarks. I was astonished to find that—once the discussion is opened to uninhibited comment—there are pockets of entrenched ill-feeling towards Canada.

I accept no responsibility for the views propounded; the ignorance often appalled me, the occasional hostility astonished me, and some of the offbeat comments—that Canadians sleep a lot, for example, or that we can't cook—struck me as simply daffy. I do accept responsibility for trying to depict, fairly and accurately, the complex range of American views about Canada.

Canadians sleep all the time. They sleep more than any other people in the whole, wide world. Every time you turn around, they're going off somewhere to have a nap.
Printer, Huntington, N.Y.

They're nice folks, not in a hurry all the time. They're like Southerners in that, though, of course, they live up north.
Farm wife, near Evergreen, Alabama

A God-fearing people, instilled and inspired of the true love of Jesus, an example to others, as the Book says.
Lay preacher, Racine, Wisconsin

Canada? I don't know nothing about it. This bus just goes to Farragut Square.
Bus driver, Washington, D.C.

They wear their hats funny. My wife's cousin, she's going with a Canadian boy, and he come over to dinner one night. Wore his hat up, right up there on the top of his head, didn't pull it down or nothing. An American wears a hat, he's

going to pull it down where it does some good. This was a winter hat, muffs for the ears, it was cold, but he didn't even have the muffs pulled down. I guess Canadians are used to that, the cold. Else this boy wasn't very smart.
Security guard, Library of Congress, Washington, D.C.

That's a very fine place, with very fine people, but they've still got a Queen up there tells them what to do. I wouldn't like that if I was them.
Warehouse clerk, Providence, Rhode Island

We should have something like that to look up to. They don't have to be smart, or do anything. They just have to be there.
Housewife, Washington, D.C.

Canadian drivers are crazy. I'm sorry, but there's no other word for it. They put their foot on the gas and their hand on the horn and look out, here I come. I wonder if it's got anything to do with their religion.
Tour guide, Williamsburg, Virginia.

Canada is absolutely vital to this country. There is no nation in the world that can compare with Canada as a safe, reliable supply of needed resources. Political stability is there, the resources are there, the friendship is there, and the need for American dollars is there. It's all there.
Research assistant, oil company, New York, N.Y.

I think if we need it and they won't give it to us, we should just take it.
National Guardsman, Fremont, Ohio

Yes, of course, problems arise in our dealings with Canada from time to time, but we can always resolve them without too much trouble. After all, you don't

operate on a pimple.
Treasury Department officer,
Washington, D.C.

I used to be all in favor of Canada. Some of my best friends, and all that. But that was up until they elected that Commie Prime Minister. Trudeau is his name. A Commie, everybody knows it. A fellow from out west, he got up in the Congress and said it right out, that the Prime Minister of Canada was a Commie. Well, I naturally expected that to be the end of Mr. Trudeau. No such thing. If they didn't go and put him right back in the next time. All I can say is that was the end of Canada, as far as I'm concerned, and I don't care who knows it.
Farmer, near Rutland, Vermont

The Canadian male is a chauvinist pig, about 10 years behind here.
TV production assistant, New York, N.Y.

"Hey, honey! Hey, you wanna go out with me?"
"No, thank you, but I'm glad you stopped me. I'd like to ask you a question."
    "What kinna question?"
    "I'm from Canada. Do you have many Canadian clients? Do you know anything about Canada?"
    "You puttin' me on?"
    "No, no . . ."
    "You a cop or somethin'?"
    "No, just a journalist, relentlessly pursuing the facts."
    "Huh?"
    "Do you know anything about Canadians?"
    "No, honey, I don't but if they all like you, they a poor bunch of peckers."
    "I'll put you down as 'Undecided."
Dialogue on L Street, Washington, D.C.

There is no rape in Canada, very little anyway. You know why? Because they electrocute the guy up there. That cools

the bastards out. It's okay by me.
High school student, Pittsburgh, Pennsylvania

Canada, that's up north, near New York state, isn't it? Only it's not a state, it's a whole country. Is that right? Do I win a prize?
Liquor store clerk, Albuquerque, New Mexico

A lot of the people speak French and a lot of the other people don't. And those that don't don't like those that do. I read that in the paper.
Security guard, Banning, California

Canadians have been trying to have it both ways for far too long. Take this matter of the draft dodgers. We had draft dodgers pouring out of this country by the thousand, by the thousand. I read someplace that there were more than 10,000 draft dodgers in Toronto alone, and what did Canada do? It got up on its hind legs, is what, and said the draft dodgers was none of its business. Well, I lost a boy in Vietnam, he was blown up by a goddamn booby trap, and I take it hard when somebody says that my boy can be killed but if some other yellowbelly wants to run off and refuse to fight, why, that's all right with them. I've never been to Canada and I never want to go; as far as I'm concerned, it's just a nation of assholes.
Independent businessman, Mobile, Alabama

Mountains, I think of mountains, and people singing.
Housewife, Austin, Texas.

Toronto's a terrific place, the police go around in little yellow Volkswagens. *Zoom, zoom,* up and down the streets. You haven't seen anything till you've seen a cop in a yellow Bug.
Secretary, Blacksburg, South Carolina

I saw a special on television all about Canada preparing for the Olympics and they had the Montreal mayor on there. He was incredible, the way he could commit the whole country to spend a billion dollars on a mess like that and nobody dares to say boo to him. You wouldn't have an American mayor getting away with a thing like that, not even [the late] Richard Daley.
Housewife, Chicago, Illinois

They speak French up in Canada, not all over the place, just in Quebec. It's a real nice city, though, Quebec City, so old and beautiful. I went there with my boss, and he kept walking around and shouting, "Lead me to somebody who speaks English," and everybody laughed.
State civil servant, Raleigh, North Carolina

Canada—just to say the name gives me goose bumps. It's so romantic. Vancouver, Canada or Montreal, Canada—when I see that in the paper it's like reading Paris, France. It has a faraway, exciting ring to it.
Typist, Albuquerque, New Mexico

I just think of Canada as that great orange expanse north of us.
Marine biology student, University of Hawaii, Honolulu

"Pardon me, but can you tell me anything about Canada, or Canadians?"
"Short hair."
"Anything else?"
"Nope."
In a barber shop, East Holden, Maine

My boy got his draft notice and said to hell with it and went up to Canada. He got a job up there, he's an English major, but he got a job working with crippled kids, for the government, not much money but he liked it. He couldn't come back here, of course, he's still on the indictment list as a deserter. He wasn't good enough for the U.S., but he was good enough for Canada, so now he's becoming a Canadian citizen. Good for him, and good for Canada, treating him right.
Pensioner, Washington, D.C.

We went up to the border once, but they wouldn't let my Dad through with his rifle and pistol, so we had to come back, 'cause he wouldn't go anywhere without a gun, he needs it for protection. Why would they do that to him?
Mechanic, Napa, California

They don't have any heroes, and not much history.
History student, University of Rochester, N.Y.

Canadian whisky is good, Canadian weather is bad, and the Canada goose is a bird. That's the sum total of my knowledge.
History student, University of Arizona, Tucson

Canadian cooking is terrible, they have the thinnest cookbook in the world. Talking about Canadian cooking is like talking about Italian war heroes.
TV production assistant, New York, N.Y.

They make the best whisky in the world, better than Scotch.
Bartender, Fremont, Ohio

I understand they grow terrific grapes up there around Niagara, but they turn them into the crappiest wine in the world.
Wine worker, French Camp, California

Walter Pidgeon comes from Canada, and Glenn Ford, so I guess they have strong culture up there.
Retired teacher, Palm Springs, California

226

Canada produced Anne Murray, what more can I say? Fantastic!
Insurance salesman, Richmond, Virginia

My mother always told me Canadians made beautiful blankets. You should get a Canadian blanket, she used to say. They really know how to make blankets up there. Well, I've seen Canadian blankets, and they look just like American blankets to me.
Waitress, Minot, North Dakota

My daughter lived with a Canadian doctor in San Francisco. He seemed real nice, he was very generous and kind, kind of a tubby fella, but friendly. He didn't marry her, though.
Saleslady, Minot, North Dakota

They took in draft dodgers, yellerbellies, and that weren't right.
Pensioner, Kearney, Nebraska

Drove up to Canada one time, just to look at the place. Along the highway, there was this big crowd, cars pulled over, regular jam-up, people all over the shoulder. Well, I pulled off, naturally, figured there was a bear or a deer or an accident or something. It was a bird, some kind of bird hopping around in a field, and everybody looking at it. I been around the world twice, been to three dog fights and a box social, but I never saw anything like that before, people lining up to gawk at a gawdamn bird.
Ranchhand, Martin City, Montana

"I don't know what to think of a country where I've never heard of a single writer from there. I've heard of British writers and German writers and Russian writers and French writers and I even know of a Swiss writer, but I have never heard of a Canadian writer."
"How abut Morley Callaghan?"
"Who?"

"You've never heard of Pierre Berton, or Farley Mowat, or Margaret Laurence?"
"Margaret Laurence is a South African. I've heard of her. She's a South African."
"She's a Canadian."
"Well, it shows. I thought she was a South African. It shows what I mean about Canada."
Literary conversation with an English Lit. Major, University of California at Los Angeles

Goods over there are starting to deteriorate, and prices are starting to skyrocket, especially labor-wise. It's not the same ball game it was five years ago; the Canadians used to knock the stuffing out of us, but we should do a lot better now.
Clothing manufacturer, New York City, N.Y.

Everything's so cheap in Canada you can't hardly believe it. There is this terrific maternity shop on Bloor Street in Toronto, the Madonna or the something Madonna, and I swore if I ever got pregnant I'd go there for all my maternity clothes. Now I've gone and had a baby, and I never did get up there to get my clothes. I think it might be worth having another baby just to go up there, but my husband says no way, he doesn't want me going near the place.
Housewife, Gaffney, South Carolina

There's your Autopact, that's Canada. Taking jobs and giving them to Canadians that we should be getting here. You can take your Autopact, if you're from Canada, buddy, and stuff it up where your granny won't see it.
Autoworker, Terre Haute, Indiana

I got nothing against the place, but what has Canada ever done? You never hear "Canadian Astronaut Lands On Moon," do you? No, really, do you? Or

Canadian-Russian troops clash, or Canada invents new medical miracle, no, really, do you? So, what kind of place is it?
National Guardsman, Cleveland, Ohio

Canada's such a terrific place, I'd move there tomorrow if I could. I'd go anywhere, even Nova Scotia.
Legal secretary, Gastonia,
North Carolina

We were assigned up in Canada for a while, my wife and I and the kids. To tell you the truth, we didn't like it much. When our kids went to school, they were subjected to a lot of anti-American propaganda. Do you know, they had to look at the Viet Cong and Red Chinese flags in school? It seemed to me the overrriding motive was to trample on our feelings.
Auto company executive, Cleveland,
Ohio

All I can think of is a railroad going through beautiful mountains. That's Canada.
Student, Boston College, Boston,
Massachusetts

A lot of people think Canada's just a big pile of snow. Not true. I been up there, up to a place called Saskatchewan where my daughter lives, in Regina, Saskatchewan. It's flatter'n hell and hotter'n hell, and I come from Texas.
Businessman, Waco, Texas

We would get along a lot better if they didn't want to play footsie with the Cubans, going down there, this Canadian Prime Minister, going down to Cuba to hold Castro's hand. They can't expect us to like that.
Army officer, Pentagon, Washington,
D.C.

Nice people, very nice. Not bright, but nice.

Tractor salesman, Fargo,
North Dakota

You never hear anything bad about Canada, that's one thing. In fact, I guess it's the only thing.
English major, University of Indiana,
Bloomington

Same as everyone else, filthy the place up, drink too much, grab your ass if they can get it, and don't leave a tip.
Chambermaid, Port Jervis, N.Y.

They're very polite, come in, sign the register—a lot of people don't sign the register—and we answer any questions, and they're real friendly. Maybe you get a better class of people when they travel, maybe all Canadians aren't like that, I'm not saying, but they seem real interested in the history of San Francisco. And they always say "thank you."
Tourist guide, San Francisco,
California

Your president's wife just had a nervous breakdown, didn't she?
Math student, University of Hawaii,
Honolulu

"Yew cain't hardly unnerstan' what Canadians say, the way they tawk."
   "What do you mean?"
   "They tawk funny, sorta mumbly an' ah donno whatall. Yew cain't harly make 'em aout."
   "Am I doing it now?"
   "Yessir, yew surely ahr."
In a restaurant, Tucker, Georgia

Canadians do some things very well, know what I mean, and other things not so hot and some things not at all. You take hockey, Canadians can really play hockey. When the Rangers were up on top, it was all Canadians, whether it was your Andy Bathgate or whoever, they wasn't hardly any Americans in the game and they still ain't. But you take your baseball, Canada isn't even in it. You got Montreal Expos, yeah, but a Canadian couldn't get on the team without he showed his passport, know what I mean? Your football, same thing, who the hell ever heard of a Canadian football player?

I don't know why it is they should be so good at hockey and not them other things. Only thing I figure is, it's so cold up there, they gotta play hockey all the time to keep warm.
Cab driver, New York, N.Y.

They play crappy football, that's all I can tell you.
Furniture dealer, Harrisburg, Pennsylvania

To me, Canada is Barbara Ann Scott whirling around on the ice, so pretty, winning all those medals. And then she married an American, of course, and moved to Chicago. Isn't that sweet?
Office clerk, Grand Rapids, Michigan

Look around here, you want to see some Canadians. Doctors. You see a lot of Canadian doctors come down here to get away from that godawful socialized medicine they've got up there. That and the weather.
Physician, Phoenix, Arizona

I think of simplicity, naturalness, ruggedness. It's wholesome, unsophisticated, vigorous and beautiful.
Minister, Grand Rapids, Michigan

I think every American dreams of having a tract of land in Canada where he could retire and retreat from the world. A mythology of the frontiers. Around the table in a saloon, you'll hear people talking about having a hunting lodge in Canada or a farm up in the Canadian hills. There's a mysticism, the cleanness, the wide expanses.
Store manager, Hays, Kansas

I don't know. All I think of, I think of Canadians going to work every day, walking across the tundra. Cute.
Law student, Washington, D.C.

They got a game up there, you ever hear of it, called curling? You have this big stone and you throw it down the ice, like bowling, really more like lawn bowling, and these other people standing around have brooms and they brush the living hell out of the ice and that's the way it's played. I saw it on the television one time. It's practically a national sport the way the guy explained it, and he said they used to play it with jam pots. What the hell? They say you can tell a lot about people by the sport, you know, they reflect what they feel in the sports they pick. Well, all I got to say is every time I think of Canada I think of these poor, dumb nuts flailing away with a broom while a rock goes whizzing by.
Hardware clerk, Cape Charles, Virginia

Canada has always stood for peace in my mind until they went and gave India the bomb. That was a very crappy thing to do and I couldn't understand it. Canada took a very major role as peacemaker in the Middle East and that in the Suez thing and here they are giving away the bomb to the Indians. Screwy thing to do. I can only assume that something's going on up there that we don't know about down here that would make them swing around like that.
Psychology major, Harvard University, Cambridge, Massachusetts

Canada can afford the luxury of straight dealing. In this country, the decisions in foreign policy are always made covertly. There is the notion that everything should give way to national security, whatever that is, everthing should be left up to the Secretary of State, he knows all, sees all, but he can't tell all because the Russians might be listening. In

Canada, there are no defence secrets to defend. At least if there are any secrets, nobody cares.

Radio news reporter, Pittsburgh, Pennsylvania

They's good fishermen, that's for sure. They know what to do with a net and a boat. Sometimes they's pushy, that's okay, we pushes back.

Fisherman, Ocean Point, Maine

Walter Stewart, a roving journalist, has worked for the Toronto *Telegram,* the Toronto *Star,* and *Maclean's.* His books are *Shrug—Trudeau in Power* (1971), *Hard to Swallow* (1974), and *Strike!* (1977). "O-Oh Say, What They See" is excerpted from *As They See Us,* by permission of The Canadian Publishers, McClelland and Stewart.

MORDECAI RICHLER

Home Thoughts

The bard of St. Urbain Street shoots again— from a safe distance.

April 29, Montreal.

Exhilaration. Ahead of me, 10 days in Europe, my home for 20 years. Nice, London, Paris. Packing my bags, I already see myself ambling down the Promenade des Anglais, pondering the Mediterranean once more. Surprising old friends in London with a telephone call. Strolling through Montparnasse with my wife again. But first there is Mirabel airport to cope with.

In years past, Montreal was favored with the most convenient of airports, Dorval, only a 10-mile run from downtown. Then Ottawa, from whom so many blessings flow, got to grieving about our city and gave us Mirabel, a $600-million fun-palace 32 punishing miles out of town. In Ottawa they pour (disinterested) honey into judges' ears, but on rainy afternoons they also think deep. Rubbing Senator Keith Davey's head and another stone together clearly sets off sparks. Ideas ignite.

The new society, for instance.

Once the Prime Minister, a man whose intelligence I greatly respect, announced the need for a new society I knew he was on to something, if only because he had managed to antagonize bankers and union leaders at the same time. And I, for one, was eager to serve. So when Trudeau's speech, which was to clarify matters, was telecast, I insisted that my wife and five children watch. This, after all, was to be an occasion. The beginning, possibly, of our Canadian Long March. Grossly overpaid doctors and lawyers might finally be ordered to spend three months of the year in the wheat fields or on an assembly line. Fat international corporations might feel the crunch. There could be a new deal for my friends in the Dene Nation. A little something for schoolteachers. Imagine my bewilderment, then, when after consid-

ASK NOT WHAT YOU CAN DO FOR YOUR COUNTRY, BUT RATHER, "WHAT CAN YOUR COUNTRY DO FOR YOU?"

erable rambling, the Prime Minister finally did get down to the crux, the sacrifices that would be called for, and solemnly enjoined us . . . not to drink and drive. Highway deaths, Trudeau declared, confusing the rest of us with the Ottawa Rotary, cost money as well as lives. The government, risking unpopularity, might just have to step in and lower the speed limit.

Ah, well, from the same Bolshevik planners, Mirabel. To be fair, 50 years from now Mirabel may indeed be a convenience. Meanwhile, we should be grateful, for had those new society futurists taken the really long view, Montreal's new airport just might have been located in Labrador.

April 30, Nice. Le Promenade des Anglais.
Ensconced on the terrace of the Hotel Ruhl, eschewing *café au lait* and *croissants* as too fattening, sipping on a low-cal cognac instead, I recalled my initial trip to the Côte d'Azur. I first saw Nice from a train window in 1952. I was returning to France after six roistering months on the island of Ibiza, in the Baleares, snottily convinced that, whatever my problems, I had to at least put picayune Canada behind me. No, no. Beneath me. Malraux, Sartre and Céline were the writers I was foolishly trying to emulate. Certainly not Leacock.

The first time I came to Nice it had been after some trouble with the Spanish cops. They took me for a spy. Immensely flattered, I was, all the same, asked to leave the country. Not immediately, mind you, but say within 48 hours. This time I was travelling more modishly, a cultural freeloader. I had been invited to Nice by *Le Festival International du Livre de Nice*. As an adjunct to the festival, the organizers were running a week of films based on novels, beginning with *L'Apprentissage de Duddy Kravitz*. Not altogether inappropriate, I thought, for

(blessed with one of the Canada Council's initial grants) I had written the first draft of the novel only 20 miles away, in Roquebrune, during the summer of 1958.

Ordering another low-cal cognac, ruminating about Canada, I reflected that in the 24 years since I had first sat on this terrace maybe not all that much had changed. At home, they were still searching the North American attic for an identity. Drilling for oil, surfacing with gas, albeit natural. Shameless Gordie Howe, after all those wasting years, was still a threat in the slot, the indestructible Dief still the country's leading stand-up comic. And out there in the Arctic they had yet to unearth Sir John Franklin's tomb, while in my native Quebec the quest for a government informed by more than avarice and incompetence, less than graft, continued.

O Canada!

If today Canada tends to raise barriers against things American (magazines, publishers) lest, as our cultural concierge, Hugh Faulkner says, we are overwhelmed, the country I thought I had put behind me in 1951 used to slap quotas against people like me, that is to say, Jews. Or, as it is sometimes more officiously put, ethnics.

According to the *Oxford English Dictionary,* "ethnic" means heathen. "A. *adj.* 1. Pertaining to nations not Christian or Jewish; Gentile, heathen, pagan 1470." But as it is commonly used in Ottawa, where language is nobody's strong suit, ethnic means Jewish, Hungarian, Ukrainian, etc., as in "the ethnic press," which is to say the *Canadian Jewish News* but not the Westmount *Examiner.* Our civil servants do indeed have a case when they protest the bilingual program. First, make them proficient in English.

Anyway, in my day, McGill would endure only so many Jews, so would Sir George Williams, and there were suburbs of Montreal where it was understood we could not buy homes or molest non-ethnic girls. And many French Canadians, who now profess to be baffled by the lack of support for the separatist cause among Quebec-born Jews, were then out painting *A bas les Juifs* on the Laurentian highway. My last summer in Canada I worked as a hotel waiter in the Laurentians and every night, after I had finished serving dinner and set the tables again for breakfast, I lay down on the lawn with a cold beer. Across the road, at another hotel called Chez Maurice, I could plainly see a sign that read RESTRICTED CLIENTELE.

Of course I didn't know then, as I do now, that when the Prime Minister of my boyhood, Mackenzie King, built his estate at Kingsmere he was careful to buy the surrounding hundred acres lest there be "a sale to Jews, who have a desire to get in at Kingsmere & ruin the whole place," possibly by opening a delicatessen.

In our day we mistakenly took Mackenzie King for a bore, a figure of surpassing blandness. We didn't realize that, taking a crystal ball for his Kissinger, he rapped with his mother's spirit nightly. Or that following Watergate, and the more recent disclosures about John F. Kennedy's philandering, we would learn that stuffy old King actually did it. With the hookers of turn-of-the-century Toronto and Chicago. Forking out as much as $1.25 a trick.

I am indebted to C.P. Stacey, author of *A Very Double Life,* for the further revelation that our Prime Minister, while still a 19-year-old-student (O shining morning face) was already a confirmed Gladstonian. Which is to say, bent on the salvation of prostitutes by day he did in fact bend over them by night and later, in his years of maturity, did enjoy a relationship with his "little angel" dog Pat ("the truest friend I ever had") which, put plainly, was just this side of sodomy. Pat died in his arms in the summer of 1941, as King, ever the campaigner, making promises he couldn't fulfil, sang aloud to him, *Safe in the Arms of Jesus.*

May 1, Nice.
Following the showing of *L'Apprentissage de Duddy Kravitz,* there is debate, and I sit on a platform bedecked with five French critics. One of them questions me pompously about *le symbolisme et la question Israélienne.*

There is no symbolism, I snap.

"Pas de symbolisme?" he repeats, affronted.

At such moments I am prone to check if my fly is properly done up. I was A-OK. Encouraged, I insisted there was no symbolism.

Shaking his head, disappointed, the critic ventured, *"C'est une tranche de vie?"*

Yes; a slice of life.

"Une tranche de vie. Simplement."

As I checked out of my hotel the next morning, the elevator operator, discovering I was a Montrealer, beamed with delight. "Ah," he said, "there is a lot of Mafia there."

Damn right.

"But it is not the same as the American Mafia, is it not?"

No, the mob, like everything else, is branch-plant.

"I know all about the Mafia there. I saw a film about the Olympics."

Even in a city with a past as exuberantly wanton as ours, there has never, in my experience, been anything quite like it. A billion four, maybe more, for two fun-filled weeks.

Enter the slippery Roger Rousseau.

Searching for a president for COJO (*Comité Organisateur des Jeux Olympiques*), Jean Drapeau required somebody with more than sports savvy; a man who would also be capable of dealing with those black African nations who, Drapeau had heard, had been so uppity during the last Olympics. Ostensibly, he found both in the person of His Excellency, Roger Rousseau. Rousseau, after twenty years with the Department of Trade and Commerce and only three years in External Affairs, had risen to the giddy heights of our Ambassador to the Cameroons.

Last winter, meeting with Rousseau, I queried him at length about the morality of spending more than a billion on stadiums when there were so many Montrealers living in squalor. The question did not give His Excellency pause. "You know," he said, his mood philosophical, "only last week a friend asked me something like that. Would you rather have a long cigar?"

"No, thanks. I prefer these little ones."

But I did not object when he refilled my enormous snifter from a magnum-sized bottle of Rémy Martin.

"Well, I said to my friend, we have our golf courses, our clubs, our country houses, but where have the poor got to go? After the Games, the marvellous facilities will remain. The poor will inherit that."

After so many centuries of war, plague and revolution, what are the poor still being offered? Bread and circuses. Not only will they inherit the facilities, but also, as it now turns out, a higher tax on health, cigarettes and drink in order to pay for it.

May 2, London.
After being rooted in London for more than 18 happy years, I quit the city with my family in 1972 to return to Montreal. I adored London then, I adore it still and my departure was not a measure of my discontent. I left out of a fear of running dry. Coming up empty. A sore-armed pitcher. Looking around, it suddenly seemed to me that other Commonwealth expatriates, writers I admired, who like me had possibly luxuriated too long in London, were suddenly writing novels set in the dim past or anticipated future. Novels uninformed by a sense of place. Clearly, it was time to come home.

Besides, the Canada I fled in 1951 was no longer the same country. There had indeed been changes, most of them heartening, much for the better, I think, but a few, embarrassing.

If, in the early 1950s, it was insultingly assumed that no mere Canadian could ever commit a work of literary excellence, now the obverse seemed true. To be a Canadian, on the present scale, was more than sufficient, many of the new nationalists overcompensating, mindlessly pronouncing just about every Canadian goose a swan.

Look out.

Canada's English-speaking writers are now a largely discontented, even fulminating, lot, given to cultural paranoia, a fire sometimes stoked by real, if not necessarily malign, fatuity, as witness the review of Margaret Laurence's last novel, *The Diviners,* in the *New York Times Book Review*. The reviewer confidently placed Mrs. Laurence's novel in Ontario, when as we all know it was set in prairie soil, and has the author dealing with the "meti" when in fact the character in question was a Métis.

Undeniably, all of us at one time or another have endured American ignorance of our country.

On a recent trip to New York, driving into town from LaGuardia airport, a taxi driver asked, "Where are you from?"

"Montreal."

"That," he allowed, beaming, "is my favourite city in the United States."

Our relationship on this continent, grudgingly shared, is tainted by a sometimes infuriating American arrogance, but if we allow that to outrage rather than entertain us, then we will be the ones to emerge deformed. The emotional waste, the loss, will be ours, not theirs. Furthermore, we risk becoming provincial, a cultural laughing stock.

Item: Only a few months ago that otherwise perspicacious Toronto book critic, William French, protested that the Canada Council had refused to underwrite the publication of a new, multi-volume all-Canadian dictionary, thereby continuing our colonial dependency on the *Oxford English Dictionary* or *Webster's*. Others, thinking the problem right through, might take the case a step further, demanding a new alphabet, Canadian to the core, on the grounds that the A,B,C, presently in use is the same one that was used by the British to exploit Africa and by the Americans in the obscene war in Vietnam.

Item: Recently, Bill Glassco, director of Toronto's Tarragon Theatre, which introduced the plays of David French and David Freeman to Canadian audiences, was driven up against the cultural wall for having the effrontery to plan two plays by foreigners—Chekhov and Wedekind—among the six he will be presenting next season. "Don't misunderstand me," he said. "We're still interested in new Canadian dramatists. But we're not going to scrounge for new Canadian work just for the sake of doing new Canadian work." Audiences, he added, "were obviously not prepared to put up with garbage. They were not prepared to patronize Canadian plays just because they were Canadian, and there's a lesson there. I don't believe you can create great art through nationalism."

Yes, indeed.

To make a political analogy, there have always, to my mind, been two kinds of socialism. One, life-enhancing; the other, contaminated by bile. On the one hand, there was that brilliant labour politician, the late Nye Bevan, who so savoured the good life (witty companions, fine books, first-rate food and wine, weekends in the country) that he fought all his days for the undeniable right of more people to have a decent crack at it. On the other, you have the socialism of the Paris *concierge*. Day after day, seething in her foul-smelling caretaker's cubicle, she watches people with more style, a better life, passing to their handsomely-appointed apartments upstairs and, like Brecht's Jenny, she dreams of sweet vengeance. A ship with eight sails and 50 cannons, a pirate freighter, coming to blast them into the sea. Alas, our new nationalism, as endorsed by some Ottawa politicians, seems to be more informed by a vengeful desire to flatten, cut off, shut out, over-inflating what is culturally available here, rather than raise our own standards. If, for instance, nobody Canadian can as yet write as beautifully as Chekhov, we simply won't perform the bloody Russian here. Put another way, a familiar nationalist argument runs that it is necessary to cultivate a good deal of manure before real indigenous cultural flowers will bloom. Yes, yes, but it is also possible that we will first drown in our own cow-shit, which is not to be construed as a comment on the novels of Richard Rohmer.

Actually, the CBC is a case in point. I salute the CBC, in principle, and, as a young writer, had reason to be grateful to it, but I cannot pretend that their highly-touted special on the October Crisis was anything but an artistic disaster, an embarrassing mixture of banal documentary and poorly acted dramatic interludes. Amateur night. There was, however, one unforgettable moment, and that was when two actors, portraying MPs, discussed the crisis over a snooker game, playing with their jackets on. Now, admittedly they were backbenchers of whom we are prepared to believe almost anything, but even I doubt there are backbenchers so dim that they would settle into a game of snooker without removing their jackets.

The CBC is such a missed opportunity. But its salvation lies not in blocking off American channels or cable, however objectionable, but in making it a service of such excellence that American border cities will gratefully tune in on us rather than the other way around. We are not so much in need of protection as an opportunity to excel. And this opportunity is not being denied us by the puerile fare proffered on American channels; it is being stifled by the craven committees of the CBC itself. We are ourselves to blame.

Unknown to the general public, and revealed here for the first time, there is a committee-sponsored behemoth who strolls the CBC corridors, a sledgehammer in hand. If he sniffs out talent or imagination anywhere it is his function to raise his dreadful hammer and instantly flatten it.

May 6, Paris.
It was here I first came to when I left Canada in 1951 and my heart leaps each time I return; I know of no other city that offers so much to delight the eye.

As part of my continuing Canadian re-entry process, I have made it my business, since 1972, to travel the country as widely as possible. Almost everywhere I went I was astonished by abundance, the natural beauty and variety of the landscape, and horrified by the cities we have made here. Most, if not all, of the towns of the Maritimes, compared with those of New England, are downright ugly. Given the natural grace of so much of New Brunswick and Nova Scotia, we have not enhanced the land, but despoiled it. And yet, and yet, in tiny Aulac, New Brunswick, opposite Fort Beauséjour, I found an excellent fish restaurant, incongruously called the Drury Lane Steak House.

Beyond magnificent Quebec City, after Montreal, now nearly ruined by developers, and nondescript but insufferably rich Toronto, there is not a proper city until Vancouver. Edmonton, like acne, is to be endured. Calgary, within reach of the Shining Mountains, looks

like it was uncrated only an hour before you got there. Me, I'd recrate and ship back.

Finally, if you must eat between Toronto and Vancouver, pack a lunch, lest in the West you are served a steak large enough for three, but uneatable, served on a platter overwhelmed by all manner of frozen or canned vegetables, each one rendered soft as absorbent cotton, equally tasty too.

May 11, Montreal.
Going through my mail, I discover a letter from Ottawa. The letter reveals a secret.

O, Ottawa, town of cultural tribunes, intellectually dazzling senators and dark secrets.

For two years after my return to Canada I travelled to Ottawa once a week, a visiting professor at Carleton U., and I still miss the conversational pleasures of the English Department luncheon table there. A fine bunch of gentlemen my colleagues were.

But, at night, prowling the town in search of more vulgar entertainment, I often met with people in or close to government in the Grill of the Château Laurier or in L'Opéra, the restaurant at the National Arts Centre. And in good time, as strangers in another city might, as a measure of affection, confide the name of a favoured restaurant or inn to the traveller, they spilled a government secret. To begin with, I leaned closer, flattered. But I soon learned that these secrets, never to be repeated, were so resoundingly boring that my problem was to appear interested. I could never understand the secret and far from passing it on, come morning, I was hard put to remember it.

In this spirit, I now offer readers an Ottawa secret. I am the chairman of the fiction committee for next year's Governor General's literary awards. Don't scoff. As this tidbit could only conceivably interest, say, 100 people in a country of more than 20 million, it is almost, if not quite, a vintage Ottawa secret. A truly vintage Ottawa secret is only of interest to five people, usually those whose jobs are directly involved.

The sad thing is the Governor General's awards, which should be widely publicized, are themselves becoming increasingly secret. No short list of candidates is published and the awards, presented at Government House, are gotten over with as quickly as possible. This year we may in fact go a step further and, once having decided on what we consider to be the best books of the year, swallow the list of authors' names, lest the news leak out and more people actually buy their books.

The reason for the secrecy surrounding the Governor General's awards, as William French has already pointed out in the *Globe and Mail,* is the fear that one of the winners, a *whisky blanc*-swilling separatist, may stand up and denounce the imperialist dogs of Ottawa even as he pockets his $5,000 cheque. The fear is misplaced. Our present Governor General, Jules Léger, is a man of such grace and stature that he could easily cope with such gaucherie.

After going through my mail, I turned to a stack of *Globe and Mails* my children had put aside for me, 12 missed Canadian days. Though I live in Montreal, I subscribe to the *Globe,* because I take it to be our only first-rate national English-language newspaper. Digging into the stack, I searched for news of the parliamentary pronouncements of young Mr. Clark, our political new face.

Watching the Tory convention on television, I had been cheered when the party eschewed crowning a menacing Claude Wagner, though they already had him on a retainer, and elected a leader instead, but now, scanning Mr. Clark's fumbling speeches, my fear was everybody's second choice at the convention might prove the people's second choice as well. If Joe Clark rang my bell, I would happily buy a *Maclean's* subscription from him. He strikes me as honest, but I'm not yet sure whether that's his *chosen* policy or merely lack of imagination. As Dorothy Parker, I think it was, once said of Los Angeles, there doesn't seem to be any there, there. Whereas Trudeau, however exasperating he is at times, is clearly a presence. When he closes the door behind him at Sussex Drive you know that somebody's home. Furthermore, I doubt that Trudeau is filled with fear when Clark confronts him across the floor of the House. More likely, he is charged with appetite.

If this saddens me, it's not because I'm a Tory, but my party, the NDP, is going nowhere, and any party that boasts the likes of Gordon Fairweather and Flora MacDonald on its front bench cannot be all bad. Even more important, I suspect that if we continue to deny the Tories office they will go bananas, falling into the hands of know-nothing cowboys, and then, my fellow Canadians, the arrogance of the Liberals will really be something to behold. Why, even as things stand, many of them seem to regard the country as their inheritance rather than their employers, and to look upon elections as a pause between acts, an opportunity for the rest of us to clap hands.

Finally, I shoved the newspapers aside in favour of more important matters. The elegant Guy Lafleur, the marvy Yvan Cournoyer, taking on the dreaded Flyers of Philadelphia. Beauty vs. Beast. This time out, beauty won.

It was good to be home again.

Mordecai Richler—essayist, short-story writer, novelist, screen writer, and author of *Jacob Two-Two,* a children's book. His novel, *The Apprenticeship of Duddy Kravitz* (1959), was made into a successful movie in 1974. "Home Thoughts" appeared originally in *The Canadian,* August 14, 1976.